Crossing Cultures

Nineteenth-Century Anglophone Literature in the Low Countries

Crossing Cultures

Nineteenth-Century Anglophone Literature in the Low Countries

Tom Toremans and Walter Verschueren,
eds.

Leuven University Press

ISBN 978 90 5867 733 4
D / 2009 / 1869 / 9
NUR: 632

Cover design: Jurgen Leemans
Typesetting: Friedemann BVBA

Contents

Walter Verschueren (Hogeschool-Universiteit Brussel) | 7
"Introduction."

PART 1

The Critical Reception and Translation of English Literature in the Netherlands

Cees Koster (Universiteit Utrecht) | 21
"Fame and Fortune in the Field of Shakespeare Translation: the Case of A.S. Kok."

Ton van Kalmthout (Huygens Instituut, Den Haag) | 35
"Eccentric Authors: Cd. Busken Huet and Taco H. de Beer on English Literature."

Kris Steyaert (Université de Liège) | 53
"Elusive Poets, Fugitive Texts: The Impact of the London Shelley Society in the Low Countries."

Anne van Buul (Universiteit Groningen) | 69
"British Influences on Dutch Book Designs: A Case Study on Dutch Bibliophilic Editions of Works by Dante Gabriel Rossetti."

Susanna De Schepper (University of Warwick) | 83
"George Eliot on the Dutch Market, 1860-1896."

PART 2

The Critical Reception and Translation of English Literature in Belgium

Lieven D'hulst (Katholieke Universiteit Leuven) | 101
"'English Literature in Belgium': Some Introductory Remarks."

Francis Mus (Katholieke Universiteit Leuven) | 107
"The Image of English Literature in Belgian Avant-Garde Periodicals."

Karen Vandemeulebroucke (Katholieke Universiteit Leuven) | 121
"Presence and Treatment of English Poetry in 19th-Century Belgian Literary Periodicals."

Liselotte Vandenbussche (Hogeschool Gent/Universiteit Gent) | 137
"The Import of English Literature by Women Translators in Flanders, 1870-1914. A Comparative Survey."

PART 3

Women's Writing in Dutch Translation

Suzan van Dijk (Universiteit Utrecht) | 159
"Researching Women's Place in the Literary Field: Anglophone Authors in the Netherlands."

Suzan van Dijk (Universiteit Utrecht) | 161
"Was Jane Austen Read in the 19th-Century Netherlands?"

Lizet Duyvendak (Open Universiteit Nederland) | 177
"English Reading in a Dutch Library for Women, 1894-1900."

Laura Kirkley (University of Cambridge) | 189
"Feminism in Translation: Re-Writing the *Rights of Woman.*"

Stephanie Walker and Suzan Van Dijk
(Universiteit Utrecht) | 201
"What Literary Historians 'Forgot': American Women Authors in the 19th-Century Netherlands."

Contributors | 216

Walter Verschueren (Hogeschool-Universiteit Brussel)

Introduction

In his introduction to *Literatuur van elders* [*Literature from Elsewhere*], a collection of essays published exactly twenty years ago, Raymond van den Broeck rejoiced at the steady rise of academic interest in translated literature and expressed his enthusiasm in terms that were at once confident and promising:

> Over the last decades the interest in translated literature within the field of literary studies has rapidly increased. Started up in the 1960s, reception studies – with its focus on the effect and the function literary texts have for the receiving audience, have greatly contributed to this. More and more literary scholars have taken an interest in the mediating role of translations in the contact between literatures and cultures, in the way translations function within the receiving culture and in the importance of translated texts for the development of national literatures.[1]

Van den Broeck's words point at a development that was just coming of age in the writings of the so-called "Manipulation School" (representatives of which were Theo Hermans, José Lambert, and André Lefevere), with which he shared an interest in embedding the study of literary translation within the larger field of literary studies. Twelve years later, the translation journal *Filter* published a survey of ongoing translation research in the Low Countries, demonstrating that attempts at reconciling the fields of translation studies and literary studies were plentiful. "A great deal of today's literary translation research," the journal's editors concluded, "takes the form of reception research, whether or not in historical perspective, using a notion of translation as a form of reception and opting for a functional point of departure."[2] Still eight years later reception studies themselves, while still flourishing, have come a long way and the field is decidedly still expanding, especially under the impulse of polysystemic theories and Bourdieusian field theory. Studies continue to abound, in other words, but behind the diversity of empirical case studies the need and desire for synthesis and a comprehensive frame of reference is becoming an urgent necessity.

The present collection does not claim to provide a conclusive answer to the question of 'framing'. Instead, these essays each add one more tessera to the grand mosaic of European literary reception. To do so, they have as their principal object the study of the individual and institutional agents and agencies that determined the reception (and non-reception) of British authors in the Dutch and Belgian literary fields in the course of the 19th century. Rather than aspiring a comprehensive survey, which in the face of the sheer wealth and complexity of 19th-century cultural life is bound to fall short, the aim of this collection is to offer a variety of 'angles' from which 19th-century literary dynamics can be studied.

With similar diffidence we have tried to avoid the pitfalls of periodization and have refused to enter the fruitless debate on what constitutes the 19th century as a cultural period. Instead, we have used an arbitrary, albeit commonsensical, 'definition' of the 19th century as a period that roughly started in 1800 and ended sometime round 1900. At either end of the time span, however, we have shown considerable flexibility. In this 'elastic' conception of the 19th century the present collection indeed covers the entire century – from the reception of Mary Wollstonecraft's *Vindication of the Rights of Woman* in its first Dutch translation from 1797 by Ysbrand van Hamelsveld to Pieter Cornelis Boutens' translation of Dante Gabriel Rossetti's *Five Poems* in 1906 and the reception and translation of Anglophone literature in Belgian avant-garde periodicals in the 1920s.

Between these limits (1800-1900), it is only fair to say that the collection reflects the traditional imbalance in critical interest between the first and second half of the 19th century. The reasons for this imbalance are well-known. Nineteenth-century Anglo-Dutch literary relations for a long time continued to suffer from the effects of the Napoleonic Wars. During the French occupation of Holland, direct import of literature from the United Kingdom, for instance, was seriously hampered by the British blockade of Dutch sea trade (1796-1814) and when trade finally picked up with the Vienna Congress (1815), English still found in French and German two languages and literatures that were far superior in social and cultural prestige. Throughout the first half of the 19th century, moreover, personal contacts with the United Kingdom were sparse. The same Napoleonic conflicts had made travelling between the United Kingdom and the Low Countries difficult and dangerous. All of this created very little 'openness' towards English literature and made it very difficult for

English literary texts to penetrate the cultural field of the Low Countries.[3] But there was more. In the newly-established United Kingdom of the Netherlands (1815) the secular and revolutionary spirit during the days of the French occupation made room for the Biedermeier values of sentimental domesticity, idyllic intimacy and contentedness, combined with a revival of Christian spirituality. In Holland this conservative backlash took the form of the Réveil movement inspired by leading literary figures such as Willem Bilderdijk (1756-1831), Isaac da Costa (1798-1860) and the literary critic Willem de Clercq (1795-1844). The low profile of Dutch culture – at least in a 19th-century European context – until the 1860s, is often attributed to the stifling parochialism of this Réveil movement. It was the 'parson mentality' of these Réveil spokesmen that was largely responsible for what Brian Downs in his commendable 1936 article on Anglo-Dutch literary relations called the "protracted [Dutch] resistance to Romanticism" (19) during most of the 19th century. This resistance certainly holds for the exponents of English Romanticism: with the exception of modest manifestations of Byronmania and Scottomania between the years 1830-1850, the overall impact of English Romantic literature (first and second generation) on cultural life in the Low Countries remained modest, if not inconsequential, during most of the period.

The introduction of Anglophone literature in the Low Countries, moreover, was hampered by the overall absence of English language teaching in the Dutch and Belgian school education, resulting in a very small elite that was able to read and understand English literary texts, and by the strong prejudices against English as a 'literary' language. In an age that idolized Goethe and Lamartine, English was considered an uncultivated and coarse language. Even in mid-century, one active promoter of English literature in Holland, B.S. Nayler (1796-1875), complained that the traditional Dutch bias against English as "the scum of all languages" was still very much alive.[4] There is evidence, however, as Lizet Duyvendak demonstrates, that towards the end of the century English began to find its way into the collections of the Dutch reading societies and started to assert itself as a competitive language in the world republic of letters.

By that time the generation of the parson poets, exemplified in Nicolaas Beets (1814-1903) and J.J.L. ten Kate (1819-1889),[5] had made room for the generation of the 'Tachtiger' poets.[6] It is much to the credit of the 'Tachtiger Movement' that the great English Romantic icons like

Keats, Shelley (see the essay by Kris Steyaert) and to a lesser extent also Coleridge and Wordsworth, were recalled from the oblivion into which they had been cast by the parson poets of the previous generation. With the ascendancy of the 'Tachtigers' and the opening up of Dutch literature towards the great international canon by a major, influential critic such as Conrad Busken Huet (see the essay by Ton van Kalmthout), Dutch literature reached an artistic height that – at least by our own 20th-century standards – was unprecedented in Dutch 19th-century literature. The retrieval of the Romantic icons in the field of poetry, moreover, coincided with the introduction of the major novelists of the great English realist tradition such as Eliot, Dickens, Thackeray and Trollope. Still, however invigorating and innovative the 'Tachtiger Movement' may have been, in some ways they were still lagging more than fifty years behind and their critical work offers remarkably little commentary on their British near-contemporaries like John Ruskin, Algernon Charles Swinburne, Lord Tennyson, Dante Gabriel Rossetti or William Morris. Generally speaking, that is, for as Anne van Buul's essay on P.C. Boutens and Dante Gabriel Rossetti makes clear, there are exceptions to this standard view.

In Belgium Anglophone literature did not fare much better. Throughout the 19th century and even at the beginning of the 20th, Anglophone literature played a minor role (see the essays by Mus, Vandemeulebroucke and Vandenbussche). Here, too, the reasons are well-known. In the newly-created Belgian state (1830) French would remain the dominant cultural language for more than a century to come. The attempt at creating a 'Belgian literature' did not result in the creation of a significant overture towards other cultures; nor did the struggle for Flemish cultural emancipation in the second half of the century lead to an increased interest in any foreign literature other than French. As Francis Mus argues in his contribution to this collection, it was precisely the overwhelming preoccupation with the 'Flemish Question', the political and cultural emancipation of Flemish culture, that prevented a genuine interest in foreign literature and in this way precluded a fruitful crossbreeding of different cultures.

Although literary life in the Netherlands and Flanders has been long and widely documented, this is not so when it comes to the mapping of transnational literary traffic. General studies of Anglo-Dutch cultural exchange are sparse. The most extensive survey of Anglo-Dutch relations, Brian Downs's still highly valuable article entitled "Anglo-Dutch Literary

Relations, 1867-1900" dates from 1936(!). Besides being in need of an urgent update, this lengthy study, though admirable in its scope, nevertheless remains focussed on the last quarter of the century.

Apart from Downs's article we should also mention a host of isolated studies on individual authors, mostly from a traditional comparative perspective. As 'mappings' go, they are mostly descriptive in nature and given the historical time span in which they appeared, they are methodologically diverse.[7]

The contributions to this volume move within the orbits of the two major directions in current reception research: the polysystemic approach, invigorated by Els Andringa's promising attempt at redefining ('psychologising') the basic concept of 'repertoire' and new developments and applications of Bourdieusian field theory. Here we should particularly mention Gillis Dorleijn and Kees van Rees's important institutional analysis of the Dutch literary field in *De productie van literatuur: Het literaire veld in Nederland 1800-2000* [*The Production of Literature: The Dutch Literary Field 1800-2000*], which offers an attractive and workable methodological frame of reference.

Although many essays in the present volume show some affinity with the analysis of the Dutch literary field provided in Dorleijn and van Rees, they differ in at least four significant ways.

(1) The aim of this collection is not so much the definition of the literary field as such, but rather its attention is geared towards one specific part of that field, i.e., the physical distribution and symbolic production of what in the given period (1800-1900) was considered to be 'English literature' within the Low Countries. For most of the 19th century, English literature – it hardly needs to be repeated – was a minor player in the French-dominated literary field, but a player nevertheless that was not entirely negligible and, along with the English language, in full ascendancy. The ways in which English literary texts penetrated the Dutch and Belgian literary fields during the 19th century (including Anglo-Dutch and Anglo-Belgian networks), as well as the different refractions in which they were consumed by the 19th-century Dutch and Flemish readership, still remain to be investigated in greater detail. It would be interesting to see, for instance, in what ways precisely

the English literary repertoire, which in polysystemic terminology would be semi-peripheral and primary, was able to challenge the central French repertoire.[8] The present collection offers a number of case studies (discussing the 19th-century reception of William Shakespeare, Mary Wollstonecraft, Jane Austen, Percy Bysshe Shelley, George Eliot and Dante Gabriel Rossetti) that uncover – at least partly – the internal workings of the literary field by pointing at the role publishers, printers, literary critics, educators and translators played in the introduction of Anglophone literature in the Netherlands and Belgium.

(2) For reasons not entirely unrelated to (1), most of the contributions in this collection deal with authors whom we nowadays consider to be canonical. To be sure, the 19th century had a more generous conception of literature that widely differed from our own essentially modernist notion of what constitutes a 'literary text'. Much of what we regard as 'high' literature (Shelley, Austen, Eliot, Rossetti) would have made little impression upon the average 19th-century Dutch and Belgian reader who was likely to show a keener interest in various sorts of religious, political, (pseudo-)scientific and pedagogical writings that all went under the name of 'literature'. Lizet Duyvendak, in her study of English readings in a Dutch Library for Women at the end of the 19th century, and Suzan van Dijk's discussion of Jane Austen's reception at the beginning of that century both draw our attention to the presence of many authors, now long forgotten, who in the 19th-century hierarchy of values ranked higher than authors whom we from our own contemporary academic interests tend to treat as 'established' or 'classic'.

(3) The specific emphasis on the reception of a foreign (English) literature also prompted a special interest in translation. Virtually all of the essays here included devote significant attention to the disseminating and often refracting role played by translations in the reception process. As argued in Laura Kirkley's contribution, Mary Wollstonecraft's *Vindication of the Rights of Woman* in Dutch translation is one example of a major political pamphlet

whose (mis)fortunes in translation turn out to have far-reaching social and political repercussions.[9]

(4) A last and perhaps most contentious difference with the collection by Dorleijn & van Rees is the geographical scope of the present collection. The Low Countries arguably do not represent a single, homogeneous literary field but rather a combination of two, possibly three autonomous, albeit historically related, fields. Dorleijn & van Rees explicitly exclude Flanders from their analysis on the grounds that "[the Flemish field] has its own status, its own history, its own institutions and agents and is moreover embedded in its own societal systems."[10] The cultural homogeneity assumed by such a definition of 'field', however, may not fully correspond to the historical reality of nations, such as Belgium or even the Low Countries more generally, that are situated at the crossroads of various cultural fields and that show a remarkably hybrid mix of cultural determinants.

***

The first part of this collection is dedicated to **the critical reception and translation of English literature in the Netherlands**. In the opening essay Cees Koster compares A.S. Kok's prose translation of Shakespeare's complete works (1873-1880) with the verse translation by L.A.J. Burgersdijk (1884-1888) in an attempt to gain insight in the various norms that govern "accepted practices in the field with respect to both translation and reception." Ton van Kalmthout's contribution focuses on two major figures of 19th-century literary criticism: Conrad Busken Huet (1826-1886) and Taco H. de Beer (1838-1923). In "Elusive Poets, Fugitive Texts", Kris Steyaert describes the impact of the London Shelley Society in the Low Countries. Starting from the question how Shelley's texts – as material commodities – reached the Dutch-speaking regions, Steyaert suggests that the London–based Shelley Society was particularly instrumental in the propagation of Shelleyan aesthetics among the members of the artistic circle of the 'Tachtigers' (Willem Kloos and Albert Verwey in particular). Anne van Buul discusses the reception of Dante Gabriel Rossetti in the translation of Pieter Cornelis Boutens and the pervasive impact of Pre-

Raphaelite aesthetics and the Arts and Crafts Movement on the later work of P.C. Boutens. A final contribution in this section is by Susanna De Schepper. In "George Eliot on the Dutch Market, 1860-1896", De Schepper explores the negotiations between the Dutch publishers of Eliot, as well as the negotiations between some of them and Eliot's UK publisher, Blackwood's, and concludes that copyright and translation right procedures played a pivotal role in the dissemination of Eliot's work in the Netherlands.

A second part is devoted to **the Belgian 'field'**. The introductory essay by Lieven D'hulst, outlining the complex correlation between various "parameters of literary communication", is followed by two contributions examining the presence of English literature in Belgian literary journals. Francis Mus analyses the place and function attributed to Anglophone literature in the literary historical avant-garde in Belgium and comparing Flemish with Francophone periodicals concludes that the former

> due to their more ephemeral character and the intranational nature of their debates [...] couldn't develop a structural dialogue with foreign literatures. The existing contacts were tied with geographically contiguous partners such as French, German and Dutch literature. Moreover, they took a keener interest in a political and cultural debate that was not strictly literary, such as the 'Flemish question'.

The more explicitly international orientation of the Francophone periodicals, he argues, allowed a relatively greater attention to Anglophone literature. Karen Vandemeulebroucke, in turn, looks into the presence and treatment of English poetry in two major 19th-century Belgian literary periodicals, *La Jeune Belgique* and *Van Nu en Straks*, and concludes with Mus that attention to Anglophone literature in both instances is rather modest. When English poems do appear in translation, they are domesticated, i.e. adapted to the dominating norms of the time and especially to the French 'model'. Finally, in "The Import of English Literature by Women Translators in Flanders, 1870-1914, Liselotte Vandenbussche suggests that much of literary transmission through translation took place "by coincidence," because of "linguistic proficiency, and rare contacts with particular editors and authors". Basing her findings on correspondences between various authors and translators, Vandenbussche concludes that in the decision to translate a given text "ideological motives with regard to politics or education, and motives concerning canon formation, whether this meant importing new authors or consolidation an existing repertoire, played a modest but actual part."

A third and final section in this collection is entirely devoted to **the critical reception of women's writings in Dutch translation**. Suzan van Dijk's contribution situates Jane Austen's immediate reception (or: non-reception) within the context of the Dutch reception of other contemporary women writers such as Charlotte Smith, Fanny Burney, Helena Maria Williams, Hannah More, Barbara Hofland, Amelia Opie, whose works were translated, commented and bought. In "English Reading in a Dutch Library for Women, 1894-1900" Lizet Duyvendak challenges some of the standard views on late 19th-century reading behaviour among women. Her analysis of the Ladies' Reading Museum in The Hague around the turn of the century shows that more women read foreign literature in the original language than is generally assumed, attesting the changing appreciation of English letters. Also the standard view that foreign literature was mainly French and German needs to be put in perspective: the list of English works purchased by the Ladies Reading Museum, Duyvendak found, was more substantial than the list of French works. In "Feminism in Translation: Re-Writing the Rights of Women" Laura Kirkley discusses Wollstonecraft's *Vindication of the Rights of Woman* (1792) in the Dutch translation of 1797 by Ysbrand van Hamelsveld. By way of comparative analysis, Kirkley demonstrates that the Dutch translation is in fact nothing but a translation of a contemporary German translation, thereby providing a fine example of the refracting power of translation: what originally was a radical and proto-typical feminist text was turned by Hamelsveld into an instrument aimed at manufacturing consent to the more conservative ideas about feminist discourses that had gained foothold in many of the German states in response to the French revolution. In the concluding essay by Suzan van Dijk and Stephanie Walker, "What Literary Historians 'Forgot'", the authors contrast the selective list of women authors included in Riewald and Bakker's *Critical Reception of American Literature in the Netherlands 1824-1900* (1982) with the number of women authors itemized in the *WomenWriters* database (since 2004). Based on the discrepancy between both listings, Van Dijk and Walker conclude with a strong plea for greater (electronic) systematization of research data.

In a final coda ("To be continued"), Van Dijk and Walker notice that with the accumulation of empirical data concerning women authors, research becomes ever more complex. Nothing could be more true about the overall project that gave shape to the collection of essays you are about to read: the attempt to 'map' Anglo-Dutch literary dynamics in the 19th-century, too, proves to be increasingly difficult and challenging. Twenty years after Raymond Van den Broeck, we feel confident nevertheless that future research, both empirical and theoretical, will help us step by step to uncover the contours of the mysterious figure in the carpet.

Bibliography

Andringa, Els. "Penetrating the Dutch Polysystem: The Reception of Virginia Woolf, 1920-2000." *Poetics Today* 27:3 (2006): 501-567.

Breedveld, Hella & Ton Naaijkens, eds. *Vertaalwetenschap anno 2000.* Special issue of *Filter* 7:2 (2000). Nijmegen: Van Tilt.

de Clercq, Martine, Tom Toremans and Walter Verschueren, eds. *Textual Mobility and Cultural Transmission*. Leuven: Leuven University Press, 2006.

Dorleijn, Gillis J. and Kees van Rees, eds. *De productie van literatuur: Het literaire veld in Nederland 1800-2000*. Nijmegen: Van Tilt, 2006.

Downs, Brian. "Anglo-Dutch Literary Relations, 1867-1900: Some Notes and Tentative Inferences." *Modern Language Review* 31 (July 1936): 289-346.

Hermans, Theo. *Studies over Nederlandse vertalingen: een bibliografische lijst.* 's Gravenhage: Stichting Bibliographia Neerlandica, 1991.

Koster, Cees. *De Hollandse vertaalmolen.* 's Gravenhage: Stichting Bibliographia Neerlandica, 2002.

———, ed. *Tussen roem en vergetelheid. Terug naar de negentiende eeuw*. Special issue of *Filter* 14:3 (2007).

Mathijsen, Marita, *Nederlandse literatuur in de romantiek 1820-1880*. Nijmegen: Van Tilt, 2004.

Schoneveld, Cornelis W., ed. *Sea Changes: Studies in Three Centuries of Anglo-Dutch Cultural Transmission.* Studies in Comparative Literature 8. Amsterdam: Rodopi, 1996.

Van den Broeck, Raymond. *Literatuur van elders: over het vertalen en de studie van vertaalde literatuur in het Nederlands.* Leuven: Acco, 1988.

Notes

1 "Sinds een paar decennia is de belangstelling voor vertaalde literatuur binnen de literatuurstudie fel toegenomen. Het in de jaren zestig op gang gekomen receptie-onderzoek, waarin de nadruk vooral op het effect en de functie van literaire teksten voor hun ontvangers kwam te liggen, is daar zeker niet vreemd aan geweest. In steeds sterkere mate zijn literatuuronderzoekers zich gaan interesseren voor de mediërende rol van vertalingen in de contacten tussen literaturen en culturen, de manier waarop vertalingen binnen de ontvangende literatuur functioneren en het belang van vertaalde teksten voor de ontwikkeling van de nationale literaturen." (7)

[2] "[...] een groot deel van het letterkundig vertaalonderzoek wordt ingevuld door receptieonderzoek, al dan niet in historisch perspectief, waarbij een notie van vertalen als vorm van receptie wordt gehanteerd, en een functiegericht uitgangspunt is gekozen." (Breedveld and Naaijkens 5)

[3] The term 'Anglophone' in the title suggests that the present volume deals with more than the reception of English literature alone. Various contributions also discuss the reception of American and Irish authors in the Low Countries. If the term 'English literature' nevertheless continues to appear in many contributions, it does so mostly as a *19th-century* reference to literature coming from the United Kingdom (including Irish and Scottish literature).

[4] See Cornelis W. Schoneveld's essay "B.S. Nayler, Promoter of English Letters in Holland, 1820-1848" in Schoneveld (139-63).

[5] Both Beets and ten Kate, however, were quite active in the translation of English poetry. Beets is particularly known for his translation of selected poems by Lord Byron and Walter Scott; Ten Kate translated works by Shakespeare, Milton, Byron and Thomas Moore.

[6] The 'Tachtiger Movement' or Movement of the Eighties was a highly influential group of poets and critics, including Willem Kloos (1859-1938), Albert Verwey (1865-1937), Frederik van Eeden (1860-1932), Lodewijk van Deyssel (1864-1952) and Herman Gorter (1864-1927). Whereas in the field of poetry, the 'Tachtigers' proved to be essentially Romantics, who strove for "the most individual expression of the most individual emotion" (Kloos), in the field of prose they paved the way for late 19th-century naturalism.

[7] For an overview of existing studies see Hermans.

[8] A good example of such a challenge is the way in which Dickens and Eliot were received in Holland and Flanders as examples of 'good' realism versus the 'bad' realism of the French authors such as Emile Zola and Gustave Flaubert.

[9] For the moment, the place of translation(s) in Dorleijn & van Rees's model for 19th-century institutional analysis remains 'invisible'. Its absence from the model, however, can be explained by the fact that translation(s) seem to have an impact on various levels. A successful translation clearly plays an important role at the level of symbolic production (the creation of values), which in turn may have ramifications on the level of material production (the success of a give translation may encourage publishers, for instance, to issue other works by the same author or similar works by other authors) and on the level of distribution outlets (booksellers, libraries, reading societies).

[10] "[het Vlaamse veld heeft] een eigen status [...] een eigen geschiedenis, eigen instituties en spelers en bovendien met eigen maatschappelijke systemen is verbonden." (23)

PART 1

The Critical Reception and Translation of English Literature in the Netherlands

Cees Koster (Universiteit Utrecht)

Fame and Fortune in the Field of Shakespeare Translation: The Case of A.S. Kok

In the second half of the 19th century, the field of reception and translation of Shakespeare's works in the Netherlands seems to have come of age, certainly when taking into consideration the situation in the major cultural centres on the continent as a criterion of maturity. In that period two complete translations were published: a prose translation of the complete dramatic works by A.S. Kok, published between 1873 and 1880, and a verse translation of the complete works (the poems included) by L.A.J. Burgersdijk, published between 1884 and 1888. The last quarter of the century also saw the rise of a modern practice of performances of Shakespeare drama and of a serious form of more academically oriented Shakespeare criticism, with some contributions to German periodicals. A final development testifying to the maturity of a Dutch field of Shakespeare activity is the publication of several school editions of some of the plays for use in a newly established type of secondary education. The latter phenomenon may be taken as an indication that, in terms of his position in the Dutch canon, Shakespeare was no longer purely reserved for the literary and cultural elite, as seems to have been the case in the first half of the 19th century. This turn was partly induced by marked changes in the socio-economic and cultural circumstances in the Netherlands in that period, particularly in the fields of printed media and education.

In my article on "Netwerken op z'n negentiende-eeuws", I dealt with the way Burgersdijk got access to the field of Shakespeare translation. I demonstrated that, with the support of the critic Anton Loffelt, he started a campaign in literary magazines and in the theatre field to establish his authority. In his articles Loffelt spoke highly of Burgersdijk's unpublished translations and published passages to prove his point. Together they found publishers willing to distribute Burgersdijk's translations and theatre companies willing to perform the plays in his translation. He got access to the field, then, on the grounds of his merits as a translator, which Loffelt helped him to establish. Changing circumstances within the field of theatre, where companies finally decided to stage Shakespeare in a modern fashion, also made it possible for him to establish his credibility. In public readings, Burgersdijk presented himself as the only true Shakespeare translator ("above everyone else"). In his private letters to Loffelt, he fiercely criticized Kok for his supposed incompetence and his choice for a prose translation.

In this article I would like to focus on the earlier of the two translators who took upon them the task of making the works of Shakespeare available to a Dutch audience: A.S. Kok. The most obvious, but still interesting question is how they came to choose such distinctly different strategies in such a short time span. Was that a matter of personal choice, a purely individual difference in translation poetics? Did Kok work from entirely different circumstances, and did he have a different set of options to choose from?

The translator as cultural mediator

My own theoretical interest here lies in exploring the possibilities of a focus on the historical dynamics of translation (and perhaps also reception), in which the translator as a cultural agent plays a central role. This is of course nothing new, although I do not know of any attempts to approach the history of translation into Dutch from this angle.

Such an approach fits in with recent developments within Translation Studies, in which a sociological approach to the phenomenon of translation is combined with literary and translational history. Whereas within Descriptive Translation Studies the study of the social and cultural aspects of translation was traditionally mainly restricted to the position of texts as objects in a system, recent approaches, inspired by the sociological paradigm of Pierre Bourdieu, are more focused on the study of translators as human mediators.[1] Within a sociological approach, "the agents of intermediation and the processes of importing and receiving in the recipient country" (Heilbron and Shapiro 95) are just one aspect of study, next to the structure of the field of international cultural exchanges and the types of constraints that influence these exchanges. Within a literary historical approach, the focus on the mediators may be particularly useful, "since the human agent necessarily brings together several social and cultural fields" (Pym "Introduction" 23). By looking at the individuals, we do not have to restrict ourselves to their actions as translators of texts, we can look into any aspect relevant to their cultural practices. The orientation towards the individual is a trend that can be found within sociology as well, in the work of Bernard Lahire, for instance, who is working towards a 'sociology of the individual', a notion which has recently been picked up within Translation Studies as well.

It must be said, however, that my focus on the individual is embedded within a reception-historical framework that is centered around a specific author. This means that not all aspects of an individual's practices are equally relevant. That need not be a problem: Kok, for instance, not only translated Shakespeare's works but also Dante's *Divine Comedy*, and his practices differ for both authors. This may be taken as an indication that both practices pertain to different (sub)fields, in which different circumstances prevail and with differing dynamics. The practices of the translator as a cultural mediator, then, will be the main focus here. And, beyond these practices, the motives, intentions and interests from which translators act; their dispositions, their social, cultural and educational backgrounds; and, finally, their status and positions within the field or fields they are active in.

Before looking specifically into Kok's practices, we should turn one more theoretical stone, concerning the use of the term 'field'. It is widely acknowledged that it is not unproblematic to apply the term in any strict Bourdieusian sense to the phenomenon of translation. In dealing with literary translation in Israel, Rakefet Sela-Sheffy remarks: "Because these translators are seen as (secondary) agents in the context of the literary field, their forming a separate, self-directed social configuration is often taken to be questionable" (10). She sidesteps the problem herself: "There is no need to try and determine to what extent literary translators operate as part of the literary field, or form a separate field of their own. Both perspectives are right". Even in a predominantly semi-professional field, she continues, translators "develop a specific 'feel of the game' that qualifies them to play in the field of translation [...], if by a 'field' we mean a stratified space of positions, with people struggling to occupy these positions driven by a specific kind of incentives and gratifications, then translators [...] also form a distinctive field of action" (11).

It may be a giant leap from 20th-century Hebrew translation to 19th-century Dutch Shakespeare translation, but it can be a small epistemological step – justified, I would argue, by the idea that in the case of the struggle between Burgersdijk and Kok we can at least speak of an emerging field or "translation space" (the term preferred by Michaela Wolf (135)). The very fact that two totally different translations of (virtually) the same work were published in such a short time may, again, be taken as an indication here: the incentive could have been the prospect of earning the title of, or being remembered as, the first Dutch translator of the complete works of Shakespeare.

A.S. Kok: teacher and translator

Kok may be a forgotten hero, whose afterlife (at least until now) consists mostly of references in footnotes and bibliographies, and his work as a translator may have been eclipsed by that of others, but as to the social and cultural upward mobility that became typically possible in Dutch society in the second half of the 19th century, he may serve as a great illustration.

In 1880, when the project of his complete translation of the dramatic works was finished and a five-volume set was published in Amsterdam by G.L. Funke, Kok's career as translator and critic already had been going on for about 20 years.

In the first five years of that career, things went fast as far as translation was concerned. In 1859, at the age of 28, Kok made his debut as a critic and a translator in the most prestigious literary periodical of the time, *De Gids*, with the article "Iets over Shaksperes sonnetten" ["Thoughts on Shakespeare's sonnets"]. This article was the first substantial piece of criticism in the Netherlands on the sonnets and also contained the first Dutch translation of a selection of them. In subsequent years, an impressive list of publications appeared. In 1860 two verse translations appeared in the series "Buitenlandsche Klassiekers" ["Classics from abroad"] published by Kruseman: *Hamlet* and *Orlando en Rosalinde* (a translation of *As you like it*). In 1861 a translation of *Richard III* was published by the publishing house of Loman (Kruseman had discontinued his series for lack of commercial success). In 1863 an educational anthology edited by Kok (under the title *English Poetry*) was published by Van Nooten, and in 1863-4 Kruseman published Kok's complete translation of Dante's *Divine Comedy* in three volumes. It may seem as if Kok's productivity as a translator was enormous, but since Kok was no professional translator, and actually had a full-fledged career in an adjacent field as a teacher in secondary education (of which more later), we may assume that he made them over a longer period of time and held them in stock.

The aspect of professionalism is an interesting matter in this context. Defining professionalism in any translation field, particularly with respect to the past, is quite complicated. With Ton van Kalmthout, we can define professionalism in the field of translation as "a daily task for providing one's means of living, for which qualifications, procedures and codes of behaviour are established, in the form of education and self-reflection" (11, my translation). In this sense, professionalism in the field of translation (and particularly literary translation) cannot have existed in the Netherlands until well into the 20th century, as there were no qualifications and forms of education specific for translation before World War II. As for the criterion of livelihood, there is no doubt that professional book translation existed as early as the 18th century,[2] though it seems to have been restricted to popular books and magazines. The main indication for the existence of such a field are the advertisements in which translators presented themselves to publishers that appeared regularly in *Het nieuwsblad voor den boekhandel*, the periodical of the Dutch association for publishers.[3] As far as professionalism is concerned, there still seemed to be a division in the 19th century between the translation of popular books, on the one hand, and the translation of canonized literature, on the other. In the latter field, mainly non-professional or semi-professional translators were active, and the grounds on which they considered themselves qualified for the task vary greatly. Access to the field was mainly given on the grounds of literary authority. J.J.L. ten Kate, one of the famous 19th-century vicar-poets and active in the same period as Kok, for instance, was a prolific translator of canonical works from German, English, French, and Italian. His main qualification, as was noted at the time, was his aptitude for versification – his educational background (an academic degree in theology) certainly did not qualify him for translating works from modern foreign languages.[4] In grammar school, modern languages were not on the curriculum, so he will have been mainly self-taught (or did not translate directly from all those languages, as has been insinuated regularly during his life by his more malignant critics).

What, then, were the qualifications that would make Kok a credible Shakespeare translator? How did he get to know his English and his Shakespeare? And how did he get to find his way into the field?

Kok's professional career as a teacher started well before 1859, and may be taken as an example for the kind of social and cultural upward mobility that was made possible by the emergence of a middle class halfway through the 19th century. The field of education underwent the most profound changes in the progress towards modernity in the Netherlands in the 19th century. Kok made his way through the entire system of elementary and secondary education. In his introduction to the "Levensbericht" ["Obituary"] that Kok wrote about himself for the yearbook of the Maatschappij der Nederlandse Letterkunde [Society of Dutch Literature], B.H.C.K. van Wijck, professor in Philosophy at Utrecht University, stated: "So his life became, once he had left his childhood behind him, a continuous self-education toward that high rank, which he conquered for himself step-by-step in the world of the mind." (79) With respect to Kok's self-image, the "Obituary" is an interesting case in itself, so a short excursion might be in place.

Every member of the Society of Dutch Literature – to which Kok was appointed in 1863 through the agency of Johannes van Vloten – was (and still is) commemorated in the yearbook, most of the time by someone close to the person in question. Some time before Kok's death the Board of the Society had complained that it was hard to find qualified and suitable authors for the obituaries, which Kok took as an invitation to write his own. After some contemplation and consultation with the widow, the Society decided that it should be published. We should be grateful, both to Kok and the Society, for there is hardly any historical documentation on Kok, no archive of his has survived, and the letters that have survived are scattered in the archives of the people he wrote to. As is the case with any ego document, the "Obituary" should be dealt with circumspectly, but it is still extremely useful, all the more since it is the main source for personal information about Kok's professional life.

Immediately after Kok finished elementary school in Amsterdam, he started working as an apprentice teacher. He does not speak highly of the elementary school he went to as a child. His family must have belonged to the protestant lower middle class. There were books in the house – Kok specifically mentions *The Pilgrim's Progress* and the Bible – but there seems to have been no money for an education at a Latin school, which would have prepared him for university. Apprentice teachers could, after taking exams for which they had to prepare by self-study, be promoted to a higher rank. Kok took all those exams and also must have acquired qualifications for teaching subjects in secondary education. During those studies he acquainted himself thoroughly with both Dutch and foreign literatures, and it is from this period that his interest in Shakespeare dates. In the "Obituary", Kok writes about his extensive walks in the rural areas around Amsterdam and recalls a visit to the dunes overlooking the ruins of Brederode Castle where he sat down and read *Hamlet* for the first time (the "Obituary" is full of romantic self-images like these). His interest in Shakespeare and the English language and literature led him to quit his job as a teacher, lend a sum of money and go to London. There he studied for months at the British Museum and visited performances of Shakespeare's plays. This was not an uncommon way for Dutch students of English to prepare for exams. Kok is never very specific about dates, so it is not clear when he went to England and how long he actually stayed there, but it must have been near the end of the 1850s. On his return, he started working as a private teacher.

In 1863 a new education law in the Netherlands provided for the establishment of a new type of secondary education: the Higher Burgher Schools (HBS), which did not prepare for university, but for all kinds of middle class jobs in trade and commerce. Modern foreign languages were a compulsory subject in this type of education (in contrast to the grammar schools and the Latin schools) and one needed teachers who were qualified for this level of education. Kok had the right qualifications (undoubtedly supported by his translations) and was appointed as a teacher of Dutch and English at the HBS of Roermond – thus landing himself in the upper middle class. He remained a HBS-teacher for the rest of his working life.

For want of an academic infrastructure in foreign languages and literatures (the first chair in English in the Netherlands was not to be founded until 1885[5]), teachers of foreign languages at the level of the HBS found their way into the fields of criticism and translation. Dutch Shakespeare criticism in the final quarter of the 19th century was dominated by critics who also worked as teachers (or had been educated to become one) at one of the Higher Burgher Schools. They had professionally acquired the knowledge of languages and literatures that provided them with the proper means to fulfil those expert positions.[6] So Kok was no exception. Still, being a teacher does not qualify one automatically to enter the field of literary translation. The social and cultural capital Kok had acquired was not necessarily in the right currency. How, then, did he actually get access to the field?

Kok's position in the field of translation

As we have seen, Kok's first publication was an article on the sonnets in *De Gids* in 1859. In the "Obituary", he relates how his professional network helped him in finding his way to a public position. Johannes C. Zimmerman, one of the editors of *De Gids*, was also on the board of governors of the school Kok worked at. He stimulated Kok in his studies and provided him with the possibility to publish and to present himself as an expert on Shakespeare. The following year, his first translation of a full play appeared (*Hamlet*). He had started out translating Shakespeare (and Dante) as part of his studies, not with the idea of publishing them. In 1852 the publishing house of Cornelis Kruseman had started the series "Buitenlandsche klassieken" ["Classics from abroad"], in which they had published reprints of earlier Shakespeare translations (*Othello*, *Macbeth*, *De Storm*, [*The Tempest*] and *Romeo en Julia*) by Jurriaan Moulijn. Moulijn's translations had originally been published in the 1830s and were metrical, philological translations, very much in the Romantic mode that was typical of German Shakespeare translation at that time, but was not current in the Netherlands. When Kruseman heard of Kok's translations, he was interested in publishing them, but did not feel qualified to judge their merits. The translations by Moulijn (a civil servant from Kampen) had been published under the supervision of Johannes van Vloten, who at that time held a chair in Dutch language and literature at the Deventer Athenaeum. It was not uncommon for men of cultural stature to lend their name to the publications of authors with less prestige. As a publishing strategy it helped to transfer the necessary prestige to the newcomer.

Kruseman applied the same strategy to Kok's translation of *Hamlet*. Not only was the supervision mentioned on the title page, a preface by Van Vloten was included in the edition, in which he praised "the important piece" on the sonnets and said to be "happy to associate his name to this honourable enterprise". In the edition of *Orlando en Rosalinde* a preface was apparently no longer needed, and the book only contains a dedication to Van Vloten. That Kok was considered to have made his own name, may be inferred from the fact that the next translations, including that of the *Divina Commedia*, did not contain any references to supervision.

Kok's position in the field is further determined by the translation strategies he opted for and the ways these strategies related to the options available in the wider field of literary translation.

The edition of his Dante translation contains an explicit self-declaration as to the kind of strategy chosen: it is announced as a "metrical translation". In the final volume Kok also included a short postscript in which he justified his way of translating. No such reflections can be found in any of his Shakespeare translations. The self-declaration of the *Hamlet* translation runs "naar het Engelsch van William Shakspere" ["after the English by William Shakespeare"]. There are extensive explanatory notes on the text, but none on Kok's translation poetics. In the bibliography added to the "Obituary" in the yearbook of the Society of Dutch literature, however, a line is added to the lemma of *Hamlet*, which runs "translated after the form of the original" (102).

For Kok the translations marked his entrance to the field of Shakespeare reception, as much as his Dante translation earned him a place in the emerging field of Dante reception. Until the early 1880s, he regularly published Shakespeare and Dante criticism in *De Gids* and *De Portefeuille* (the journal edited by Taco de Beer, his fellow HBS teacher). Among his contributions in *De Gids* was an extensive and sympathetic review in 1867 of a school edition of *Hamlet* by Anton Loffelt, whom he also knew from HBS circles. As far as translation was concerned, however, nothing much happened in the years following the early surge. In the early 1870s, Kok edited two school editions in English, *Julius Caesar* and *Richard III*.

In 1872, however, things changed rapidly. Kruseman had discontinued his series in 1864 and sold the rights of the books to the Amsterdam publisher G.L. Funke, who was interested in publishing all the plays in translation. In the introduction to the first volume of the 1880 complete edition Kok speaks of an "invitation" of the publisher to translate the complete plays of Shakespeare. Between 1872 and 1879 Kok published translations of all the plays – this time, however Shakespeare's verse was transformed into prose. Funke did not put much effort into making sophisticated looking books of this series. The volumes were slim, the quality of the paper was poor – the idea must have been to keep it cheap.[7] Only at the end of the project, in 1880, the translations appeared together in seven bound volumes. Unfortunately no documentation survives of the contact between Kok and Funke, which means that we can only speculate on the reasons why Kok made this dramatic poetical turn. Everything Kok has said on the subject dates from well after the publication of the translations, and must be interpreted as a reaction to the public discussion generated by his translation.

The prose translation goes against anything Kok publicly stated in relation to his Dante translation, i.e. that the form of the original should be retained to guarantee the integrity of the work of art, even though readability should be a factor too – a view on translation that at that time had begun to establish itself in the wider field of literary translation in the Netherlands.[8] We must assume that the publisher convinced Kok to do it otherwise and let readability prevail. Apparently the publisher must have thought that there was no market for metrical and poetical translations of Shakespeare plays, which was not an uncommon idea among cultural brokers.[9] Kok did not have the power, nor felt the need, to resist his publisher, or must have felt that he could get away with it – the decision to comply (if that was the case) was fully his.

One might say that Kok did get away with it, as there was hardly any critical reaction to the project – in fact, there seems to have been hardly any reaction at all. As early as 1873, after the first nine instalments, C. Stoffel (teacher of English in secondary education) wrote a philological review, full of amendments and micro-criticism in the literary periodical *Vaderlandsche Letteroefeningen*. In 1878, however, Loffelt – by then no longer a teacher and working his way into the field of literary and theatre journalism – in a discussion of several translations of separate plays published the years before ("Shakespeare-vertalingen"), publicly chided Kok for his prose translations, after praising him for his metrical translations:

> Kok's translations may boast on a high degree of accuracy as to meaning, but his use of Dutch is not always as fluent as one might wish. […] Of late Kok has agreed to continue his translations in prose, presumably to more easily fulfil a task already undertaken, namely providing us with a complete Shakespeare in Dutch. This effort does not testify to the same accuracy that we have come to expect of this meritorious man of letters. […]
> We do not believe that Kok's prose translations will last very long.[10]

In a letter to Loffelt, Kok reacted furiously to what he called the "ungentlemanlike insinuation" that he had changed to prose to make it easier for himself. He did not, however, give reasons for his turn to prose and made no attempt to defend his choice.

Only in 1880, in the introduction to the seven-volume edition, did Kok undertake an effort tot defend himself. In a rather elastic discourse, he simultaneously argued that he did not want to follow the iambic pentameter because he did not intend to make a translation for the stage, *and* denied that one can speak of a prose translation:

> By way of information for those who might believe that the translator has let himself be guided by a somewhat elastic conscience, may serve the fact that separate plays or passages, that already existed in manuscript, has been reworked by him since he established his opinions on these point.
> Now, an altogether different question is whether one has the right to speak of a prose translation, as has been done. This I deny. In some passages, who are distinctly lyrical in nature, I did follow the metre. I felt that the requirements of form were so tangibly predominant that the spirit of the original forced the metre. I did however stick to my original principal by not painstakingly transforming ten syllables of the original into the same amount of Dutch syllables.[11]

That Kok felt forced to defend himself in such strained discourse may be taken as an indication that he felt marginalized. Loffelt went on to praise Moulijn (by thirty years Kok's predecessor) over Kok and in the next issue of *De Nederlandsche Spectator* started his campaign to promote Burgersdijk, who by that time already had translated several plays and all of the sonnets.

Conclusion

For Kok the moment had passed. He had entered the field on a glorious note, on the authority of others, gained prestige on his own merit (after all Loffelt still did call him a "meritorious man of letters") and achieved a central position as translator and critic. He might have been in the position to make a lasting impression. If he had continued to produce verse translations, his work may have lasted longer and it might have been Kok and not Burgersdijk who would have been remembered in the field as *the* 19th-century translator of Shakespeare's works.

But the decision to change to prose translations turned him into a marginal figure. That is, as far as Shakespeare translations are concerned. When studying Kok's bibliography of criticism, one of the striking features is that he gradually writes less and less about Shakespeare and at some point even falls silent. Dante criticism, in contrast, is something he remained active in throughout his life. Although in Kok's lifetime four other translations of the *Divine Comedy* appeared, nobody doubted his position. He proved to have "the feel of the game", but in the Shakespeare field decided to play by different rules.

Perhaps Kok was not powerful enough to overrule or convince his publisher, or perhaps he didn't even try. Either way he must have been uncomfortable with the result, both in terms of his translation ethics and of his prestige.

In the "Obituary", his tone is no longer defensive, but outright defeatist. And perhaps one of the reasons that he wrote his own obituary was to take one last opportunity to respond to his critics and from the grave to try to modify the image as Shakespeare translator he felt existed of him: "Whatever one may find fault with it, the labor was undertaken and fulfilled with love, even though the form differed from my other Shakespeare translations I mentioned earlier." (99)

Bibliography

Colmjon, Gerben. *De oorsprongen van de renaissance der litteratuur in Nederland in het laatste kwart der negentiende eeuw*. Arnhem: van Loghum Slaterus, 1947.

Heilbron, Johan and Gisèle Shapiro. "Outline for a Sociology of Translation. Current Issues and Future Prospects." *Constructing a Sociology of Translation*. Eds. Michaela Wolf and Alexandra Fukari. Amsterdam/Philadelphia: John Benjamins, 2007. 93-108.

Kok, A.S. "Iets over Shaksperes sonnetten." *De Gids* 23.1 (1859): 252-268.

———. "Levensbericht van A.S. Kok. 10 Juni 1831–15 Januari 1915. Autobiografische aanteekeningen. Met een inleidend woord van Jhr. Dr. B.H.C.K. van der Wijck." *Jaarboek van de Maatschappij der Nederlandse Letterkunde, 1915*. 78–108. 1 April 2008. <http://www.dbnl.nl/tekst/_jaa003191501_01/_jaa003191501_01_0013.htm>.

Korpel, Luc. *Over het nut en de wijze der vertalingen. Nederlandse vertaalreflectie (1750-1820) in een Westeuropees kader*. Amsterdam: Rodopi, 1992.

Koster, Cees. *De Hollandsche vertaalmolen. Nederlandse beschouwingen over vertalen 1820-1885*. Den Haag: Stichting Bibliographia Neerlandica, 2002.

———. "Netwerken op z'n negentiende-eeuws. A.C. Loffelt en L.A.J. Burgersdijk als pleitbezorgers van hun Shakespeare." *Filter, tijdschrift over vertalen en vertaalwetenschap* 14.3 (2007): 23-38.

Kuitert, Lisa. *Het ene boek in vele delen. De uitgave van literaire series in Nederland, 1850-1900*. Amsterdam: Buitenkant, 1993.

Lahire, Bernard. "From the Habitus to an Individual Heritage of Dispositions. Towards a Sociology at the Level of the Individual." *Poetics* 31 (2003): 329-355.

Leek, Robert. *Shakespeare in Nederland: kroniek van vier eeuwen Shakespeare in Nederlandse vertalingen en op het Nederlands toneel*. Zutphen: De Walburg Pers, 1988.

Loffelt A.C. "Nieuwe Nederlandsche Shakespeare-vertalingen." *De Nederlandsche Spectator* (27 juni 1878): 172–174.

———. "Shakespeare-vertalingen." *De Nederlandsche Spectator* (3 juli 1878): 178–179.

Ploeger, Lieke. "Tussen christendom en poëzie – J.J.L. ten Kate als vertaler." *Filter, tijdschrift over vertalen en vertaalwetenschap* 13.2 (2006): 49-54.

Pym, Anthony. *Method in Translation History*. Manchester: St. Jerome Publishing, 1998.

——— "Introduction." *Sociocultural Aspects of Translating and Interpreting*. Eds. Anthony Pym et al. Amsterdam/Philadelphia: John Benjamins, 2006. 9-25.

Rössing, J.H. *De Koninklijke Vereeniging Het Nederlandsch Tooneel. Bijdrage tot de geschiedschrijving van het tooneel in Nederland, gedurende meer dan een halve eeuw*. Amsterdam: N.V. De erven H. van Munster & Zoon, 1916.

Sela-Sheffy, Rakefet. "How to Be a (Recognized) Translator. Rethinking Habitus, Norms, and the Field of Translation." *Target* 17.1 (2005): 1-26.

Shakespeare, William. *Shakespeare's dramatische werken*. Vertaald en toegelicht door A.S. Kok. 5 vols. Amsterdam: G.L. Funke, 1873-1880.

——— *De werken van William Shakespeare*. Vertaald door Dr. L.A.J. Burgerdijk. 12 vols. Leiden E.J. Brill, 1884-1888.

Stoffel, C. "Shakespeare's Dramatische Werken. Vertaald en toegelicht door A.S. Kok, Leeraar aan de Rijks Hoogere Burgerschool te Roermond. Afl. 1-9. Amsterdam: G.L. Funke." *Vaderlandsche Letteroefeningen, bibliografisch deel* (1873): 383-396.

van Kalmthout, Ton. "Middelaars tussen de grote volken. Literatuuronderwijs en vertaalwezen in Nederland, 1880-1940." *Filter, tijdschrift over vertalen en vertaalwetenschap* 14.3 (2007): 5-12.

Wilhelm, F.A. *English in The Netherlands. A history of foreign language teaching 1800–1920. With a bibliography of textbooks*. Nijmegen: Radboud Universiteit, 2005.

Wolf, Michaela. "The Female State of the Art: Women in the 'Translation Field'." *Sociocultural Aspects of Translating and Interpreting*. Eds. Anthony Pym at al. Amsterdam/Philadelphia: John Benjamins, 2006. 129-141.

Notes

1 See, for example, Pym's *Method in Translation History* and his "Introduction" to the volume on *Sociocultural Aspects of Translating and Interpreting*.

2 For a more detailed discussion of this period, see Korpel's *Over het nut en de wijze van vertalingen*.

3 See Colmjon's *De oorspong van de renaissance*.

4 On ten Kate, see Ploeger's "Tussen christendom en poëzie".

5 See Willhelm's *English in the Netherlands*.

6 Other notable examples include Anton Loffelt and Taco de Beer (see Ton van Kalmthout's contribution to the present volume).

7 See also Leek's *Shakespeare in Nederland*.

8 For a more detailed discussion of the translation poetics at the time, see my *De Hollandsche vertaalmolen*.

9 H.J. Schimmel, for instance, at that time playwright and managing director of one the most prestigious Dutch theatre companies, considered himself an admirer of Shakespeare, but kept his plays off the stage because in his mind the Dutch theatregoers were not ready for such complicated matter. See Rössing's description of the Dutch theatre scene in his *De Koninklijke Vereeniging Het Nederlandsch Tooneel*.

10 "Wel kunnen Koks metrische vertalingen op vrij groote nauwkeurigheid van zin bogen, maar het Nederlandsch is niet immer zoo vloeiend als men het wenschen zou [...]. In den laatsten tijd heeft Kok goedgevonden zijn vertalingen verder in proza voort te zetten, waarschijnlijk om zoodoende gemakkelijker een aanvaarde taak te volbrengen, namelijk

een volledigen Shakespeare in 't Nederlandsch te bezorgen. Die arbeid getuigt niet van de dezelfde nauwgezetheid waaraan die verdienstelijke letterkundige ons gewend had [...]. Wij gelooven niet dat de proza-vertalingen van Kok lang het veld zullen behouden." (172)

[11] "Tot naricht van hen, die soms mochten meenen, dat de vertaling zich door een enigszins ruim geweten heeft laten leiden, diene overigens dat onderscheiden stukken of gedeelten, die reeds lang in handschrift bestonden, door hem opnieuw bewerkt zijn, sedert zijn meening op dit punt zich vestigde.

Een andere vraag is nu, of men hier het recht heeft van een prozavertaling te spreken, gelijk gedaan is. Dat ontken ik. In enkele gedeelten, die een stellig lyrisch karakter hebben, heb ik wel degelijk het metrum gevolgd. Ik meende dat daarbij de eischen van den vorm zoo tastbaar overheerschend waren, dat de geest van het oorspronkelijke het metrum noodzakelijk maakte. Daarbij bleef ik echter mijn aangenomen beginsel getrouw, door juist niet angstvallig een tiental lettergrepen van het oorspronkelijke in een zelfde aantal Hollandsche lettergrepen over te gieten." (35)

Ton van Kalmthout (Huygens Instituut, Den Haag)

Eccentric Authors: Cd. Busken Huet and Taco H. de Beer on English Literature

At the time of his sudden death, Conrad Busken Huet (1826-1886) was working on an essay in which he wrote: "No Dutch author in the last fifty years has written any Dutch book, whether in prose or in verse, that is valued by the rest of Europe."[1] In the light of this opinion, it is not surprising that Busken Huet's interests had become increasingly international in the course of his career. His name is bound to crop up in any study of literary relations between the United Kingdom and the Netherlands. In his home country he is regarded as one of the foremost literary critics and cultural historians of the 19th century and his essays are deemed to have established not just a national literary canon, but also an international one. More incidentally, Busken Huet was also responsible, together with his wife Anne, for the translation of a number of English-language novels into Dutch.[2]

A second name worth noting in this context is that of Taco Hajo de Beer (1838-1923). In the late 19th century, he was also regarded as an important literary critic. Indeed, his opinions carried such clout that in 1883, when he published a review in a weekly magazine called *De Portefeuille* appearing to cast a shadow on the reputation of the popular author Louise Stratenus, she accused him of making it well-nigh impossible for her to get her work published in the future.[3] His role as a heavyweight on the cultural scene of the time is also clear from his appearance in Willem Paap's 1884 roman à clef, *De Bombono's* [*The Bombono Family*]. The novel is a satire on the Dutch literary establishment of the day and the protagonist is based on de Beer.[4]

Like Busken Huet, de Beer managed to reconcile cosmopolitan interests with a nationalist frame of mind. But what exactly did the two of them have to do with English literature? This article discusses their respective views on English literature and the ways in which they brought it under the attention of Dutch readers. It sets out to explore the part both critics played in the reception of English literature in the Netherlands and the types of English literature involved. Since far less is known about de

Beer,[5] he is the chief focus of attention. My remarks are based not only on his published works, but also on a selection of his surviving letters. I begin, however, by discussing Busken Huet's discussion of English authors in the 26-volume collection of his main critical writings, entitled *Litterarische fantasiën en kritieken* [*Literary Fantasies and Criticisms*].

Conrad Busken Huet's critical view

In the history of Dutch literature, Conrad Busken Huet is famous primarily as an ambassador for French literature.[6] However, he also wrote at least fifteen essays about English literature.[7] True, he thought Britain was producing no new young writers of any importance, but then he thought that about France too. And he admired the leading English authors of an earlier generation – authors such as Byron, Dickens and Eliot.[8] Most especially, Busken Huet had a life-long admiration for George Eliot, believing that her objective and psychologically convincing realism was unsurpassed by any other modern writer. His one – not insignificant – reservation on this point concerned the portrayal of the young married heroine of *Middlemarch*: he was dismayed at Eliot's refusal to pursue her otherwise detailed exploration of Dorothea Brooke's emotional life into the bedroom and to address the young woman's repulsion at sexual relations with her much older husband. "So great is the tyranny of English prudishness, to the detriment of art", he was forced to conclude.[9]

This reservation about Eliot suggests the ambivalence of his general attitude towards 19th-century England. He condemned the prudish society of Victorian Britain for trying (albeit in vain) to banish memories of the boisterous immorality still openly displayed in the 18th century (4: 15, 21: 58 and 114). On the other hand, he was impressed by the vitality, fighting spirit and patriotism that had powered the expansion and defence of the British Empire (4: 39-40, 12: 157). Through British history and literature, he wrote, "other nations have come to know the English as a powerful, enterprising, freedom-loving and prosperous nation, inclined to vainglory, eccentric, but high-spirited, hospitable and devoted to their own institutions, their own land, and their own way of life".[10] More recently, however, the English could boast only the glories of the past: "The blood of the nation had turned to milk, tea and sugar".[11] And hypocrisy ruled supreme: "no other society in Europe is so thoroughly permeated with hypocrisy as the English."[12] When he said that the English nation differed from the Dutch in its eccentricity,[13] it was clearly a polite way of expressing his general disapproval of British society. However, his views on the English were considerably more favourable than those he held on the United States, where he feared that the young, culturally impoverished democracy heralded the end of aristocracy and hence of Western civilisation.[14]

Like many people of his time, Busken Huet assumed that developments in a particular language and literature were a close reflection of the moral health of the nation concerned. It is hardly surprising, therefore, that he was as critical of recent English literature as he was of the nation that had produced it. The documentary value he ascribed to works of literature shows just how closely he thought the two were related.[15] He admired Disraeli's novel *Lothair* (1870) as a "slice of English life"[16] and felt that a comedy by Oliver Goldsmith made "a splendid contribution" to knowledge of 18th-century England.[17] Like many contemporary critics, he felt that the success of the best English authors in drawing such a faithful portrait of their nation was due to the fact that they themselves were products of it. Additionally, such authors also devoted themselves to selflessly serving the community.

Milton had likewise set out to serve his native land. Busken Huet felt that *Paradise Lost* marked the close of a period in British history and prophetically announced the role that England was soon to play on the world stage. It was also an inspirational work, in that the outlook on life that it expressed

> appears to have entered the very blood of the English over the last two centuries. […] To think as Milton thought, to feel as Milton felt, to believe, to hope, to love as Milton did, has been perhaps the most distinctive characteristic of the English nation […].[18]

Busken Huet had great respect for such writers, who moved beyond expressing the current preoccupations of their nation so as to play a role in inspiring their society and prophesying new developments in it. Yet he seems to have had a particular sympathy with authors who also criticised mainstream society – authors such as Charles Dickens. Busken Huet certainly did not turn a blind eye to what he saw as the limitations of Dickens' work, but he admired the author as "an opponent of national weaknesses, a reformer of social abuses, a man of the people" and also as "a full-blooded radical, in the English sense of the word".[19] He saw and presented Byron in the same light. In him, he said, English society had encountered an "enemy" who had entirely distanced himself from his native land in order to attack it from overseas – an attitude which Busken Huet felt was tantamount to a "declaration of war" (4: 104-105).

The rebel poet's *Don Juan* was, to his mind, a unique work of unequalled merit. Busken Huet called it, without reservation, the "greatest and most immortal work of English literature in modern times".[20] He was grateful to Byron for exposing "fictitious piety, whitened moral sepulchres, schoolboy learning masquerading as science, and the degeneration of patriotism into self-glorification". But, equally, he understood that anyone who had attacked society as the poet had done could expect outrage and rejection. To be treated as a pariah was the inevitable price to be paid by a genius like Byron (27: 110-111).[21] Moreover, "we think that he was too little of a saint himself to make such a to-do about the lack of true saintliness in others".[22] The question is whether such an 'eccentric' writer could have expected any better treatment at the hands of Taco de Beer.

Taco H. de Beer as a literary mediator

De Beer pursued a teaching career which culminated in a post in English and German at a non-classical grammar school (HBS) in Amsterdam.[23] For a period he also taught history of drama at the theatre school.[24] Like many other teachers of his day in the Netherlands, he supplemented his earnings by producing educational books. In his case, these included lexicographical works, scholarly editions (for example in the short series of foreign works published under the name *Bibliotheek van Buitenlandsche Schrijvers* [*Library of Foreign Authors*][25]), anthologies and histories of literature. His contribution to Jan ten Brink's *Geschiedenis der Noord-Nederlandsche letteren* [*History of Dutch Literature*] is still relevant.[26] In this article, however, we will mainly focus on de Beer's English-language anthology *The Literary Reader*, which will be discussed in more detail below.

Many of his contemporaries will have known de Beer at least in part as a founder and editor of periodicals – of which he edited not less than fourteen. Most of these periodicals were devoted to theatre and the performing arts, language and literature, or the teaching of these subjects. Some, like the weekly magazines *De Amsterdammer* and *De Portefeuille*, covered subjects of wider social and cultural interest.[27] The most important professional journal that de Beer edited was undoubtedly *Noord en Zuid* [*North and South*], which was designed for teachers and student teachers and concentrated mainly on Dutch language and literature. For English literature, readers turned to *Taalstudie*, a periodical that appeared between 1879 and 1891.[28] De Beer supplied copy for all the magazines he edited but he still found time and energy in the course of his career to contribute a stream of poems, novellas, studies, critical pieces and reviews to at least thirty-five other daily, weekly and monthly publications – many of them also relating to education, language and literature.[29] To all this he added a number of prose works, plays for amateur dramatic societies, pamphlets on social and literary issues and, towards the end of his life, a book on the Shakespeare-Bacon theory, discussed at greater length below. Finally, he also produced Dutch translations of novels and plays by past and present French, German and English authors (for clients including what was then the leading Dutch theatre company, the Koninklijke Vereeniging Het Nederlandsch Tooneel).[30] It is perhaps hardly surprising that in 1902 he suffered a nervous breakdown and resigned his teaching post.

That same year, he launched himself as a certified translator with a translation office in Amsterdam (the "Bureau voor Translaten"). Even before this, however, he had apparently acquired something of an international reputation as a go-between in this field. In 1880, the American writer Wendell P. Garrison had asked him to help find a Dutch publisher to issue one of his books in translation.[31] Probably nothing came of it, but Garrison's request shows that de Beer at the time already had a network outside the Netherlands. Garrison was literary editor of the well-known New York weekly *The Nation* and had himself made contact with de Beer two years earlier.[32] This had led to a correspondence and an exchange of periodicals, engravings and even their own portraits.[33] Another foreign contact around this time was J. Stuart Bogg, secretary of the recently established Dramatic Reform Association in Manchester. The association's aims were shared by the Nederlandsch Tooneelverbond ["Dutch Theatre Federation"], whose periodical *Het Nederlandsch Tooneel* was at the time being edited by de Beer. Bogg discussed the efforts of his Association in detail and in return de Beer informed Bogg about the dramatic reform movement in the Netherlands, perhaps also contributing an article to the *Journal of Dramatic Reform* (for which he certainly provided material).[34] The relationship never became particularly close, but it was sufficiently friendly for de Beer to contact Bogg again five years later, when he was trying to arrange an English theatre engagement for a Dutch actress.[35] This was not a one-off incident: de Beer made a practice of acting as an intermediary for people trying to establish themselves abroad. When successful, of course, his reward was yet another informant in a foreign country.[36]

One such person was Johanna Rittner Bos, who helped de Beer to obtain American literary journals. In 1897 she wrote to him from the United States expressing her gratitude for the help he had given her during her student days.[37] At the time of writing she was trying to earn a living in the US as a translator and correspondent for the Dutch press. She was managing to find work in journalism but finding it difficult to obtain attractive literary material to translate. De Beer advised her on how to find a publisher, on copyright matters and on how to establish a claim to translate works by promising authors like rising star Rider Haggard, on whom she had set her sights. He even acted on her behalf in registering an official claim to first refusal on the translation of one of Rider Haggard's novels and in pursuing a payment due from the Bolle publishing company. That firm at least offered her some prospect of translation work, probably once again as a result of de Beer's intervention.[38] In this way, de Beer was gaining experience in the quest for books to translate. His archive includes a postcard from the famous playwright George Bernard Shaw which suggests that de Beer may have enquired about the possibility of translating his work.[39]

It is not clear whether de Beer was successful, but he did make it into the foreign press from time to time, for example with an annual review of recent Dutch literature in the London magazine *The Athenaeum*. And in 1889 the celebrated Dutch translator of Shakespeare, Leendert Burgersdijk, thanked de Beer for an article about his work that had been published in a magazine called *The Comedy*.[40] Through activities like these, de Beer built up an extensive network. He made deliberate use of this network in 1900, when he tried to intervene in the appointment of the new professor of English Literature at the University of Groningen by lobbying on behalf of Francis J. Curtis, an Austrian-based academic.[41] De Beer was unable to whip up support for his candidate and Curtis later obtained a chair in Frankfurt instead. But he felt he owed de Beer a favour and wrote to him that, if he needed a recommendation for his new book, he would comment on it.[42]

The Literary Reader

Despite this plethora of activities, de Beer's most important contribution to the reception of English-language literature in the Netherlands was undoubtedly the anthology mentioned earlier. *The Literary Reader. A Handbook for the Higher Classes in Schools and for Home Teaching* was first published in 1874. It was a multi-volume anthology of extracts from English literature accompanied by historical and biographical notes intended to give "a tolerably accurate idea of the conditions under which these works were composed and the leading characteristics of their author's genius" (de Beer and Irving i) The publication offered samples of the literary heritage "from the remotest times" right up to the present day. In 1882-1883 a second edition,[43] said to be "entirely rewritten", was published in collaboration with Elisabeth Jane Irving, co-editor of de Beer's *Bibliotheek van Buitenlandsche Schrijvers* and an English teacher working in Amsterdam. She would continue to be listed as co-author in later editions, all of which (including a German one) were said to have been "revised and rewritten". By 1907 the anthology consisted of five parts, each containing around 500 pages, and a sixth in manuscript. Four were devoted to the 19th century and two to earlier periods.[44]

The Literary Reader was intended mainly for pupils in the two top years of grammar school education, but was also thought suitable for student teachers. The idea was that one volume should be used in each academic year, although this meant that users had to make choices, given that the relevant school curriculum included only two hours a week on English literature. In any case, the classroom repertoire had to be tailored to pupils' sensibilities. De Beer and Irving stated: "Our aim has been to give a fairly representative selection from English literature, as far as could be done without admitting anything unsuitable for young readers of either sex; either from a moral point of view, or as tending to excite class prejudice, or religious controversy" (1882: II). This posed two problems, especially in relation to the very early periods: "an occasional freedom of expression and allusion intolerable to modern taste, and the necessity of touching, however lightly, on the religious movements that contributed so powerfully to determine the course of English Literature". In the latter respect, they were careful "not to 'construe an author into vice', or to weaken his utterances and dim his pictures by reckless tampering with the text". The other problem was solved "by the uncompromising and silent removal of every word and passage unmistakeably objectionable" (1883: III)

Another consideration was that the teaching of literature should not be a matter of merely memorising passages:

> not that we expect everything in the book to be got by heart, or even studied so as to be mastered in all its details; our intention is to offer a choice of good exercises in English reading: supply something to suit, as far as possible, every taste.

But the choice of pieces was dictated, above all, by nationalism: "as no history of literature can be satisfactory unless it embodies the history of the nation, so no national history can be complete and trustworthy unless it takes into account the literary productions of the master-minds of the era, and their share in moulding the national destiny." (1882: II).

There is little information on how *The Literary Reader* was received and used in classrooms. A German reviewer of the German edition, writing in 1907 about one of the volumes devoted to the 19th century, commented

> that it is certainly not as thorough and reliable as it should be and beginners should watch out for pitfalls; however, the chief merit of the book is still that it conveys an amazing amount of information and opinion at a low price.[45]

In 1883 a brief review published in *De Gids* gave a warmer recommendation and indicated that the volume on the 19th century was already in regular use in Dutch grammar schools and was "one of the best in this field" (*De Gids* 1883: 597).[46] An anonymous reviewer writing in *De Nieuwe Gids* five years later confirmed this opinion, but thought that a later edition was even better – "This is an unusually good book" – and called it "a sound and original study". Its originality lay in two particular features. Firstly, Irving's introductions to the selected texts offered a contemporary re-appreciation of them. According to *De Nieuwe Gids*, she "knew that the aesthetic evaluation of the schools of poetry of the past was in urgent need of review, that she could not adhere to a presentation based on the views of fifty years ago, but that her book must be in accordance with the more refined taste and more accurate judgement of [the] younger generation". Secondly, the book paid at least equal attention to contemporary English literature, "about which little is yet known in Holland, and which has so far hardly been used in the service of education".[47]

One may wonder whether de Beer was particularly pleased with this review by a member of the progressive camp, given that it systematically avoids mentioning his name and totally ignores his share in the book.[48] Nor did the volumes on the previous centuries, which he had edited largely single-handedly, invariably bring him satisfaction, although he recorded in 1920, in the last volume to appear, that it had been of service not only to Dutch students, but also at the universities of Bonn, Jena and Vienna.[49] "I am glad to hear your books are so successful", Francis Curtis wrote in a reply to de Beer's suggestion that the book should also be prescribed in Frankfurt. But this time he was apparently less keen to oblige his old acquaintance. He not only took a year to reply, but wrote in his letter that the high import duties on books and the current severe economic difficulties meant that post-war Germany was cut off from foreign literature. Anyway, he thought the book was now out-dated: "it seems to me that the work requires a pretty thorough revision to bring it up to date and make it suitable for our students".[50]

"The drunken butcher's boy of Stratford-upon-Avon"

It is not immediately clear whether de Beer was discouraged by Curtis's response, but he continued right to the end of his life to pursue his interest in the history of English literature. He was particularly fascinated by Sir Francis Bacon. On the title page of the last volume of *The Literary Reader* to appear, de Beer presents himself as a "Member of the Board of the Austrian Shakespeare-Bacon Society". From the very start of his career he had been interested in Shakespeare, at that stage producing several educational booklets on the subject.[51] But from 1913 onward he became absorbed in the "Shakespeare-Bacon theory". This theory was at the time widely credited throughout the Western world, particularly between 1880 and 1930, and de Beer became one of its most fanatical champions in the Netherlands.[52]

The theory (which still has its adherents) was first articulated in the 1850s and was one of many that attempted to remedy the lack of biographical information about Shakespeare. It started from the basic assumption that, as the son of a butcher in Stratford-upon-Avon, the playwright was a man of modest social origins. In his youth he had led a licentious life – including drunkenness and a forced marriage – and had received little or no formal education. Consequently, he could not have possessed the large vocabulary and breadth of knowledge necessary to create the complex literary works that for centuries had been ascribed to him. The Baconians were even convinced that the historical Shakespeare was illiterate. They explained the association of his name with a complete literary oeuvre by arguing that he was a humble theatre employee who allowed himself to be used as a straw man by somebody who wanted to remain anonymous. And that somebody was his contemporary, Bacon. The proponents of this theory based their claims not only on a certain similarity between the two oeuvres, but also on cryptograms, anagrams, and numerical and textual codes that they found in the masterpieces written under the name of the Stratford rustic. (They also thought that Bacon was the real author of Cervantes' *Don Quixote*.)

De Beer helped to spread this mystification theory by publishing a series of brochures and articles in the Dutch (and sometimes even foreign) press.[53] These activities culminated in 1917 in the publication of *Shakespeare… een pseudoniem*, a rather incoherent book in which he reworked the content of his main publications on the question and at the same time sought to put forward new information and ideas. The book was apparently also intended to provide the initial impetus for a manifesto. "This little book is an introduction", he wrote in his preface, "it is a part of our (Baconian) programme, preceding and blazing the trail for a publication written in German, to serve Baconians in Germany, Austria and the Netherlands, and which will be perused possibly in Scandinavia and certainly in England and America."[54]

One of the main pillars in de Beer's argument is a book called *The Great Cryptogram* by an American Baconian called Ignatius Donnelly.[55] As late as 1895 de Beer had condemned this book, but now he referred to studies of this kind, which seemed to him much more thorough than those of the Shakespeareans, who – he claimed – tended to be too stupid and slow-witted to do any research of their own. He preferred, therefore, to refer to them as "those who still believe in Shakespeare". It was mental laziness, he argued, that made even professors and other scholars adhere to the traditional view that Shakespeare was simply Shakespeare. "But during his lifetime every professor is infallible", he sneered, "and when a proposition has been regarded as valid for 300 years, it must be hard for a professor to have to humbly admit that for 300 years people have been wrong".[56] He often adopted a scornful and indignant tone to reinforce his arguments. For example, he tried wherever possible to avoid using the name Shakespeare, preferring to speak of "the man from Stratford", "the Stratforder", or even "the drunken butcher's boy of Stratford".

His attitude probably did nothing to muster support for his view.[57] He pointed the finger at Groningen professor J.H. Kern, holder since 1900 of the chair for which de Beer had supported Curtis's candidacy, as one of those who refused to recognise the validity of the Baconian theory. In 1914 he succeeded in persuading seventeen daily papers to publish an announcement drumming up public support for the theory[58] but when he sent a hundred reprints of one of his Bacon articles to major daily papers, periodicals and professors and teachers of English, he received no more than a handful of polite acknowledgements.[59] Nevertheless, he clung to his position and continued his correspondence on the subject. Shortly before his death, for example, he was still writing about the theory to publisher and theatre historian Leo Simons, one of his successors as lecturer at the theatre school.[60] He was no more successful in persuading him than he was with the American writer George Seibel, who had sent de Beer his brochure *Bacon versus Shakespeare*[61] in an attempt to convince him of "the essential absurdity of Baconism":

> You need not feel surprise[d] that your name is known in Pittsburgh – it is not only known here, but highly esteemed, though we do not permit our admiration to its bearer to lead us into following him blindly through the maze of error that is known as the Baconian theory.

Seibel warned de Beer that he risked being discredited by his association with the Baconians: "Your solid scholarship is out of place in such company". He signed his letter with the assurance "of my unshaken conviction that Shakespeare was Shakespeare".[62]

Conclusion

Even if, towards the end of his career, de Beer became enmeshed in Baconian speculations, the surviving letters show that he continued to correspond about English literature with colleagues at home and abroad almost right up to his death in 1923. However, he was undoubtedly taken more seriously prior to the First World War. Not that he ever enjoyed the same literary status as Busken Huet. De Beer's often sloppy use of language and careless structuring of texts revealed him as Busken Huet's inferior, both intellectually and stylistically. But it should not be ignored that, despite the size of his readership at the time of his death in 1886, Busken Huet was also a controversial figure. He held strong opinions and was not afraid of expressing them. He had no time whatsoever for the United States and major reservations about the English nation, past and present. These were reflected in a marked preference for authors who took a critical view of British society. In this respect, he differed from de Beer and his co-author Jane Irving, who selected and edited the texts in *The Literary Reader* with a view to causing the least possible offence. Unlike Busken Huet, de Beer seems to have preferred to avoid conflict.[63]

This enabled him to continue for decades as "a major figure in the literary life of the Netherlands"[64] by virtue of his talents as an organiser and intermediary. He was important as a founder, editor and administrator of countless periodicals and associations, as a speaker and language teacher, and as an extremely prolific writer. But he also possessed a great ability to popularise the ideas of the literary establishment. Whether he took ideas directly from Busken Huet I have not been able to establish. Certainly, by his own admission, he consulted other people's work in relation to *The Literary Reader*.[65] With this school anthology and his other work, de Beer probably reached at least as large a readership as Busken Huet. The latter may have gained more lasting fame, but it is doubtful whether many people in the Netherlands or elsewhere were persuaded by his views during his own lifetime. More moderate critics like de Beer, whose ideas were closer to those of the average reader, may well have done more to influence the general public.

Even so, de Beer certainly cannot be accused of preaching to the converted. While Busken Huet offered his personal views on a small number of leading English authors who were already regarded by his Dutch readership as part of the international canon, de Beer tried – especially in

The Literary Reader – to offer a far wider and more representative selection of English literature, including something for every taste. And whereas Busken Huet found hardly any younger British authors worth reading, de Beer chose – with the vigorous backing of Jane Irving – to pay particular attention to the contemporary literary scene. As a result, a number of English writers probably owed their first mention in the Netherlands to Taco H. de Beer.[66]

Bibliography

Busken Huet, Conrad. *Litterarische fantasien en kritieken*. 26 vols. Haarlem: Tjeenk Willink, 1881-1888.

Colmjon, Gerben. *De beweging van tachtig. Een cultuurhistorische verkenning in de negentiende eeuw*. Utrecht/Antwerpen: Het Spectrum, 1963.

de Beer, Taco H. *The Literary Reader. Handbook of English Literature for the Higher Classes in Schools and for Home Teaching*. Kuilenburg: Blom and Olivierse, 1887.

———. “De Baco-bacil.” *Algemeen Handelsblad* (9 June 1895): Avondblad, Derde blad, 1-2.

———. “Ph.J. Olivierse.” *Noord en Zuid* 30 (1907): 366-368.

———. “Shakespeare of Bacon?” *Het Vaderland* (25 July 1914): Tweede avondblad B, 1-2.

———. “Shakespeare of Bacon?, II” *Nederland* 68.1 (1916): 18-42.

———. *Shakespeare... een pseudoniem. Bacon is de auteur van ‘Shakespeare’s’ werken*. Bussum: Schueler, 1917.

de Beer, Taco H. and Elizabeth Jane Irving. *The Literary Reader. A Handbook for the Higher Classes in Schools and for Home Teaching. Part II: The Nineteenth Century*. 2nd ed. Kuilenburg: Blom & Olivierse, 1882.

———. *The Literary Reader. A Handbook for the Higher Classes in Schools and for Home Teaching. Part I-1: From Caedmon to Milton*. 2nd ed. With introductory notices by Elizabeth Jane Irving. Kuilenburg: Blom and Olivierse, 1883.

———. *An Epitome of Early English Literature B.C. 55 – A.D. 1509. A Handbook for Students (Pages 1-177 of ‘The Literary Reader’, 2nd ed., I.i.)*. 3rd ed. Rev. by Taco H. de Beer. Amsterdam: Hollandsche Uitgevers-mij. Amsterdam, 1920.

Kroder, Armin. “Chrestomathien.” Review of: Taco H. de Beer & E. Jane Irving, *The Literary Reader. A Handbook for the higher classes in schools and for home-teaching, III: The Nineteenth Century, part II*. (4th ed. Halle a.S.: H. Gesenius, 1905). *Englische Studien* 38 (1907): 127.

Meijer, J. *Willem Anthony Paap 1856-1923. Zeventiger onder de Tachtigers. Het levensverhaal van een vergetene*. Amsterdam: Meulenhoff, 1959.

Noordegraaf, Jan. “De Afrikaanse connectie van Taco H. de Beer [I-III].” *Trefwoord*. March, April and October 2004 <www.fa.knaw.nl/fa/uitgaven/trefwoord/jaargang-2004/mansvelt.pdf>, <www.fa.knaw.nl/fa/uitgaven/trefwoord/jaargang-2004/pannevis.pdf> and <www.fa.knaw.nl/fa/uitgaven/trefwoord/jaargang-2004/debeeriii.pdf>.

Praamstra, Olf. *Gezond verstand en goede smaak. De kritieken van Conrad Busken Huet*. Amstelveen: Ernst & Co., 1991.

——— “Droom of nachtmerrie. De visie van E.J. Potgieter en Conrad Busken Huet op de Verenigde Staten.” *Literatuur* 14.4 (1997): 213-218.

———. *Busken Huet. Een biografie*. Amsterdam: SUN, 2007.

Tibbe, Lieske. "Nieuws uit nergensoord. Natuursymboliek en de receptie van William Morris in Nederland en België." *De Negentiende Eeuw* 25.4 (2001): 233-251.

Tielrooy, Johannes. *Conrad Busken Huet et la littérature française. Essai de biographie intellectuelle.* Harlem: Tjeenk Willink/Paris: Librairie Ancienne Edouard Champion, 1923.

van Loghem, M.G.L. "Levensbericht van Taco Hajo de Beer, 18 Nov. 1838 – 12 Sept. 1923." *Handelingen en mededeelingen van de Maatschappij der Nederlandsche Letterkunde te Leiden, over het jaar 1923-1924.* Leiden: Brill, 1924. 7-16.

Wester, Rudi. "Busken Huet en de Franse literatuur." *Maatstaf* 34.4/5 (April 1986): 66-70.

Wilhelm, F.A. *English in the Netherlands. A History of Foreign Language Teaching 1800-1920, with a Bibliography of Textbooks. Een wetenschappelijke proeve op het gebied van de letteren.* [diss. Nijmegen, 2005].

Notes

1 "Geen hollandsch auteur heeft in de laatste vijftig jaren een hollandsch boek geschreven, proza of verzen, hetwelk door Europa als eene aanwinst beschouwd is." (22: 201)

2 See also Praamstra's *Busken Huet* (216-220, 575, 785).

3 Letter from Louise Stratenus to Taco H. de Beer, 4 July 1883. Unless otherwise specified, all letters to de Beer cited in this article are preserved in Leiden University Library, sign. LTK 1721 and 1735.

4 See Meijer (78-93) and Colmjon (246-247).

5 In particular some of his activities concerning South African lexicography have been discussed recently. See Noordegraaf.

6 See Tielrooy (vii-viii, 287-292) and Wester's "Busken Huet en de Franse literatuur".

7 Busken Huet tended to discuss editions in the Collection of British Authors published by the Tauchnitz company of Leipzig, "outside England and the English colonies, available all over the world at the reasonable prices for which they are well-known" ["buiten Engeland en de engelsche kolonien, in alle landen der wereld voor den bekenden matigen prijs te bekomen"] (5: 132).

8 See Praamstra's *Gezond verstand en goede smaak* (263) and his *Busken Huet* (577).

9 "Zoo ver gaat, tot schade der hoogere kunst, de tyrannie der engelsche preutschheid." (8: 129)

10 " [...] heeft het buitenland de Engelschen leeren kennen als een krachtig, ondernemend, vrijheidlievend, welvarend volk, geneigd tot zelfverheffing, excentriek, maar levenslustig, gastvrij, gehecht aan eigen instellingen, eigen bodem, een eigen stijl van leven [...]" (17: 163).

11 "Het bloed der natie was melk, was thee, was suiker geworden [...]" (21: 90).

12 "[...] geen maatschappij in Europa zoo doortrokken is van den zuurdeesem der farizeën, als de engelsche." (4: 65)

13 "Eccentricity – the quality that otherwise most distinguishes the English from the Dutch – was inborn in him [Bilderdijk]." ["Excentriciteit – de eigenschap die anders het meest scheiding maakt tusschen Engelschen en Nederlanders – was hem aangeboren."] (4: 109)

14 See Praamstra's "Droom of nachtmerrie".

15 This is not to say that Busken Huet uncritically assumed literature to be mimetic. He wrote, for example, that "[m]odern English criticism, seldom very discerning, has almost invariably blundered by unthinkingly identifying Disraeli with the protagonists of some of his novels." ["De moderne engelsche kritiek, zelden scherpzinnig, heeft bijna altijd de fout begaan Disraëli plompweg te vereenzelvigen met de hoofdpersonen van sommige zijner romans."] (21: 85)

16 "[...] greep uit het engelsch leven [...]" (4: 43).

17 "[...] eene kostelijke bijdrage [...]" (4: 19).

[18] "[...] schijnt in den loop der jongste twee eeuwen den Engelschen als in het bloed gevaren te zijn. [...] Te denken als Milton, te gevoelen als Milton, te gelooven, te hopen, lief te hebben als Milton, is misschien het eigenaardigst kenmerk der engelsche natie geweest [...]." (12: 157-158)

[19] "[...] een bestrijder van nationale ondeugden, een hervormer van maatschappelijke misbruiken, een volksman [...]", "[...] in den engelschen zin van het woord een volbloed radikaal [...]." (4: 52-53)

[20] "[...] grootste en onvergankelijkste werk der engelsche letterkunde van den nieuweren tijd [...]" (17: 117, 139; 168-169, 176 and 21: 114-116). On Busken Huet's appreciation of the poem, see also Praamstra's *Busken Huet* (716-717).

[21] See also (4: 105) and (21: 80, 115).

[22] "[...] wij vinden dat hijzelf te weinig een heilige geweest is, om over de schijnheiligheid van anderen het zoo druk te mogen hebben [...]" (21: 113).

[23] From 1868 to 1870 he taught German and geography at the HBS in Breda and from 1870 to 1877 German and English at the HBS in Goes. He then taught in Amsterdam from 1877 to 1902. Unless otherwise specified, all biographical information about de Beer is drawn from van Loghem.

[24] Letter from Taco H. de Beer to Leo Simons, 19 April 1922 (Letterkundig Museum, The Hague).

[25] For example volume 4: "[Charles] Dickens, *The Chimes*, met aanteekeningen en toelichtingen uitgegeven door T.H. de Beer." (Maassluis: Van der Endt, [1875]). This 'Library of Foreign Authors' series was launched in 1875 and continued at least until 1877.

[26] Jan ten Brink, *Geschiedenis der Noord-Nederlandsche letteren in de 19e eeuw in biographieën en bibliographieën,1830-1900*, grootendeels herzien door den auteur, verder verzorgd en bijgewerkt door T.H. de Beer. 3 vols. (Rotterdam: Bolle, 1902-1904).

[27] *De Amsterdammer* was founded in 1877; de Beer left the editorial board within a year, following financial squabbles. *De Portefeuille* appeared from 1879 to 1895.

[28] In the case of this two-monthly periodical for modern language studies, de Beer assumed responsibility for editing the German section, while F.J. Rode had French in his portfolio and C. Stoffel took care of English. See Wilhelm (203 n. 317).

[29] See van Loghem (15-16) for a (rather partial) bibliographical overview.

[30] I know of the following translations from English: Charles H. Ross, *Een lief weeuwtje*, naar het Engelsch van – door T.H. de Beer (Amsterdam: Kraay, 1868) [original title: *The Pretty Widow*]; Babington White (Miss Braddon), *Circe. Drie bedrijven uit het leven van een kunstenaar*, naar het Engelsch van – door T.H. de Beer. (Zutphen: Wansleven, 1869) [original title: *Circe*]; Thom. Bailey Aldrich, *Prudence Palfrey*, uit het Engelsch door T.H. de Beer. (Amsterdam 1875) [original title: *Prudence Palfrey*]. Now and then de Beer also translated non-fiction, such as Edward Jenkins' *Glances at Inner England*, to which he added material of his own in relating Jenkins' observations to the political situation in the Netherlands. (Edw. Jenkins, *Van Westminster naar het Binnenhof. Blikken in het innerlijk leven van Engeland en Nederland. Klachten, opmerkingen ... opgedragen aan bestuurders en volksvertegenwoordigers en aan hen, die dat zullen worden*, vertaald uit het Engels en bewerkt door T.H. de Beer. (Maasluis: Van der Endt, 1875))

[31] Letter from Wendell P. Garrison to de Beer, 18 March 1880.

[32] Letter from Wendell P. Garrison to de Beer, 8 April 1878.

[33] Letters from Wendell P. Garrison to de Beer, 15 May 1878 and 20 Feb. 1880. Although the correspondence seems to have petered out after 1880, Garrison still turned to his Dutch counterpart in 1898 when he needed a correspondent to cover the Dutch coronation for *The Nation*. See the letters written by Wendell P. Garrison to de Beer on 28 March and 10 Aug. 1898. In the latter, Garrison says that he has heard that Dutch nationals are barred from acting as representatives for foreign news media at the coronation.

[34] Letters from J. Stuart Bogg to de Beer, 25 and 30 April 1878 and 19 July 1880.

[35] Letter from J. Stuart Bogg to de Beer, 7 May 1885.

[36] Like Louise Stratenus, already mentioned in this article, who tried in 1883 to earn a living and pay off her debts by doing translation work in London (letters from Louise Stratenus to de Beer, 4 July and 10 Dec. 1883). Two years later, when she had moved to Paris, she wrote to de Beer to inform him "in complete confidence" of the plagiarism repeatedly committed by the successful Dutch author Justus van Maurik, one of the new editors of *De Amsterdammer* – for example by publishing under his own name a story already presented elsewhere by a different writer as a translation from the English (letter from Louise Stratenus to de Beer, 11 Jan. 1885).

[37] Letter from Johanna Rittner Bos to de Beer, 22 Jan. 1897.

[38] Letters from Johanna Rittner Bos to de Beer, 5 Jan. 1893, 2 and 29 April, 12 and 20 Sept., and 8 Oct. 1895.

[39] Postcard from George Bernard Shaw to de Beer, 3 Aug. 1906: "'John Bull's Island', 'How He Lied to Her Husband' (in one act only) and 'Major Barbara', my three last plays, are not yet published. They will appear in print before Christmas, I hope. I am sorry I cannot lend you a copy of John Bull: the only one I have is wanted by the printer. You will find the names of my other plays in the list of my works at the end of any of my published plays, I am writing to my publishers to send you one of them. You will find 'who's who' much more useful for your purpose than the Literary Year Book."

[40] Unfortunately, however, Burgersdijk had spotted a series of errors in it. In a postcard of 23 March 1889, he wrote to de Beer that he regretted the evidence of haste in the article but that he appreciated de Beer's good intentions.

[41] Letters from Francis J. Curtis to de Beer, 27 Aug. and 22 Sept. 1900.

[42] Letter from Francis J. Curtis to de Beer, 20 March 1902.

[43] Leiden University Library has two copies of Part I, one bound in red (sign. Bolland 8 A 25) and the other in grey (sign. 1265 C 18).

[44] De Beer "Ph.J. Olivierse" (367). I have come across a total of eleven editions (or mentions of editions) of various volumes, with numbers ranging from I.1 to IV.1. They include special versions, such as a condensed "one volume edition" of 1887, designed exclusively for use in schools. The first edition was published by D.A. Thieme in Arnhem. Most of the later editions were produced by de Beer's regular publishers, Blom & Olivierse in Culemborg, but in the early 20th century some were published by Hermann Gesenius of Halle (Germany). The last edition was published by the Hollandsche Uitgevers-Mij. Amsterdam in 1920.

[45] "[…] dass es an der richtigen gründlichen durcharbeitung allerdings mangelt, anfänger mögen sich also für fussangeln hüten; deswegen bleibt dem buch aber doch sein hauptvorzug: für billiges geld eine erstaunliche fülle von wissen und anschauung zu vermitteln" (Kroder 127).

[46] The review appeared in *De Gids* (1883), vol. I: 596-597.

[47] "Dit is een zeldzaam goed boek"; "een degelijke en oorspronkelijke studie"; "Zij wist dat het aesthetisch oordeel over de oude dichterscholen dringend herziening behoefde, dat zij zich niet mocht houden aan een voorstelling, gebaseerd op een oordeel van voor vijftig jaar: maar dat haar boek in overeenstemming moest zijn met den fijneren smaak en het juistere oordeel van dit latere geslacht"; "waarvan nog maar weinig in Holland is bekend, en die allerminst ten dienste van het onderwijs werd gebruikt" (*De Nieuwe Gids* 1888: 320-321).

[48] Reading between the lines, the review seems to include a couple of gibes at de Beer, who was a member of an older generation. Apart from the passage cited, see the closing sentence of the review: "We very much hope that Miss Irving's book will come to replace other, increasingly obsolete, books of the same sort, even more than is now the case" ["Wij hopen van harte dat Miss Irving's boek andere, verouderende boeken van dezelfde soort, nóg meer dan nu het geval is, moge vervangen"] (*De Nieuwe Gids* 1888: 322). The review appeared in *De Nieuwe Gids* 3 (1888), vol. I: 320-322.

[49] De Beer & Irving *An Epitome of Early English Literature* (3). Van Loghem adds not only Gotha and Weimar to the list, but also "Belgium (e.g. the Military Academy)" (10).
[50] Letter from Francis J. Curtis to de Beer, 25 Oct. 1921.
[51] T.H. de Beer, *A Short Account of the Plots or Fables of Shakespeare's Plays, Edited with Chronological Tables and a List of Characters* (Arnhem: Thieme, 1871); [Taco H. de Beer], *Verklarende aanteekeningen ten gebruike bij de lezing van Shakespeare's Richard II / Explanatory Notes Illustrative of Shakespeare's King Richard II* (Amsterdam: Hassels, [1872]) (Bibliotheek voor Hoogere Burgerscholen 2).
[52] There is a vast literature on the Shakespeare-Bacon theory. Some introductory resources can be found at http://www.ull.ac.uk//specialcollections/baconshakespeare.shtml.
[53] Apart from the brochures *Shakespeare oder Bacon* (Hamburg: Weltwissen, 1914) and *Eye-openers, Respectfully Dedicated to Serious Stradfordians [sic] and Disdainfully to Propagandists of Unfounded Assertions* (Amsterdam: Heijnes, 1914), also: "Shakespeare of Bacon? [I]" (in: *Nederland* 65 (1913), vol. III, 33-46), "Shakespeare of Bacon?" (in: *Het Vaderland*, 25 July 1914), "Van waar de naam Shakespeare?" (in: *Het Vaderland*, 2 Aug. 1914), "De werken van Shakespeare werden door Bacon geschreven" (in: *Het Vaderland*, 23 April 1916), "Shakespeare of Bacon? II" (in: *Nederland* 68 (1916), vol. I, 18-42), "Shakespeare's Errors" (in: *Baconiana* 16 (1921), 53). In addition, de Beer produced the translation of an article by Alfred von Weber Ebenhof on the current state of Baconian studies, which was published in *Wetenschappelijke Bladen*, Nov. 1915, 246-271, under the title "Over het Shakespeare-Bacon-vraagstuk. De tegenwoordige stand der Shakespeare-onderzoekingen en haar betrekkingen tot den grooten Lord-Kanselier van Engeland, Francis Bacon van Verulam-St. Alban".
[54] "Dit boekje is eene inleiding, het is een deel van ons (Baconian) programma, de voorloper en wegbereider van een orgaan in de Duitsche taal geschreven, ten dienste van Baconians in Duitschland, Oostenrijk en Nederland, waarvan ook wellicht Skandinavië en zeker Engeland en Amerika zal [sic] kennis nemen." (12)
[55] Ignatius Donnelly, *The great cryptogram. Francis Bacon's cipher in the so-called Shakespeare plays*. 2 vols. (London: Sampson Low, Marston, Searle & Rivington, 1888 [repr. 1972]).
[56] "Maar bij zijn leven is elke professor onfeilbaar. Het moet dan ook hard vallen voor een professor als een stelling 300 jaar voor waar gegolden heeft, deemoedig te moeten erkennen, dat men zich 300 jaar lang vergist heeft." ("Shakespeare of Bacon?"). It can be noted that de Beer lauded his contemporaries L.A.J. Burgersdijk, A.S. Kok, A.C. Loffelt, C. Stoffel and even the Shakespearean Edward B. Koster as outstanding experts on Shakespeare and translators of his works, while casting doubt on the competence of younger colleagues like Jacobus van Looy and Arthur van Schendel.
[57] For example, de Beer's colleague Smit Kleine was puzzled by it, as witness a letter from F.S.K. [= Frits Smit Kleine] to de Beer, 25 March 1922. The only Dutch fellow-Baconian named by de Beer was a Utrecht professor of law, J. d'Aulnis de Bourouill.
[58] Probably it was a letter to the editor along the lines of "Bacon of Shakespeare" (in: *Nieuws van den Dag*, 22 May 1914).
[59] De Beer "Shakespeare of Bacon?, II" (37 n. 1).
[60] See letters from Taco H. de Beer to Leo Simons, 19 April and 2 May 1922 (Letterkundig Museum, The Hague), and from L. Simons to de Beer, 30 April 1922.
[61] George Seibel, *Bacon versus Shakespeare. Who wrote the plays?* (Pittsburgh: Lessing, 1919).
[62] Letter from George Seibel to de Beer, 18 July 1920.
[63] See, for example, the letters from Louise Stratenus to de Beer, 4 July and 10 Dec. 1883 and 11 Jan. 1885. Faced with her initial indignation and accusations, de Beer made immediate efforts to appease her and the relationship quickly became extremely warm.
[64] "[...] eene figuur in het letterkundig leven van Nederland" (Van Loghem 7).

[65] More specifically: Thomas B. Shaw's *A History of English Literature*, Stopford A. Brooke's *English Literature* and a work by 'Chambers and Spalding', probably the *Cyclopaedia of English literature. A history, critical and biographical of British authors from the earliest to the present times*, edited by Rob Chambers (de Beer 1887: VIII).

[66] Examples include William Morris and Dante Gabriel Rossetti. On the former, see Tibbe (322) and on the latter the article by Anne van Buul, elsewhere in this publication.

Kris Steyaert (Université de Liège)

Elusive Poets, Fugitive Texts: The Impact of the London Shelley Society in the Low Countries

In 1995, Ton Naaijkens published his essay "De slag om Shelley", in which he examined the literary debate initiated by the publication of a number of ambitious Dutch Shelley translations.[1] This debate, he argued, was driven by personal agendas, deep-seated rancour, and calculated strategies of self-interest. I would like to put Naaijkens's arguments to the test by bringing into the picture an aspect of the reception of Shelley not covered in his essay. Like him, I will take Dutch Shelley translations as my main starting point but I will then shift my attention to the possible source texts and their dissemination. It is my belief that a better knowledge of the editions used by the translators will increase our understanding of both the ensuing debate and the reception of Shelley's works abroad. More particularly, in what follows I wish to develop the idea that the London-based Shelley Society and its activities constituted a determining factor in the response to and distribution of the poet's writings in the Low Countries. By zooming in on a few episodes in the reception history, I want to illustrate how the Shelley Society helped shape, albeit indirectly, the Dutch literary climate at the end of the "long" 19th century.

A tentative start

The very first Shelley translation to appear in Dutch was published in the literary periodical *De Gids* in June 1864. There was no introduction by the translator, who hid behind the pseudonym "W. D–s", nor any explanation or comment as to why he had chosen to translate a poem that even today will be unknown but to the most dedicated Shelley enthusiast. The rationale behind the translator's choice, his motives, and intentions remained as elusive as the characters whose adventures are described in the poem in question, "The Fugitives" (or "De vlugtenden" as the Dutch rendition has it). Fourteen years later, in an index published in *De Gids* in 1878, "W. D–s" was revealed to be a pseudonym of the famous critic E.J. Potgieter.[2] For some time, Potgieter's Shelley translation remained an isolated occurrence. It was not until the 1880s that other Dutch Shelley translations began to see the light. Soon, Shelley's works gained such a prominent position in the literary discourse that later commentators have referred to the phenomenon as something resembling a Shelley cult. Dutch poems were written on Shelleyan models and the *Defence of Poetry* (translated in Dutch by Albert Verwey in 1891) was drawn upon to formulate a new set of poetological principles with which a new generation of poets tried to break free from what they considered the shackles of backward-looking provincialism.

The first more or less systematic analysis of this obsession with Shelley was undertaken in 1926. In that year the South African scholar G. Dekker wrote his doctoral dissertation *Die invloed van Keats en Shelley in Nederland gedurende die negentiende eeu* [*The Influence of Keats and Shelley in the Netherlands in the 19th Century*], more than half of which is devoted to the so-called Tachtigers, the poets of the Eighties Movement, named after the decade in which they first rose to prominence. The writers most often associated with this Dutch Shelley cult are Willem Kloos, Albert Verwey, Frederik van Eeden and Herman Gorter. Concluding his dissertation and paraphrasing the English Romantic, Dekker writes how many of Shelley's own words and ideas "are pregnant with a lightning which *did* find a conductor [...] in die tagtigers". In many respects, it was Shelley's poetry "which formed the basis of the artistic views and the art itself of the Tachtigers".[3] The central position occupied by Shelley and his works for this generation of writers has also been recognized by scholars from across the Channel. In his essay "Anglo-Dutch Literary Relations 1867-1900" (1936) Brian W. Downs posits:

> With greater or less intensity and with longer or shorter persistency all these writers, who between them refashioned Dutch poetry and advanced it to the front rank in contemporary Europe, were haunted by Shelley. They made him more than a household word; in no other country has he, thanks to them, been accepted so unreservedly as the supreme exemplar of poet, critic and thinker combined [...]. (304)

James Anderson Russell arrived at a similar assessment in his *Dutch Poetry and English. A Study of the Romantic Revival*. In this monograph from 1939 two entire chapters are devoted to the influence of Keats and

Shelley in the Netherlands.[4] In sum, the importance of Shelley's work for the development of Dutch letters has been acknowledged right from the beginning. This is not surprising, given that someone like Willem Kloos, in his own essays and literary critiques, never stopped promoting Shelley as the pre-eminent model for Dutch writers.

One further manifestation of this interest in Shelley is the appearance of various Shelley translations. These too have been the subject of study. B.M. Baxter examined *Albert Verwey's Translations from Shelley's Poetical Works* in her MA dissertation written in 1963. Then we have to wait for more than thirty years before the subject is taken up again in Ton Naaijkens's essay mentioned above. My own contributions in the field deal with the context and ideological thrust of specific Shelley translations.[5] These (case) studies are primarily concerned with the quality of the translations (Baxter) or try to reconstruct the discursive context in which they functioned as weapons in fierce translation battles (Naaijkens, Steyaert). In his analysis Naaijkens introduced the phrase "literary territoriality" to characterize the nature of the debate:

> Shelley is the subject of a contest of literary territoriality. The weapons deployed in the battle are discourses that are hardly distinguishable from fiction. This does not only apply to the translations themselves but also to the reflections on translation and the translation critiques. Things are not presented in a logical or 'correct' way by the parties involved. Rather, there is an obfuscation of ideas.[6]

We know how Shelley's originals fared in the hands of their Dutch translators and we know which texts were favoured over others. Yet, in the relevant literature, the actual transfer of Shelley's works to the Low Countries is still largely unexplored territory. Through which channels, for instance, did the Dutch avant-garde come into contact with Shelley's writings in the original English? In what guise did the English texts come to them and how did this affect the distribution and reception of the Dutch translations?

Before we can answer these and related questions, we need to focus on the periodical associated with the Dutch avant-garde for whom Shelley played such an important role. This periodical is *De Nieuwe Gids*, founded in October 1885. Six months later, Shelley's name was mentioned in its pages for the first time. The following, which appeared over the initial "G.", is taken from the periodical's "Varia" ["Miscellaneous"] section:

> Shelley Society. Many will be happy to learn that a society has been founded in London with the aim to 1° increase the knowledge of Shelley's works and life, 2° have Shelley's plays put on stage, 3° reprint in facsimile the rare first editions of his works [...]. Anyone who becomes a society member by paying one guinea (21 shillings) will receive a free copy of all its publications.[7]

De Nieuwe Gids was not the only foreign journal to cover the foundation of what was soon to become an influential literary society. Notices also appeared in *Le Figaro* (17 April 1886) and *The Boston Evening Transcript* (12 April 1886), to mention just two other examples. The almost haphazard manner in which the Society had come into being was made public in an anecdote shared during the inaugural meeting at University College London on 10 March 1886. The speaker, Dr F.J. Furnivall, reminisced about his father, a physician, who had known Shelley personally. I quote from the minutes:

> The poet would often run down to Windsor [...] and come and sit on the surgery counter to have a chat with Mr. Furnivall [...]. Although the doctor did not believe in Shelley's theories, [...] he was delighted with Shelley's society. Having therefore heard so constantly of Shelley during his boyhood, the Chairman [i.e. Furnivall junior] observed that when Mr. Sweet said to him barely three months ago, "Why not found a Shelley Society?' he replied, 'By Jove! I will. He was my father's friend." (*Note-Book* 7)

This was not the most felicitous way to legitimize the foundation of a literary society and several critics were quick to lampoon Furnivall's account. Andrew Lang, in the *Saturday Review*, even turned his hand to poetry:

> "By Jove, I will: he was my father's friend!"
> Thus Dr. Furnivall, in choice blank verse,
> Replied [...]
> "And what that question?" Briefly, it was this –
> "Why do not you a new communion found –
> "'Shelley Society' might be the name –

> "Where men might worry over Shelley's bones?"
> "By Jove, I will; he was my father's friend,"
> Said Furnivall; and lo, the thing was done!
>
> (*Note-Book* 33)[8]

Despite the barbed comments, the new Shelley Society was a great success. During the year of its foundation, membership numbers increased steadily: "The Society numbers [...] 144 members, a most promising beginning", the secretary recorded in June 1886 (*Note-Book* 8). A few months later, that number had already risen to about four hundred. Browsing the membership lists for that year we encounter a familiar name, that of Willem Kloos. There were only three other members from Mainland Europe, a Professor Brandl residing in Prague, Gustav Maier in Frankfurt, and Gabriel Sarrazin, a teacher at the Lycée in Nancy who translated Shelley in French. Others before me have mentioned Kloos's membership of the Society but its significance has never been fully appreciated. As the earlier notice in *De Nieuwe Gids* made clear, members received copies of the many editions published on the Society's behalf. In its fairly short existence,[9] dozens of titles were issued, easily recognizable by their uniform design with gothic lettering on a distinctive blue-green paper cover. They would have formed the cornerstone of Kloos's impressive private Shelley library, very likely to have been one of the largest in the country.

The notice in *De Nieuwe Gids* had listed as one of the Society's main goals the staging of *The Cenci*, which had not been allowed by the Censor during Shelley's lifetime because of the play's seditious content. The plot, based on historical sources, involves incestuous rape, parricide, simony, and papal corruption. A public performance was still out of the question in the 1880s, but the Society had gained enough clout, also financially, to secure a private staging. After a few frantic weeks of preparation the play was premiered at the Grand Theatre in Islington on 7 May 1886. The event was widely covered in the press, also abroad. In the Low Countries, the periodicals *Nederland* and *De Nederlandsche Spectator*, as well as the newspaper *Opregte Haarlemsche Courant*, devoted some column space to the premiere, but not *De Nieuwe Gids*. The review in *Nederland* was written by Abraham Seyne Kok (1831-1915), the well-known Shakespeare translator, and it was followed by a Dutch translation of three scenes from the play.

The brilliance of *Alastor*

I will return to *The Cenci* later but first I wish to present another text, printed for the Shelley Society in 1886: *Alastor or the Spirit of Solitude*. Bertram Dobell, who sat on the Shelley Society Committee, was responsible for the preface and editorial comments. This poem held special significance for the most vocal Shelley enthusiast in the Low Countries, Willem Kloos. Kloos considered the work a poignant self-portrait of the author and a supreme example of his poetic talents. In the 1880s, he had contemplated doing a translation of the work, but his deficient knowledge of English proved too great an obstacle, as he explained in one of his letters to Albert Verwey. It was not until 1905 that the poem appeared for the first time in Dutch: *Alastor of de geest der eenzaamheid*. Its plain design and unassuming size (102 x 138 mm) belies the historical importance of this publication, for it is the first complete Shelley poem to appear in Dutch as a separate book. The author of the translation was not Kloos but a close friend of his, Kornelis Herman de Raaf (1871-1948). Kloos sanctioned the enterprise by writing a programmatic introduction, outlining the importance of Shelley for the renaissance of Dutch literature in general and for the Tachtigers in particular. In his preface, Kloos referred repeatedly to the ethereal quality of Shelley's poems. The allure of his art, he explained, is similar to the sheen on a piece of satin: "Shelley's art and mental life sometimes look more like a soft-coloured, shape-changing palace in the clouds rather than like an immovable construction made from solid materials. The appeal of his art is often like the appeal of the sheen on satin."[10] Shelley was an elusive poet whose mercurial essence, to some extent, had been captured in his verse. To do justice to the almost unsubstantial character of his writing is a challenge any Shelley translator must face. According to Kloos, De Raaf had passed the test successfully.

De Raaf's *Alastor* was reviewed by Alex Gutteling in *De Beweging*, the journal founded by Albert Verwey in 1905, and by A.S. Kok in *De Nederlandsche Spectator*.[11] Though Kok admires the translator's courage for tackling such a difficult poet, he points out several metrical deficiencies in De Raaf's pentameters and deplores the occasional sloppiness in the phraseology. But for our purposes, the most interesting feature of the review is Kok's critical assessment of Shelley, especially since he had already outed himself as an enthusiastic Shelley translator back in 1888, when he had published a translation of three scenes from *The Cenci* in *Nederland*.

In his *Alastor* review, Kok "is critical of Shelley, holds him in high esteem but also quotes from the reactions in England that emphasize the esoteric aspects of especially *Alastor*." Though Naaijkens does not probe further, it is clear there is more to Kok's critical attitude than meets the eye. Whereas Kloos had likened Shelley's poetry to the sheen on a piece of satin with its "kaleidoscopic, multi-coloured" ["millioenen-lijnige, duizend-tintige"] quality (De Raaf, *Alastor* 11), Kok summarized earlier critiques of *Alastor* and pointed out "a lack of light and shadow, which renders the depiction too flat, too monochrome".[12] The wording seems to suggest that Kok was deliberately positioning himself against Kloos. How may we account for this apparent antagonism?

Kok's critical remarks, I suggest, may stem from his irritation towards Kloos, who had written disparagingly of Byron's poetical talents, especially when compared to Shelley's. Indeed, in the preface to the Dutch *Alastor*, Kloos had dismissed Byron as a rhymester, only capable of producing almanac-like poems that collapsed under the weight of their own banality. Kok must have felt aggrieved, for as he was reading Kloos's negative assessment of Byron, he would have been applying the finishing touches to his own metrical translation of Byron's *Cain*, published the following year (1906). Viewed from this perspective, one passage in Kok's *Alastor* critique suddenly acquires additional meaning:

> [The] glorification of Shelley has been growing constantly, often not without exaggeration, characterized by an injudicious running down of the fame of others, which is always a fateful sign for the party or factions which are guilty of such practices.[13]

Here, personal sensibilities are articulated as literary considerations. In other words, Kok's reservations about Shelley's poetry can be interpreted as Kloos's comeuppance for his earlier attack on Byron. Once again we are confronted with the truth that the reception history of Shelley's works in the Netherlands cannot be separated from the resentment and literary rivalry that existed between the writers involved.

When Kok's critical review of the Dutch *Alastor* was published, Kloos immediately jumped to De Raaf's defence in *De Nieuwe Gids*. He did so by stripping Kok of his credibility as a literary historian. He argued that flaws in Kok's historical overview were proof of the reviewer's gross incompetence on the subject of Shelley, and this ineptitude necessarily invalidated his aesthetic value judgements about the original poem and the translation. In his review of De Raaf's rendition, Kok had dwelt on the genesis of *Alastor* in 1815 and its subsequent reception, and had made the following claim: "When the poem first appeared it attracted little attention".[14] Only in 1824 did a second edition appear as part of the *Posthumous Poems* edited by Mary Shelley. A facsimile edition, so Kok had informed his readers, was published by the Shelley Society in 1886.[15] Incidentally, it was probably this last remark which brought Naaijkens to the mistaken conclusion that Kok was a Shelley Society member.[16] In his reaction in *De Nieuwe Gids*, Kloos expressed his outrage at Kok's claim that the original *Alastor* had been ignored by contemporary critics. He quotes from two English periodicals which had reviewed *Alastor* on its first publication in 1816 and accuses Kok of "fantasizing off the cuff". Because of this factual error, he condemns Kok's piece as "a rash idea committed to paper without much thought".[17]

It is here that the Shelley Society and its activities can help us to put things in their proper perspective and expose the underlying deception. If we compare Kok's review in *De Nederlandsche Spectator* with Dobell's preface in the *Alastor* facsimile edition, we notice many similarities. It is evident from the material that Kok used Dobell's preface as a blueprint for his own text. One representative example will suffice here. Kok praises Shelley "for its flawless, melodious versification, as for its greatness of conception, and, one could almost say, luxurious fantasy."[18] Dobell's preface eulogizes the "melody of versification, the nobility of conception, and the inexhaustible wealth of imagination" (Shelley, *Alastor* xii). If we continue our reading of Dobell's preface, we encounter this statement: Shelley's poem "attracted, upon its first appearance, no public attention" (Shelley, *Alastor* xxxvii). Compare this to Kok's phrasing ("When the poem first appeared it attracted little attention"), and again the similarities are obvious. Kloos's accusation that Kok's historical overview was just a piece of fantasy written off the cuff suddenly loses much of its validity. True, Kok's statement is incorrect but only because the reviewer relied on an outdated source, not because he was making things up.

The story does not end there. In his preface to De Raaf's *Alastor* translation, Kloos had commented on the poem's special status in the Shelley canon and compared it to the overtly didactic *Queen Mab*:

> Yes, it is good that a translation of Shelley has appeared, a literal translation of his first actual poem. The more famous 'Queen Mab' is Shelley's first substantial literary attempt in verse, but it hardly counts as a poem. The poet had not yet found himself and his art, and so, as a nineteen-year-old boy, he started making enthusiastic speeches and abstract asseverations as had been fashionable in the rhyming treatises from the end of the 18th century. No, *Alastor* is Shelley's first real poem in which his youthful spirit suddenly reveals itself in abundant beauty, like a bud blooming into a large, beautiful flower.[19]

A similar, explicit comparison between *Queen Mab* and *Alastor* can be found in an English source published nineteen years prior to Kloos's preface:

> *Alastor* is, by the general verdict of Shelley's critics, admitted to be the work in which his peculiar excellences were first exhibited. *Queen Mab* indeed, [...] with all the audacity of thought, declamatory force, and enthusiasm for humanity by which it is characterised, [...] yet shows few or no traces of the melody of versification, the subtlety of conception, and the inexhaustible wealth of imagination which distinguished the poet's later works. In *Queen Mab* Shelley treads in the footsteps of his predecessors and contemporaries, [...]; but in *Alastor* he first struck out a pathway of his own on which he was henceforth to travel, and which led him to ever fairer regions of splendour and delight.

Kloos is more disparaging about *Queen Mab* but for the rest both passages are remarkably alike. Part of the English quotation may have rung a bell for we have already encountered the reference to the melody of Shelley's versification and the wealth of his poetic imagination. Indeed, the entire passage is lifted from Dobell's preface to the *Alastor* facsimile edition (Shelley, *Alastor* xi-xii). Do the similarities between the two quotations, both in form and content, not suggest that Kloos too drew on this particular Shelley Society publication when composing his foreword to De Raaf's translation?

Whatever the case may be, when Kloos admonished Kok for fantasizing off the cuff, he was less than fair. As a Shelley Society member Kloos would have received a copy of the *Alastor* facsimile with the preface by Dobell. And as his own foreword suggests, he probably used the same edition when writing down his own thoughts in 1905 on the respective literary value of *Alastor* and *Queen Mab*. He would have known, therefore, that Kok merely repeated what he had found elsewhere. All this reinforces Naaijkens's argument about Kloos's territorial urge in connection with Shelley and the sometimes underhand way in which he fought for supremacy. Extrapolating his findings about the translation battle, Naaijkens makes this general pronouncement:

> In the search for conceptions of translation, one cannot subordinate biographical and individual aspects to the whole. True enough, the reflection on translation constitutes a world in itself [...] but at the same time it is a phenomenon that is very much part of the world, connected to various motives, interests and intentions, a world also of gossip, affairs and calumniation. [...] That is why in the reflection on translation one cannot neglect the importance of fabrications.[20]

When we include the Shelley Society and its publications in the general picture we begin to understand even more the partisan nature of the critical exchange related to the distribution of Shelley's works in the Low Countries. A picture emerges of highly personal agendas steering the distribution and reception of an author whose intrinsic literary qualities often appear to be of secondary importance for the participants in the debate.

De Cenci and a private Shelley library

After his Dutch *Alastor* translation, De Raaf decided to tackle Shelley's play *The Cenci*. His translation of the first act was published in *De Nieuwe Gids* in April 1907. The complete text appeared as a book the next year (1908).[21] It is here that we see further evidence of the impact of the Shelley Society on Dutch Shelley translations. A facsimile edition of *The Cenci* had been published by the Society in 1886. In this edition, the text of the play is followed by an Appendix bearing the title "Relation of the Death of the Family of the Cenci". This is a biographical account of the Cenci family written by Shelley and based on historical documents. To this text, the editors appended the following note: "The omission of this literal version of the story from the two editions of *The Cenci* published during Shelley's life may perhaps have arisen from the consideration that, to the public of that day, the bare horrors of the story might, if given, negative that very delicacy and reticence to which Shelley refers" (Shelley, *The Cenci* 92). De Raaf included a Dutch translation of this Appendix in *De Cenci*. Interestingly, his Appendix contains the only editorial comment in the entire volume: "Though in some editions this account is left out or only partially included for reasons of decency, the Translator felt he ought to reproduce it in its entirety."[22] There can be little doubt as to where De Raaf had found the inspiration for this note. Furthermore, the design of De Raaf's *De Cenci* closely resembles the earlier edition issued by the Shelley Society. Did De Raaf perhaps borrow the copy Kloos would have received as a Society member?

The question above leads us to a rather uncomfortable realization. So far, all proof of the impact of the activities generated by the Shelley Society has been indirect. Only Kok mentioned in his review of De Raaf's *Alastor* translation that he had consulted the English facsimile edition as distributed by the Society. Is there any more concrete evidence to link the Shelley Society publications with writers in the Low Countries? We know for instance that Kloos had an extensive Shelley library of which he was justifiably proud. The library, which numbered over one hundred titles, was broken up after his death but some of it remains. One of the works that is still part of the Kloos collections at the Literary Museum and Documentation Centre in The Hague happens to be the *Alastor* facsimile edited by Dobell. A stamp on the title page, however, appears to cast doubt on the assumption that Kloos had a (personal) copy at his disposal when he wrote his programmatic preface to De Raaf's *Alastor* translation. The stamp reads: "Mr. D. Spanjaard / Wagenaarweg 10 / 's-Gravenhage / Telef. 51749". David Spanjaard (1862-1935) was another Dutch Shelley enthusiast and a personal friend of Kloos's.[23] He died in April 1935 and one could advance the hypothesis that his widow, the artist Rosa Spanjaard, passed on the book to Kloos. At any rate, the friendship between the Spanjaard and Kloos families only began in the 1920s, long after the publication of De Raaf's *Alastor* translation. It was also around 1920 that Rosa and David Spanjaard settled in The Hague (Denekamp 14), the city mentioned on the stamp. We can rule out, therefore, that Kloos came into the possession of Spanjaard's copy before the Dutch *Alastor* rolled off the press.

This chronology certainly threatens to invalidate the argument developed in the previous paragraphs. How are we to make sense of the fact that Kloos's Shelley library does not contain a single facsimile edition printed for the Shelley Society?[24] Bearing in mind the Shelley Society issued dozens of publications which were sent to all its members, the notable absence in Kloos's collection of any such title – apart from Spanjaard's *Alastor* copy – is disturbing. However, the mystery of the fugitive texts is solved when we turn to an unpublished letter written by Spanjaard on 12 February 1931 and addressed to Kloos:

> Amice, Your letter has given me much joy and I have read with great pleasure about the time when you had to dispose of the Shelley Society papers (I assume you will not have entertained any illusions about the profit at that time [...]).[25]

Kloos suffered many financial difficulties in his life and we can safely assume he sacrificed part of his book collection to make ends meet.

All this confirms that Kloos, as a Shelley Society member, must have had privileged access to Shelley editions and facsimiles which he acquired at a very advantageous price. These editions followed one another in close succession, so Kloos's later claims that he was breathing Shelley at the time are given added credence. Moreover, the Shelley Society publications furnished Kloos with critical commentaries and ideas which he could use in his efforts to establish himself as the foremost Shelley expert in the Low Countries. It is undoubtedly in this context that we need to understand Kloos's decision in 1934 to reproduce in *De Nieuwe Gids* a one-line letter written almost half a century earlier (13 Feb. 1887): "Sir, I send you by this post the sum of one guinea as contribution for the second year of my membership of the Shelley society" (Kloos, "*Nieuwe Gids*-correspondentie" 643). As I argued elsewhere: "Why did Kloos publish this otherwise [...] unremarkable letter but to prove his own mettle as a serious, well-informed critic" on all matters Shelleyan (Steyaert, "Willem Kloos" 159)? Anyhow, on more than one occasion it was the Shelley Society which provided the source texts for some of the most ambitious Shelley translations to appear in Dutch. Yet, because of the low visibility of the Shelley Society Publications abroad, their role in the spread of Shelley's fame outside Britain has received scant attention. Though the small, blue-green volumes made only a fleeting appearance in the Low Countries, they evidently reached the hands of those who were most active in shaping the reception history of Shelley's works.

Bibliography

Baxter, B.M. *Albert Verwey's Translations from Shelley's Poetical Works: A Study of Their Style and Rhythm and a Consideration of Their Value as Translations*. Leidse Germanistische en Anglistische Reeks No. 3. Leiden: Leiden University Press, 1963.

Dekker, G. *Die invloed van Keats en Shelley in Nederland gedurende die negentiende eeu*. Groningen and The Hague: J.B. Wolters, 1926.

Denekamp, Paul. "David Spanjaard en zijn letterkundige ambities." *Mishpagazette* (Dec. 1996): 14-15.

De Raaf, Kornelis Herman, trans. *Percy Bysshe Shelley: Alastor, of de geest der eenzaamheid. Met een voorrede van Willem Kloos*. Rotterdam: W.L. & J. Brusse, [1905].

———, trans. *Percy B. Shelley: De Cenci. Een treurspel in vijf bedrijven*. Amsterdam: S.L. van Looy, 1908.

Downs, Brian W. "Anglo-Dutch Literary Relations 1867-1900: Some Notes and Tentative Inferences." *Modern Language Review* 31.3 (July 1936): 289-346.

G. "Varia: Shelley-Society." *De Nieuwe Gids* 1.4 (Apr. 1886): 159.

Kloos, Willem. "Literaire kroniek." *De Nieuwe Gids* 21 (Apr. 1906): 287-93.

———. "*Nieuwe Gids*-correspondentie." *De Nieuwe Gids* 49 (June 1934): 639-49.

Kok, Abraham Seyne. "Drie tooneelen uit Shelley's treurspel *De Cenci*." *Nederland* (1888): 213-45.

———. "Shelley's *Alastor*." *De Nederlandsche Spectator* 27 Jan. 1906: 25-27; 3 Feb. 1906: 33-35.

Naaijkens, Ton. *De slag om Shelley en andere essays over vertalen*. Nijmegen: Vantilt, 2002.

Note-Book of the Shelley Society. Ed. by the Honorary Secretaries. London: Reeves and Turner for The Shelley Society, 1888.

Potgieter, Everhardus Johannes. "De vlugtenden. (Naar Percy Bysshe Shelley)." *De Gids* 28 (June 1864): 524-27.

Russell, James Anderson. *Dutch Poetry and English: A Study of the Romantic Revival*. Amsterdam: H.J. Paris, 1939.

Shelley, Percy Bysshe. *Alastor or the Spirit of Solitude and Other Poems*. Ed. by Bertram Dobell. London: Reeves and Turner for The Shelley Society, 1886.

———. *The Cenci. A Tragedy in Five Acts*. Ed. by Alfred Forman and H. Buxton Forman. London: Reeves and Turner for The Shelley Society, 1886.

Steyaert, Kris. "Shelley in travestie: De vertaalstrijd om *Alastor*." *Filter: Tijdschrift voor vertalen en vertaalwetenschap* 6.3 (Sept. 1999): 28-36.

———. "A 'Massive Dramatic Plumpudding': The Politics of Reception in the Antwerp Performance of Shelley's *The Cenci*." *Keats-Shelley Journal* 50 (2001): 14-26.

———. "Willem Kloos and Percy Bysshe Shelley: The Rationale behind a Posthumous Friendship." *The Low Countries: Crossroads of Cultures*. Eds. Ton Broos, Margriet Lacy and Thomas F. Shannon. Studies in Dutch Language and Culture No. 1. Münster: Nodus Publikationen, 2006. 151-163.

———."'Love for a Godhead due': Shelley in the Low Countries." *The Reception of P.B. Shelley in Europe*. Eds. Susanne Schmid and Michael Rossington. The Athlone Critical Traditions Series. London and New York: Continuum, 2008. 169-185, 345-348.

Notes

[1] The essay first appeared in *Vertalen historisch bezien: Tekst, metatekst, theorie* (Eds. Dirk Delabastita and Theo Hermans. 's Gravenhage: Stichting Bibliographia Neerlandica, 1995). A revised version appeared in a collection of essays in 2002. It is to the latter version that I will refer in the rest of this article.

[2] Potgieter used the pseudonym as a tribute to the poet Willem Arnoldus Dwars (1793-1855).

[3] "wat ook ten grondslag gelê het aan die kunsopvattinge en aan die kuns self van die tagtigers" (242).

[4] Several sections from this study had been serialized in *De Nieuwe Gids*. The book was dedicated to Willem Kloos, who had died the year before (1938), and Lodewijk van Deyssel.

[5] See the bibliography for a selection. My chapter on the reception of Shelley in the Low Countries will appear in *Shelley in Europe* (Eds. Michael Rossington and Susanne Schmid. London and New York: Continuum, to be published in 2008).

[6] "Shelley is de inzet van literaire territoriumdrift. De wapens die in de strijd worden gegooid, zijn vertogen die nauwelijks te onderscheiden zijn van fictie, en dit geldt niet alleen voor de vertalingen zelf, maar ook voor de vertaalreflectie en de vertaalkritieken. De zaken worden door de betrokken partijen niet logisch of 'juist' voorgesteld. Er is eerder sprake van vertroebeling van ideeën." (178)

[7] "Shelley-Society. Velen zeker zullen met genoegen vernemen, dat er te Londen een genootschap is opgericht om 1°. de kennis van Shelley's werken en leven te vermeerderen; 2°. Shelley's drama's te doen vertoonen; 3°. de zeldzame eerste uitgaven zijner werken in facsimilé te herdrukken [...]. Wie voor een guinea (21 sh.) lid van het genootschap wordt, ontvangt gratis een exemplaar van al hare uitgaven." (G. 159)

[8] Andrew Lang's poem was originally published in *The Saturday Review*, 13 March 1886: 354.

[9] The demise of the Shelley Society is clothed in mystery and it is not clear when the organization ceased to exist. Already in the 1920s, Newman Ivey White and Walter Edwin Peck were engaged in a polemic in *Modern Language Notes* about the date of and the circumstances surrounding the Society's final activities.

[10] "Shelley's kunst en gedachteleven lijken soms meer op een zachtkleurig, vormenwisselend wolkenpaleis, dan op een onwrikbare constructie van stevig materiaal. De bekoring zijner kunst is dikwijls als die van een glans op satijn" (De Raaf, *Alastor* 11).

[11] Alex Gutteling produced translations of Shelley's *Adonais* and *Prometheus Unbound*. Both were published in *De Beweging*. *Prometheus ontboeid* was subsequently issued as No. 127 in "De Wereld-Bibliotheek" in 1910.

[12] "gebrek aan licht en schaduw, waardoor het schilderstuk te vlak, te eentonig wordt" (33).

[13] "[De] verheerlijking van Shelley [is] steeds stijgende gebleven, vaak niet zonder overdrijving, die zich vooral kenmerkte door een onoordeelkundig afbreken van anderer roem, wat altijd een veeg teeken is voor een partij of richting die zich daaraan schuldig maakt." (26).

[14] "Toen het gedicht verscheen, trok het weinig aandacht" (25).

[15] As a rule, the Shelley editions published by the Shelley Society were not facsimiles of the autograph but of the first printed edition.

[16] "But already the first reaction to De Raaf, by the veteran and Shakespeare translator Dr A.S. Kok in *De Nederlandsche Spectator*, fellow member of the Shelley Society, is harsh." ["Maar meteen de eerste reactie op De Raaf, van oudgediende en Shakespeare-vertaler dr A.S. Kok in *De Nederlandsche Spectator*, medelid van de Shelley Society overigens, valt fel uit"] (Naaijkens 185). However, Kok's name does not feature in the membership lists, and as Kok pointed out himself in his review, he had received the *Alastor* facsimile edition directly from the editor and not through the Society.

[17] "voor-de-vuist-weg fantaseeren" (Kloos, "Literaire kritiek" 288); "een haastige inval, ondoordacht op 't papier gegooid" (292).

[18] "om de onberispelijke, melodieuse versificatie, als om de ongemeenheid van opvatting en, men zou haast zeggen, weelderige fantasie" (25).

[19] "Ja het is goed, dat er een vertaling van Shelley is gekomen, een woordgetrouwe vertaling van zijn eerste eigenlijke gedicht. Het bekendere "Queen Mab" toch is wel Shelley's eerste, grootere, in versmaat geschrevene letterkundige proeve, doch telt als gedicht nagenoeg

niet meê. De dichter had toen zichzelf en zijn ware kunst nog geenszins gevonden, en zoo ging hij, als negentienjarige jongen (1812), daar aan 't geestdriftig speechen en 't abstract verzekeren, gelijk dit in de rijmende geschriften van het eind der 18e eeuw de mode was geweest. Neen, Alastor is Shelley's vroegste wezenlijke dichtwerk, en zijn jonge ziel breekt daar plotseling open in overvloedige schoonheid, gelijk een knop die uiteenspringt tot een groote, mooie bloem." (7)

[20] "Je kunt bij het achterhalen van vertaalopvattingen biografische en individuele aspecten niet ondergeschikt maken aan het geheel. Vertaalreflectie is enerzijds inderdaad een wereld op zich [...] maar tegelijk een fenomeen dat volledig in de wereld staat, verbonden met uiteenlopende motieven, belangen en intenties, de wereld ook van de achterklap, de affaires en de zwartmakerij. [...] Vandaar dat aandacht voor verdichtsels in vertaalreflectie nodig is." (194)

[21] A second edition of *De Cenci* was printed in 1911 as volume 26 in the so-called Roo-Rozen Series. Apart from a different cover and a slightly different title page, both editions are identical.

[22] "Hoewel in sommige uitgaven dit verhaal wordt weggelaten of kieschheidshalve slechts besnoeid wordt opgenomen, meende de Vertaler het in zijn geheel te moeten geven" (De Raaf, *De Cenci* 113).

[23] Spanjaard published a translation in verse of Shelley's *Epipsychidion* in 1927. It was dedicated to his wife, Rosa.

[24] Though Kloos's library was broken up after his death, it is possible to reconstruct his collection of Shelleyana as a hand-written catalogue, compiled by Kloos in the 1930s with his wife acting as his amanuensis, has been preserved.

[25] "Amice, Je brief heeft me veel genoegen gedaan, en de bijzonderheden over de tijd, toen je de papers van de Shelley-Society mo[es]t van de hand doen (over de opbrengst, in *dien* tijd, zul je je wel geen illusies hebben gemaakt, dunkt me [...]) heb ik met plezier gelezen". This letter is part of the Kloos collections at the Literary Museum and Documentation Centre in The Hague (class mark K533 B2).

Anne van Buul (Universiteit Groningen)

British Influences on Dutch Book Designs: A Case Study on Dutch Bibliophilic Editions of Works by Dante Gabriel Rossetti*

In August 1905 the Dutch poet P.C. Boutens (1870-1943) mentioned in a letter to his friend J.M. Kakebeeke (1881-1958) that he was working on a translation of the poem "The Blessed Damozel" by the Pre-Raphaelite poet, painter and translator Dante Gabriel Rossetti (1828-1882). By winter, he hoped, he would have completed several stanzas and sent them to his friend. A later letter shows that Kakebeeke did indeed receive Boutens's translation and was much impressed by Rossetti, as Boutens praises him with the words: "How good of you, to love him so!" ["Hoe goed van je, dien zoo te beminnen!"] (Goud, "Brieven van P.C. Boutens" 37, 42). This translation of "The Blessed Damozel" was the first in a series of four Rossetti-translations published by Boutens in the literary journal *De Gids* in December 1905 and October 1906. In February 1905, Boutens's translation of Rossetti's "The Portrait" had appeared in the journal *De Beweging*.[1] A final translation was to follow in 1910 and in 1912 all six translations were put together in the volume *Carmina,* which contains, besides Boutens's own poems, a section with eighteen translations (135-189). Boutens is one of the few who translated Rossetti into Dutch.[2] Until recently, Rossetti's fame in the Netherlands was based more on his original works and articles about his work. It wasn't until 2004 that a book with a large number of sonnets from the cycle *The House of Life* appeared, translated by Ike Cialona.

Boutens's interest in and admiration for Rossetti is indicated by the two lectures on Rossetti he delivered in 1908 (Goud, "Residentienieuws" 69, 70). He also wrote a "Sonnet aan D.G. Rossetti voor zijn portretstudies naar Mevr. Morris" ["Sonnet to D.G. Rossetti for his portraits of Mrs. Morris"] included in the volume *Carmina* (65-66). We know that Boutens still read and admired Rossetti at the end of his life, because, as a member of the "Residentietoneel" in The Hague, he recited one of his poems on the occasion of a special afternoon devoted to "unknown poems" on 2 December 1939.[3]

P.C. Boutens as a publisher

In 1906, Boutens conceived a plan to publish the five poems of Rossetti he had translated up until then in a bibliophilic edition. Boutens is well-known for the extraordinary attention he paid to the bindings of his volumes of poetry. He often asked artists to design a cover or initials, and a few copies of each edition were printed in a more luxurious form. This was in keeping with his exalted notion of the poetic genius and the superior role he awarded to poets. Boutens was convinced "that if ever God's secret in its sublime simplicity will be deciphered, it will be a poet who will be allowed to speak the words of deliverance." The luxurious bindings of his books underlined the exclusive and sublime character of the content of his poetry. It was directed at "the happy few". Boutens aimed to "in an indifferent world, lure a few readers along on his path to higher beauty."[4] In his opinion, only a select company of insiders was really able to understand his edifying poetry. This explains the limited print run of his editions.

The most famous example of Boutens's bibliophile activities is the volume *Naenia* from 1903. This elegy for Willem van Tets – one of the pupils who attended Boutens's course on the classics at the boarding school "Noorthey" at Voorschoten – was printed in just fourteen copies.[5] A few of these have hand-painted embellishments and initials by the famous Dutch symbolist painter Jan Toorop (1858-1928). The book is one of the rarest and most exceptional books printed in the Netherlands in modern times, and is typical not only of Boutens's love of books but also of the revival of the art of printing at the end of the 19th and the beginning of the 20th century. Although Boutens's bibliophilic interest seems to fit in with his poetical ideas, a number of questions arise as to why he chose to publish the Rossetti-volume in this particular form.

Rossetti and Morris as forerunners

Dante Gabriel Rossetti was a poet, a painter, and a translator. In 1848 he established the Pre-Raphaelite Brotherhood, a society of young artists that also William Morris (1834-1896) came to be identified with. The Pre-Raphaelites wanted to modernise art by turning back to the art of the Middle Ages, before Raphael (1483-1520). They wished to return to the beauty of the handiwork of medieval craftsmen, partly as a protest against mechanization and industrialization. At the end of the 19th century, these ideas were propagated by the Arts & Crafts Movement.

The Pre-Raphaelites derived inspiration for their work from the Italian primitive painters. Medieval manuscripts and old printed books served as examples for their own bibliophilic editions, which they had printed in limited editions and with traditional techniques. Originally, Rossetti had his first two volumes of poetry, *Poems* (1870) and *The Blessed Damozel* (1874), printed in a limited edition for his own circle of friends. He also made designs for books by friends and family. He aimed to integrate the written word with the decorative possibilities of the book as a physical object, and thus create a "total artwork". He often used simple geometric shapes derived from small hand-made books dating from the 15th century. Rossetti also paid special attention to the covers. The pastedowns and flyleaves show floral patterns that would return in the ornaments designed by Morris in the 1890s.[6]

In 1891, William Morris set up the Kelmscott Press, which printed and published 53 works over a period of seven years.[7] The editions were richly decorated with ornaments, and several typefaces were designed specially by Morris, such as the Chaucer Type for the edition of medieval works and the Golden Type for more recent literature. In 1898, all types designed by Morris were used posthumously for the publication of the *Note by William Morris on his aims in founding the Kelmscott Press*. Here Morris summarized the aims of the Kelmscott Press as follows:

> It was the essence of my undertaking to produce books which would be a pleasure to look upon as pieces of printing and arrangement of type. Looking at my adventure from this point of view then, I found I had to consider chiefly the following things: the paper, the form of the type, the relative spacing of the letters, the words and the lines; and lastly the position of the printed matter on the page. (*The Ideal Book* 75-76)

The first English printer, William Caxton, was a great example to Morris, but he indicated more than once that his book designs were influenced by Rossetti as well. We may safely assume that Morris prepared the three Kelmscott editions of Rossetti's works – *Ballads and Narrative Poems* (1893), *Sonnets and Lyrical Poems* (1894) and *Hand and Soul* (1895) – in his spirit.

In his edition of five translations of Rossetti's poems, Boutens also gives the impression of having worked deliberately in Rossetti's spirit. The question then arises whether Boutens followed Rossetti's work just with respect to content, or whether he was also influenced by the philosophy of Rossetti and his circle with regard to the outer appearance of his editions.

Three Dutch scholars have expressed their views on this matter, but it turns out that they contradict each other. In 1996 Sjoerd van Faassen claimed that Boutens's library furnished no proof that Boutens was familiar with the ideas or works of editors-publishers such as Morris and Charles Ricketts (128). Two years later Dick van Vliet claimed the opposite:

> Boutens's bibliophilic activities may have coincided in part with the revival of the art of printing in the Netherlands, they were essentially determined by the aestheticism of the English Pre-Raphaelites, in particular by the poet and painter Dante Gabriel Rossetti, whom Boutens greatly admired, [...] and by William Morris.[8]

In the same year, Paul van Capelleveen agreed with this hypothesis by stating that "the British influence on his [Boutens's] ideas on typography clearly stems from Morris."[9] Whereas Van Faassen had stressed two years previously that no proof for any influence exists, neither van Vliet nor van Capelleveen provides proof for their hypotheses. In what follows, I will underpin the assumptions of both scholars with reasonable arguments.

Boutens's acquaintance with British book designs

First of all, the claim that proof of Boutens's knowledge of the work of Morris and other English editors of his circle via his library is lacking, must be refuted. Marco Goud, Boutens expert and biographer, made an inventory of Boutens's library for his own use. This shows that Boutens possessed four editions of Rossetti's work. Three of these date from before his own Rossetti edition of 1906: the *Sonnets and Lyrical Poems* (printed on Morris's Kelmscott Press in 1894), *The Early Italian Poets* (a volume of Rossetti's translations, published in 1904 by Dent) and a reprint of *The Blessed Damozel* (published in 1906 by T.N. Foulis). The latter edition derives stylistically from the work of private presses such as Morris's. The Kelmscott edition is printed in black and red ink in the Golden Type designed by Morris, and is bound in vellum. Boutens could only have deduced the style of English private presses from this edition.

The assumption that innovations in the art of book printing by English printers inspired Boutens's own private editions (and his edition of the five Rossetti translations in particular) acquires a more solid basis now that we know that Boutens owned these bibliophilic editions at one time or another. Moreover, around 1900, William Morris and the Kelmscott Press were the subject of vivid interest in the Netherlands, for instance in journals such as *De Kroniek* and *De Gids.* It is very likely that Boutens took note of this, considering his own publishing activities and bibliophilic interests. His good friends Lodewijk van Deyssel and Jan Toorop, too, may have contributed to his knowledge. Jan Toorop met William Morris during his stay in England in 1889 and was influenced by the latter's critique of materialism and mass industry and his ideas on the pursuit of naturalness.[10] Van Deyssel visited the printers Charles Ricketts and Charles Shannon, who worked in the tradition of Morris, in England in 1894.

What is more, one or more copies of Boutens's translation of Plato's *Symposion* (1901) were bound according to a special binding technique invented by Morris. Alexandre Stols, himself a publisher of exclusive books, describes it as follows:

> As one knows, this [method of binding] consists of sewing the pages onto two coloured ribbons; the ribbons are stuck through the limp velum binding at the spine, pass between parchment and pastedown up to several centimetres from the long end of the book, where they emerge again from the cover (the binding) and are then tied into bows so as to close the book.[11]

The application of Morris's binding method demonstrates that Boutens moved in circles of printers and publishers who studied Morris's techniques and worked in his spirit.

When Boutens's own volume of poetry, *Praeludiën*, appeared in 1902, the choice of binding again reveals English influences. The binding was designed by the illustrator Herbert Granville Fell (1872-1951), whose work is characterized by a stylish combination of Pre-Raphaelite, symbolic and art-nouveau-like elements. Fell designed the 14-volume series *The Lyric Poets,* published by Dent in a cheap and a luxury edition between 1894 and 1900. The luxury edition served as a model for the binding of *Praeludiën*: both bindings are almost identical.[12] In 1901 Boutens had visited England, where he may have gained inspiration for the editions of his own poems, although the preferences of his publisher, Joh. Enschedé and sons in Haarlem, will also have played an important role.

Boutens's Rossetti-edition

When in 1906 Boutens went in search of a suitable printer for his edition of the five Rossetti-translations, he chose to cooperate with the Belgian printer Eduard Verbeke, based in Bruges. How Boutens found this printer we do not know, but it will not have been by accident. Verbeke established the "Imprimerie Sainte-Cathérine" in 1905 and thus was a newcomer to the business. He was educated in England and anglicized his name to Edward (Bonneure 155). In some of Boutens's editions he also anglicized the name of his press to "The Saint Catherine Press Ltd.". Perhaps Verbeke or Boutens wished to create the impression of a private press à la Morris, of which there were many in Britain at the time – at the very least, it appears they wished to place themselves in this tradition. From the foundation of his printing business onwards, Verbeke ventured bibliophilic editions of contemporary Flemish writers such as Guido Gezelle, Karel van de Woestijne and Stijn Streuvels. Between 1906 and 1913, Boutens had ten editions printed by Verbeke: two volumes of his own poetry, five translations and three editions of poetical works by others. Four of these books were original English works by Oscar Wilde, Rossetti and Lord Alfred Douglas. This, too, may point to a deliberate choice for a combination of content and exterior stemming or deriving from British examples. As it happens, most of Boutens's Plato translations were printed elsewhere.

The first edition printed by Verbeke for Boutens, immediately after the founding of his printing business, was the Rossetti edition *Vijf gedichten van Dante Gabriel Rossetti, in het Nederlandsch overgebracht door P.C. Boutens,* printed in December 1906 in a print run of 32 copies. The volume contains 44 pages, consists of three quires, and measures 225 x 175 mm. Initially Boutens left the edition unbound. It is unclear whether the edition was bound at his initiative at a later stage or whether he left this task to the collectors and friends who acquired copies. The edition was printed in black and red ink, on smooth Japanese paper. The typeface used was the 18th-century Caslon type, and the layout is generous. The lettering on the title page is filled in with small decorations. Several aspects of this edition imitate the work of English book printers of the 1890s.

The 18th-century Caslon type regained popularity in England in the 19th century. In 1844 the original Caslon old-face Roman was put into use again by the Chiswick Press in London. From then on, the Caslon type was widely used in England, especially for fine books given a semblance of old print. Because of its frequent use in England in the late 19th and early 20th century, the Caslon type became closely identified with Englishness. William Morris liked the primitive crudeness of Caslon and used it for his commercially printed books. After him, Bernard Shaw used the type in the late 1890s. This had the effect of bringing the Caslon type into even wider general circulation (Peterson 22-25). Because of its great popularity in England around 1900, it is not surprising that Edward Verbeke, who was partly educated in England, introduced the type in Belgium by using it for many luxury editions. By choosing Verbeke as a printer, Boutens placed himself deliberately in the English tradition, as the Caslon type was the only type on Verbeke's press. This raises the question whether there is a relation between text and choice of type. It is not unlikely that Boutens took it for granted that such an out-and-out English poet as Rossetti should be printed in a corresponding type.

The decorations Verbeke used in Boutens's Rossetti translation appear to derive even more strongly from William Morris and the style of his Kelmscott Press. Rossetti used a floral pattern on the pastedowns and flyleaves of his books as early as 1870. Morris's works are always decorated with leaves and flowers. He liked to fill in any white space on a page with small ornaments and usually filled out lines with the shapes of small leaves to form a closed block on the page. In Boutens's Rossetti translation, we see the same filling of a block of text on the title page, with the same – be it simplified – shape of leaf. As Morris was identified with this ornament, just as the Caslon type was with English books of the *fin-de-siècle*, Verbeke and Boutens evidently followed in Morris's footsteps.

Three other Rossetti-editions

Boutens was not alone in the Netherlands in publishing Rossetti's works according to the typographical principles of the author and his circle. Towards the end of the 1920s, three editions of Rossetti's works appeared with three different publishers-printers. They all belonged to the traditionally oriented vanguard to whom William Morris's editions presented a shining example. They, too, had a love of craftsmanship and detested the tasteless commercial books that had been produced ever since the industrial revolution. However, this later generation paid less attention to decorations than Morris did, and concentrated rather on a book's readability. Key figures in this context are Sjoerd de Roos, Alexandre Stols and Charles Nypels – all of whom were connected to each other and, in one way or another, to Boutens.[13] Nypels was a pupil of de Roos and a friend of Stols, who in his turn was on friendly terms (and cooperated) with Boutens. Stols wrote about Boutens as a publisher during the latter's lifetime. Of the Dutch typographers to have worked in Morris's spirit, De Roos is the best-known, namely as the editor of a collection of William Morris's lectures in translation entitled *Kunst en Maatschappij* (1903), by some regarded as the first modern book in the Netherlands.

It appears that all four editors had the same reason for choosing Rossetti's work for their bibliophilic editions: his aim to achieve a perfect match between text and image, content and appearance is exemplary of the tradition of late 19th-century British book innovators in which they wanted to situate their work.

The first to print original work by Rossetti in a bibliophilic edition in the Netherlands was Charles Nypels, on the press of the publishing house Leiter-Nypels in Maastricht in 1927. He made a selection of poems for an edition of *Sonnets and Songs towards a work to be called The House of Life*, containing the first 28 sonnets and the first 7 songs of the cycle *The House of Life*, published by Rossetti during his lifetime in various compilations. Nypels printed 200 copies, part of which, according to the colophon, he exported to the United States and France. In the Netherlands, private patrons could subscribe to a copy printed in their name. Among the subscribers were the artist Richard Roland Holst and his wife Henriette, as is shown by the copy in the possession of the Dutch Royal Library in The Hague. The inventory of Boutens's library indicates that he, too, ordered a copy. The typeface used for this edition is Grotius, designed a year earlier by Sjoerd de Roos, who was highly influenced by Morris – his most famous type is the "Hollandsche Mediæval", based on a combination of 15th-century types and Morris's Golden Type. In 1928, also in Maastricht, an edition of Rossetti's prose story *Hand and Soul* (1849) was printed by Alexandre Stols on his own Halcyon Press, in cooperation with Joh. Enschedé and sons. Like Boutens, Stols had several copies printed in a more luxurious form: on Japanese paper and, in some cases, on vellum.

The layout was designed by Stols himself and is unique in its funnel-like shape of the text of the prologue. In this Rossetti edition, too, a striking typeface is used. At the end of the book the following "typographical note" was added in English:

> This book is printed in the Roman type said to be made by Peter Schoeffer of Gernsheim (1420–1502). His descendants preserved the matrices more than two hundred years. In 1768 these belonged to Jacobus Scheffers, printer at Bois-le-Duc. On the 26th of August of that year the collection of about sixty matrices came into possession of Joh. Enschedé who only used them for experiments to study the oldest methods of type-founding. Early in the 20th century a suitable fount and a reproduction of the lost matrices were made.

Whereas Enschedé had only studied medieval type-founding, the medieval craftsmanship of printing had become so popular in Stols's day that he, in imitation of the English private presses, started to reuse it. A connection of Pre-Raphaelite, mystical and medieval content with a medieval type, must have seemed extremely appropriate to him.

In 1929 the fourth Rossetti edition appeared in the Netherlands: a bibliophilic edition of *Hand and Soul* by the typographer Sjoerd de Roos. In line with Morris, his main concern was the overall impression of a page, which had to be balanced and harmonious. Since 1926, De Roos had owned a small printing press in Hilversum, which he called "Heuvelpers". *Hand and Soul* was the press's third publication (from a total of four) and was printed in 125 copies, partly bound in vellum. De Roos not only designed the page layout, but also the type, "Meidoorn", and the initials. The newspaper *Nieuwe Rotterdamsche Courant* published the following comment on 19 December 1929:

> one should read [the story] in this noble form of page and letter in order to feel how well printer-artist S.H. de Roos has succeeded again in arranging the letters on the pages and the decorations of the text in harmony with the spirit of the story.[14]

It is not surprising that two of the publishers opted for an edition of Rossetti's only prose text, as the title of this work expresses the philosophy behind bibliophilic editions. In *Hand and Soul* a medieval painter paints his own soul, which reveals itself to him in the guise of a woman. He thus invests his inner self, his soul, with a perceptible physical manifestation. In the same manner Stols and De Roos express the soul of the book, the content of *Hand and Soul*, through their hand-made, exclusive designs which resemble the printing practices of Morris and Rossetti inspired by medieval printers.

Conclusion

Even though the Rossetti editions of Nypels, Stols and De Roos came about well over twenty years later than Boutens's edition of five Rossetti translations, and even though they had more developed and therefore perhaps more sophisticated ideas regarding the art of printing, their ideas about which literary work should be placed in which typographical context turn out to be remarkably similar. In comparison to the others, Boutens may have been early in his interest in Rossetti and his private-press-like editions. Nonetheless, it is very likely that Boutens was thoroughly aware of the English innovations and the tradition in which he placed himself through his choice of printers, type, covers and binding methods.

Solid proof for influence is always hard to give, but even though this article only provides a critical exploration of the field in question, it does demonstrate that Boutens and his circle were well-informed about the British innovations in the art of book printing. Richard Roland Holst, who met Morris and Shannon and Ricketts in England in 1893 and 1895 respectively, also played an important role in the propagation of Morris's ideas.[15] The binding he designed in 1895 for the volume of poetry *Sonnetten en Verzen in Terzinen geschreven*, written by his future wife Henriette van der Schalk, has many of the characteristics aimed at by English private presses: a lineation that resembles medieval manuscripts, hand-cut initials and decorations. A more extensive network analysis may shed light on the precise ways in which the ideas of Rossetti and Morris and their practical execution reached Dutch bibliophiles and was reflected in their work. It will be clear that Boutens, with his bibliophilic edition of his five translations, has been one of the forerunners.

Thanks to Jan Gielkens,
Adriaan van der Weel
and Marco Goud.

* The Dutch version of this article contains pictures of the books mentioned. See Anne van Buul, " 'Scheppers van het schoone boek.' De invloed van Engelse boekvernieuwingen op P.C. Boutens en andere bibliofiele uitgevers van het werk van Dante Gabriel Rossetti." *De Boekenwereld* 24.5 (2008): 287-299.

Bibliography

Barber, G. "Rossetti, Ricketts, and Some English Publishers' Bindings of the Nineties." *The Library* 25 (1970): 136-149.

Bonneure, Fernand. "Brugse drukkers in de 20ste eeuw." *Vlaanderen* 43.252 (1994): 154-158.

Boutens, P.C. *Naenia. Tot de nagedachtenis van Willem van Tets, waarbij zijn herdrukt de strofen* In Memoriam, *geschreven van 12-18 juni 1900 en nu gegeven aan George van Tets.* [Voorschoten: P.C. Boutens], 1903.

———. *Vijf gedichten van Dante Gabriel Rossetti, in het Nederlandsch overgebracht door P.C. Boutens.* ['s-Gravenhage: P.C. Boutens], 1906.

———. *Carmina.* Amsterdam: Van Kampen, [1912].

———. "Vorm en vormeloosheid in de dichtkunst. Bezorgd door Karel de Clerck." *Verslagen en mededelingen van de Koninklijke Vlaamse Academie voor taal- en letterkunde* (1964): 359-370.

"Dante Gabriel Rossetti's "Hand and Soul". Uitgaaf van de Heuvelpers te Hilversum." *Nieuwe Rotterdamsche Courant,* 19 December 1929.

de Clerck, Karel. *Uit het leven van P.C. Boutens.* Amsterdam: Polak & Van Gennep, 1964.

Goud, Marco. "'Neem nooit een molenaarsdochter!' Brieven van P.C. Boutens aan zijn vriend J.M. Kakebeeke." *Jaarboek. Letterkundig Museum* 7 (1998): 21-58.

———. "Residentienieuws." *De Parelduiker* 5 (2000) 5: 69-72.

———. *Een ondraaglijke drukfout. De ontstaansgeschiedenis van P.C. Boutens' Naenia, gevolgd door acht brieven van Boutens aan Joh. Enschedé en Zonen.* Woubrugge: Avalon Pers, 2005.

Hefting, V. *Jan Toorop 1858-1928.* Den Haag: Haags Gemeentemuseum, 1989.

Lommen, Mathieu. *De Grote Vijf. S.H. de Roos, J.F. van Royen, J. van Krimpen, C. Nypels en A.A.M. Stols.* Amsterdam: M.M. Lommen, 1991.

McGann, Jerome. *Dante Gabriel Rossetti and the Game That Must Be Lost.* New Haven & London: Yale University Press, 2000.

Morris, William. *The ideal book; essays and lectures on the arts of the book.* Ed. William S. Peterson. Berkeley: University of California Press, 1982.

Peterson, William S. *The Kelmscott Press. A History of William Morris's Typographical Adventure.* Oxford: Clarendon Press, 1991.

Prick, Harry G.M. *Een vreemdeling op de wegen. Het leven van Lodewijk van Deyssel vanaf 1890.* Amsterdam: Athenaeum/Polak & Van Gennep, 2003.

Purvis, A.W. en C. de Jong. *Nederlands grafisch ontwerp van de negentiende eeuw tot nu.* Arnhem: Terra Lannoo, 2006.

Rossetti, Dante Gabriel. *Sonnets and lyrical poems.* London: Kelmscott Press, 1894.

——— *The Early Italian poets. Together with Dante's Vita nuova.* London: J.M. Dent and Co, Aldine House, 1904.

———. *The Blessed Damozel.* London/Edinburgh: T.N. Foulis, [1906]. Roses of Parnassus.

———. *Sonnets and songs towards a work to be called The House Of Life.* Maastricht: Leiter-Nypels, 1926 [1927].

———. *Hand and Soul.* Maastricht: The Halcyon Press, 1928.

———. *Sonnetten.* Vertaald uit het Engels door Ike Cialona. Amsterdam: Athenaeum-Polak & Van Gennep, 2004.

Stols, A.A.M. "P.C. Boutens als uitgever." *Halcyon* 3.11/12 (1942): 1-11.

ter Braak, Menno. "J.C. Bloem over onbekende gedichten. Leden van het Residentietoneel dragen voor." *Het Vaderland,* 3 December 1939.

van Capelleveen, Paul. "P.C. Boutens en de band van *Praeludiën.* (een bibliografische voetnoot)." *Jaarboek. Letterkundig Museum* 7 (1998): 59-84.

van Faassen, Sjoerd. "'Een zeker amateurisme.' P.C. Boutens als boekverzorger." *Ik heb iets bijna schoons aanschouwd. Over leven en werk van P.C. Boutens 1870-1943.* Eds. Jan Nap et al. Amsterdam: Athenaeum-Polak & Van Gennep, 1993. 126-149.

van Halsema, J.D.F. "Van oorsprong naar oorsprong. Van Royens letters en zijn boeken." *Disteltype, corps 15. Over de Disteltype van J.F. van Royen en L. Pissarro, en de literatuur van de Zilverdistel.* Amsterdam: De Buitenkant, 2000. 77-94.

van Vliet, H.T.M. "Estheticisme en mystiek bij P.C. Boutens." *Tijdschrift voor Nederlandse Taal- en Letterkunde* 114.1 (1998): 34-47.

Notes

1 "Het portret" (*De Beweging* 1.1 (1905): 318); "De zalige jonkvrouw" (*De Gids* 69.4 (1905): 430-434); "Doods geboorte", "Herfstliedje" and "Bewolkte grenzen" (*De Gids* 70.4 (1906): 47-52); "Verloren dagen" (*De Gids* 74.4 (1910): 372).

2 In 1889 the poet Augusta Peaux translated a couple of fragments for her sister's article about Rossetti in *De Tijdspiegel* (A.-J. Peaux, "Dante Gabriel Rossetti." *De Tijdspiegel* 46.3 (1889): 151-169). The author Albert Verwey translated two sonnets named "Willowwood" but did not publish them (Albert Verwey, "Ik zat met liefde…" *Dichtspel. Oorspronkelijke en vertaalde gedichten*. Bezorgd door Dr. Mea Nijland-Verwey. Amsterdam: De Arbeiderspers 1983. 461). J.F. Kunst translated and published "The Blessed Damozel" again in his volume *Langs den weg* in 1928. (J.F. Kunst, *Langs den weg.* [S.I.: s.n.] 1928. 113-120.) The poet Adriaan Roland Holst published his versions of seven poems in different periodicals between 1920 and 1936 (A. Roland Holst, *Verzameld Werk. Poëzie II.* Amsterdam: G.A. van Oorschot, 1981. 1260, 1261, 1267-1271). In 1941 Simon Vestdijk published a translation of "The Moonstar" in *Groot Nederland* (39 (1941): 2, 94).

3 Menno ter Braak commented on this evening in the newspaper *Het Vaderland,* 3 December 1939.

4 "dat, wanneer ooit Gods geheim in zijn sublieme simpelheid zal worden geraden, het een dichter is, die het verlossende woord zal mogen spreken."; "in een onverschillige wereld enkelen meê te sleepen of meê te troonen op zijn weg ter hoogere schoonheid." ("Vorm en vormeloosheid" 365)

5 The exact number of copies is still uncertain. See Goud's *Een ondraaglijke drukfout.*

6 For further information on Rossetti's printing activities, see Barber and McGann.

7 For the history of the *Kelmscott Press* and more about the English book renewals, see Peterson's *The Kelmscott Press.*

8 "Boutens' bibliofiele activiteiten mogen dan deels samenvallen met de opleving van de boekdrukkunst in Nederland, zij zijn echter wezenlijk bepaald door het estheticisme van de Engelse Preraphaëlieten, en dan met name van de door Boutens zeer bewonderde dichter en schilder Dante Gabriel Rossetti en […] William Morris." (36)

8 "de Engelse invloed op zijn [Boutens'] ideeën over typografie is duidelijk via Morris tot hem gekomen." (73)

9 On Toorop's meeting with Morris, see Hefting (9-10). On van Deyssel, see van Faassen (137) and Prick (423-424).

10 "Deze [bindwijze] bestaat, zoals men weet, uit het naaien der vellen op twee gekleurde linten; deze linten worden bij den kneep even door den slappen perkamenten omslag gestoken, loopen tusschen perkament en schutblad tot op enkele centimeters van de lange zijde van het boek door, komen daar weer uit het omslag (den band) te voorschijn en dienen dan om het boek met strikken te sluiten." (5)

[11] See also Van Capelleveen.

[12] For general information about these printers see Lommen, and Purvis and De Jong.

[13] "men zou [de vertelling] moeten lezen in dezen edelen vorm van bladzijde en letter om te voelen hoe goed ook weer ditmaal de drukker-kunstenaar S.H. de Roos in harmonie met den geest van het verhaal zijn arrangement van de letters op de bladzijden en de schikking en versiering van den tekst heeft getroffen." ("Dante Gabriel Rossetti's 'Hand and Soul'. Uitgaaf van de Heuvelpers te Hilversum." *Nieuwe Rotterdamsche Courant,* 19 december 1929.)

[14] This hypothesis is also mentioned by, among others, Van Halsema.

Susanna De Schepper (University of Warwick)

George Eliot on the Dutch Market (1860-1896)

Although a surprising number of Dutch 19th-century translations of George Eliot's works can be found in the Dutch Central Catalogue, very little scholarship *about* these translations has been published. William Baker and John Ross mention most studies on Eliot's reception in the Low Countries in their thorough *George Eliot: A Bibliographical History* (2002), but they clearly suffer from a language barrier, proof of which are the many misprints in the transcription of the Dutch title pages. There also seems to be an additional geographical barrier, as most of the mentioned translations are held in libraries that they apparently consider out of their reach – which they dutifully acknowledge by stating that the edition in question was "not seen". Apart from Diederik Lüch van Werven's *Dutch Readings of George Eliot 1856-1880* (2001), Baker and Ross also occasionally refer to Brinkman's late 19th-century catalogue. Although Van Werven includes an overview of the translations in an appendix, he mainly focuses on the key reviewers of Eliot's fiction in the Netherlands (such as Conrad Busken Huet, Johannes van Vloten and Allard Pierson) and their affinity with Eliot's philosophical background. Hence, his treatment of the actual translations is limited and on some points incomplete. Van Werven's overview of translations is based on a similar list in Clazien Verheul's "Ethisch realisme: de ontvangst van de romans van George Eliot in Nederland in de periode 1860-1881" (1984). Yet again, her main focus is on the *reception* of Eliot's ideas rather than on material evidence.

The present contribution aims to fill this lacuna by turning to the published translations themselves, as well as to the most important contemporary sources Brinkman's *Catalogus* and the *Nieuwsblad voor den Boekhandel*. Before discussing Eliot's Dutch translations and the agreements between publishers in more detail, I will briefly sketch Eliot's publishing situation in the UK.

Eliot in the United Kingdom

George Eliot's financial success was in part determined by the time in which her novels were written. As Sutherland clearly states, "1850-1880 [was] one of the richest periods that fiction has known" (39). According to Sutherland, this was the result of a combination of four factors: high prices, multiple outlets, wide sales and abundant creative genius. I will not go into detail about the UK publishing world in the second half of the 19th century; in the present context, it should suffice to indicate that the business of books was booming, which resulted in many experiments in publication form, sales strategies and library policies. The firm that played an undeniable role in Eliot's career is Blackwood and Sons, which Finkelstein describes as "the house that George built" (34). They were one of the most successful publishing houses at the time, based in Edinburgh and well-known for their periodical *Blackwood's Edinburgh Magazine*. Eliot was introduced to them through her partner, George Henry Lewes. Though Eliot and the firm had occasional disagreements – most notably about her pseudonym and true identity – they developed a cordial working relationship. As a result, all of Eliot's novels but one was published by Blackwood's – George Smith, from Smith & Elder, managed to secure publication rights for Eliot's *Romola* by offering the then unheard of sum of £10,000. John Blackwood handsomely accepted the fact that he could not exceed this offer, as is evident from the following letter to Eliot on 20 May 1862: "I am of course sorry that your new Novel is not to come out under the old colours but I am glad to hear that you made so satisfactory an arrangement" (Haight, *The George Eliot Letters* IV: 35). In all, Eliot was a successful author and generated immense profits for Blackwood's firm until the turn of the century, when the market was saturated and desperately on the look-out for something new.

When it came to copyrights, they were usually sold for a particular work as a lump sum. "Extra profits" from reprints would simply go into the publisher's pockets. They had no legal obligation to share it with the author. Copyright was recognized within the UK (and the British Colonies) by the Copyright Act of 1842. However, it applied only to domestic authors and was powerless on the international scene. The situation was rectified slightly in 1887 when many European countries signed the Berne Convention, which stated that "a book which is copyright in any signatory state is also copyright in all the other signatory states under exactly the same conditions (except legal deposit) as a book first published in that country" (Feather 174). The Netherlands, however, only signed the Berne Convention in 1911.[1] This meant that no official agreement between the UK and the Netherlands existed when it came to reciprocal acknowledgement of copyright. Consequently, publishing translations of British works, whether authorised or not, was completely legal in the Netherlands. There was no obligation to pay the British publisher, let alone the author.

Within the Netherlands though, there were agreements when it came to translation rights. These were regulated by the "Vereeniging ter Bevordering van de Belangen des Boekhandels" (VBBB) ["The Association for the Promotion and Interests of Booksellers"], founded in 1815. In 1857, a Translations Committee was established which would specifically handle and organise the translation requests. Though there was a general consensus on this policy, some people were notorious for blatantly disregarding the regulations. Such a public enemy of the VBBB was Ter Gunne, who will be discussed further below.

In the UK, publishers and authors were well aware of the peculiarity of "free translation" in the Netherlands, where it caused some controversy. Though there was no legal necessity for remuneration, there was a gradual "*de facto* Dutch recognition of English copyright" (Van der Weel, "Dutch Nineteenth-century Attitudes to International Copyright" 37), which can be traced in Eliot's Dutch publishing history.

Eliot in Dutch translation

With regard to published Dutch translations in book form, Eliot is an exceptional case when compared to other canonical women novelists of that period. Not only were *all* of her novels translated into Dutch during the 19th century – and even some of her poetry –, also a five-volume edition of her collected works was issued, all of which appeared in multiple editions. These books are the product of six translators and six publishers, cooperating in varying combinations.

The first work to be translated in the Netherlands was not Eliot's first publication, *Scenes of Clerical Life* (1858), but her novel *Adam Bede* (1859). The translation right was registered by A. C. Kruseman in 1859 (*Nieuwsblad*, 24 Feb 1859), soon after the UK publication. He published the work [01][2] a year later at his firm in Haarlem (*Nieuwsblad*, 10 May 1860). Similar to the UK three-decker, it was issued in three volumes, each containing a steel engraving by J. H. Rennefeld, based on drawings by Jozef Israëls. The translator was Anna Dorothea Busken Huet-Van der Tholl (1827-1898), wife of Conrad Busken Huet and friend of Kruseman. Previous to *Adam Bede*, she had translated other stories from both English and French. *Adam Bede* would be her last big translation project, as soon after this publication her son was born and she devoted all her attention to him and her husband (Molhuysen and Blok X: 1022-1024). Rights for this edition were bought on a stock sale two years later by Van Druten & Bleeker, a young publishing firm from Sneek (*Nieuwsblad*, 6 Nov 1862). They were responsible for many reprints of this translation, and included the work in their series "Goedkope bibliotheek voor alle standen" ["Cheap library for all classes"]. Before the turn of the century, *Adam Bede* appeared in at least 8 more editions [06, 11, 18, 22, 24-27], making it a bestseller. Eliot herself was aware of the translation as early as 1860, as is evident from a letter that Lewes sent to his eldest son, Charles, on 17 March: "Adam Bede is translated into Hungarian, Dutch, German, and French – so you see we are becoming quite European celebrities" (Haight, *The George Eliot Letters* III: 274).

Translation rights for Eliot's *Scenes of Clerical Life* were also registered by Kruseman in 1859 (*Nieuwsblad*, 23 Feb 1859), yet he published them only in 1861 (*Nieuwsblad*, 8 Aug 1861). It appeared under the title *Herders en schapen: Drie novellen* [02] and comprised all three stories that originally appeared in *Blackwood's Magazine*.[3] They were translated into Dutch by Conrad Busken Huet himself. This time, Kruseman opted for a two-volume octavo edition, again each with a steel engraving. The title page of both volumes announces Eliot as the "schrijver" ["male author"] of *Adam Bede*, showing that the pseudonym was still intact in the Netherlands at this time even though the truth about Eliot's identity was already out in the UK. Again, Kruseman sold the rights at a stock sale in Amsterdam (*Nieuwsblad*, 6 Nov 1862; *Brinkman* 339). This work was only reprinted once, namely in the first volume [12] of the collected works edition by Van Druten & Bleeker.[4]

1861 was a very productive year in the Netherlands. Not only did the aforementioned *Scenes of Clerical Life* appear, but also translations of *The Mill on the Floss* (1860) and *Silas Marner* (1861). The latter were published by P. N. van Kampen from Amsterdam, and translated by Jacoba Westrheene-van Heijningen (1821-1900), probably Eliot's most important Dutch translator. She was a teacher, governess and later principal of a school for girls. She was married to Tobias van Westrheene, a painter, writer and editor. To add to the family income, Jacoba Westrheene-van Heijningen translated novels from English into Dutch. After her husband's death, she published original novels under the pseudonym Hester Wene. From Eliot she translated *The Mill on the Floss*, *Silas Marner*, *Felix Holt, the Radical*, *Middlemarch* and *Daniel Deronda* (Molhuysen & Blok III: 1414-1415). The translations of *The Mill on the Floss* and *Silas Marner* were published by Van Kampen in, respectively, three [03] and one [05] octavo volumes. Each volume was headed by a lithographed title vignette, representing key moments of the story. Here, too, Eliot is still announced on the titlepage as the "schrijver van Adam Bede". Both translations were reprinted later in the collected works edition [12, 13] by Van Druten & Bleeker.

Van Kampen is the first Dutch publisher to pay Eliot – or, rather, Blackwood's – for his translations. Both Baker and Ross's *Bibliographical History* (124) and Haight's *Biography* (318) list a received payment of £10 for a Dutch translation of *The Mill on the Floss* [03] in 1861. Presumably, this was done by Van Kampen since he was the only publisher of such a translation at this time. For *Silas Marner* [05], Blackwood's received a cheque for £20 from the Netherlands, again, presumably by Van Kampen, as is evident from a letter George Henry Lewes sent to John Blackwood on 16 April 1861: "Thanks for the cheque; but you have been hasty in sending me the whole of 20£ from Holland since you have an account *against* me for binding of m.s.s. of Mill and Silas as well as for some other things" (Haight, *The George Eliot Letters* VIII: 281n.4). Although Baker and Ross refer to this letter, they also state that Eliot received but "£10 for the rights (*Journal* 88)" (127). It is possible that Eliot had already deducted some other costs to be settled with Blackwood when she wrote this figure down in her journal, as Lewes's letter seems to suggest. Or, since the registration date with the Translations Committee and the date of the receipt of the cheque in the UK are so close together, Van Kampen perhaps came to an agreement beforehand with Blackwood already for the "right of early sheets".

It is true that this new novel, *Silas Marner*, was highly anticipated by Dutch publishers. The Translation Committee received requests from three different firms within mere days of each other.[5] Van Kampen was first, however, and published the translation within three months. It is here that Ter Gunne's name emerges on the scene again. Almost simultaneously with

Van Kampen's publication and thus completely ignoring the Committee's policy, Ter Gunne issued a translation [04] as well, also entitled *Silas Marner, de wever van Raveloe* (*Nieuwsblad*, 4 July 1861). It was, like Van Kampen's, a one-volume octavo edition bearing a lithographed title vignette. It is not known who the translator was. However, Ter Gunne definitely knew what he was doing when he priced it decidedly lower than Van Kampen. When *Silas Marner* was reprinted in the collected works edition by Van Druten & Bleeker, Ter Gunne, too, issued a reprint and, again, sold it at a lower price (*Nieuwsblad*, 27 Jan 1871). Sadly, no copy of a *Silas Marner* edition published by Ter Gunne has survived in a public collection.

The translation of *Romola* (1863), the only book not brought out by Blackwood's, seems to have been a very straightforward affair. It was published in 1864 [07], soon after its original appearance in the UK, by Kruseman (*Nieuwsblad*, 18 Feb 1864). The translator this time was not Busken Huet, nor his wife, but his brother-in-law, Julius Christiaan van Deventer (1824-1892). Van Deventer was very active in the field of education, contributed to several periodicals and was known for a few other translations.[6] This was again a three-volume edition, containing three lithographs, and later reprinted in the collected works edition [14]. Similar to Kruseman's other publications, *Scenes of Clerical Life* and *Adam Bede*, there appears to be no material evidence of any payment for *Romola*.

Apart from Kruseman, Van Kampen and Ter Gunne, also a fourth publisher, Van Druten & Bleeker, played an important role. The first novel they published was *Felix Holt, the Radical* (1866), translated by Jacoba van Westrheene-van Heijningen in two volumes in 1867 [08]. From lithographer to artist to translator, this is exactly the same group of people as Van Kampen employed for his Eliot editions.[7] What is new about this publication, though, is that the title page announces Eliot for the first time as the "schrijfster" ["female author"] of *Adam Bede*. Again, no trace could be found of a payment for this translation. This novel was also later reprinted as part of the collected works edition [09, 17].

These collected works were published by Van Druten & Bleeker over a period of more than three years. First sold in 48 parts at regular intervals, the publisher aimed at a large audience, which is evident from the very low price per instalment.[8] Eventually, all parts were gathered into five volumes, published in 1871-1872. These instalments were not issued chronologically: *Novellen* [12], for example, was published simultaneously with *Felix Holt* [09, 17], one (and later two) instalments of each appearing at regular intervals. Similarly, *Romola* [14] was published in parts alongside the remainder of *Felix Holt*.[9] Consequently, also the volumes did not appear in a logical order: first volume V (*Felix*) [09, 17] was published, then volume I (*Novellen*) [12], IV (*Romola*) [14], III (*Molen*) [13], and finally volume II (*Adam Bede*) [18]. Van Druten wrote to Blackwood's to ask for a photograph of "Miss Evans", probably to include it in this collection, entitled *George Eliot's Romantische Werken* [10]. He did not receive one though, as Lewes wrote 1 December 1871: "Touching the Dutchman please inform him that Miss Evans has ceased to exist as Miss Evans for 18 years; and that no photograph of her exists" (Haight, *The George Eliot Letters* V: 223). This, however, did not affect the working relationship, as the Dutch firm remunerated Eliot in the following way, as she writes to Blackwood 3 January 1873, "My friendly Dutch publishers lately sent us a handsome row of volumes [...] with an introduction in which comparisons are safely shrouded for me in the haze of Dutch, so that if they are disadvantageous I am not pained" (V: 362).

To return to our first publisher, Kruseman, his last contribution to the Eliot translations is a collection of selected extracts published in 1872, entitled *Uit George Eliot* [15]. This is a shortened version of the Blackwood publication *Wise, Witty, and Tender Sayings* (Baker and Ross 479-480). The translation was by Pieter Jacob Cousijn (1840-1899), though published under the female pseudonym of Marie Neve. He was not a prolific translator and probably took this on as a favour to Kruseman and a means of earning something on the side of his professional work in several educational institutions (Molhuysen & Blok VIII: 321-322).

While Van Druten & Bleeker were in the midst of publishing their collected works edition in instalments, they also registered the translation rights for *Middlemarch* (1871-1872), which were granted to them 27 October 1871 (*Nieuwsblad*, 31 Oct 1871). That this was an uncontested decision for such a bestselling novel is probably due to the fact that Van Druten & Bleeker had come to an earlier agreement with Blackwood for the amount of £25.[10] The translator for all four volumes was Jacoba van Westrheene-van Heijningen. This edition [16] was heavily advertised in the Netherlands from 1871 onwards, with the four volumes appearing over the course of the next two years.

Given this successful cooperation between Blackwood's and Van Druten & Bleeker, it is not surprising that this small Dutch firm also published a translation of *Daniel Deronda* in 1876. This time, however, there was a Dutch competitor, De Erven F. Bohn from Haarlem. Bohn wrote the following to Eliot 9 October 1875:

> Having read in the Atheneum it is your intention to publish shortly a new novel, we beg to apply to you the kind request to transfer to us the right of translation into Dutch. In case your answer is favourable we would be very glad to hear from you on which condition you would be so kind to sell us the right. Of course it is our meaning to get one copy some weeks before publication for the purpose of preventing all concurrence, as it will be known to you that translation is free in our country. (UL, Bohn Archive, BOH C3, fol. 254)

Blackwood's replied, asking a sum of £50 for the right of early sheets. Bohn declined, again drawing attention to the peculiar Dutch situation: "Perhaps you are not aware that, though having received from you the right of early sheets, every bookseller in our country may publish another translation, which is not seldom the case" (UL, Bohn Archive, BOH C3, fol. 261). He obviously did not want to run the risk of someone like Ter Gunne beating him to it at a lower price. Instead, Bohn countered the offer and proposed £20, which was not accepted by Blackwood. In this case, Van Druten was more successful in his negotiations with Blackwood, perhaps on the basis of their earlier cooperation, but more likely because of the fact that they offered £40. As soon as this deal was agreed, Van Druten & Bleeker registered the translation rights in the Netherlands,[11] and widely advertised this forthcoming publication, referring to the success of the novel in the UK. Again, the translation [19] was by Jacoba Westhreene-van Heijningen. In a letter of 21 December 1875 to his business relations, Van Druten wrote

> I hereby announce to you that, as a result of an agreement with the British publishers, on 1 Feb, the first part of the Dutch translation of Daniel Deronda will appear with me SIMULTANEOUSLY with the first part of the original work.[12]

The date and contents of this letter indicate clearly that, as in the case of *Middlemarch*, Van Druten had come to an agreement with Blackwood before officially registering the translation right in the Netherlands.

When after *Daniel Deronda* no new Eliot novel appeared, Van Druten & Bleeker used this as an opportunity to publish untranslated older work by Eliot. They gathered two short stories, "The Lifted Veil" (1859) and "Brother Jacob" (1864) and published them in one volume in 1878 [20], respectively 19 and 14 years after their initial publication in the UK. As far as I know, the firm did not give Eliot or Blackwood any form of payment, possibly due to the fact that this was older work. For some reason, these stories were not translated by Van Druten's usual translator, Jacoba van Westrheene-van Heijningen, but by Jacoba Berendina Zwaardemaker-Visscher (1835-1912). Not much is known about her, aside from her marriage to Cornelis Zwaardemaker, who was a bookseller, publisher, and, most importantly, editor of the *Nieuwsblad voor den Boekhandel* (Molhuysen & Blok VII: 1354).

Eliot's last work, a collection of essays entitled *Impressions of Theophrastus Such* (1879), appeared in the Netherlands in 1879 in a one-volume edition [21]. It is not indicated who the translator was, but the publisher was De Erven F. Bohn. In a competitive struggle similar to that leading up to the publication of *Daniel Deronda*, both Van Druten and Bohn expressed an interest in this title and requested early sheets. Eliot was in doubt: Van Druten was, in her words, "a man to deal with", yet Bohn made an attractive offer of £20 (Haight, *The George Eliot Letters* VII: 145). Blackwood sent details to both Dutch publishers but did not receive the expected response, as he writes to Eliot 14 May 1879: "Van Druten declines our terms for translation and Bohn reduces his offer from £20 to £10 as it is not a story [...] Bohn's offer you will I suppose decline" (VII: 148). Bohn explains his reasons for reducing his offer in a letter to Blackwood 9 May 1879: "As we thought it to be a novel and not a 'series of philosophical essays' we regret our offer of £20,- because the Dutch public will not receive the book with the same intrest [sic] as a new novel would" (UL, Bohn Archive, BOH C5, fol. 356). Having not much of a choice, Eliot decided to accept Bohn's reduced offer after all.[13]

Given that *Theophrastus* is Eliot's final title, this brings us to the end of Dutch translations of her work, except for one late publication. In 1888, the poem "Jubal" (1874) was translated into Dutch and published 14 years after its initial publication, as part of a collection entitled *Dichterlijke navolgingen van François Coppee, Louis de Ronchaud, George Eliot, John Keats* [23]. This volume was published by Rössing in Amsterdam, and the translator was C. van Kempe Valk, bringing us to our sixth publisher, as well as our sixth translator. All in all, Eliot's Dutch publications amount to 27 books, of which 23 can be found in public collections.

Conclusion

To conclude, while the reception of Eliot's poetics in the Netherlands has been dealt with by, amongst others, Van Werven and Verheul, the specific and limited focus of these studies leaves an entire field yet to be analysed. The same holds for this article, which has mainly aimed to provide an overview of Dutch Eliot translations. When it comes to copy and translation rights, Eliot offers a good example of the growing business relations between the UK and the Netherlands. Whereas publishers such as Kruseman did not negotiate with the UK, others spent a good portion of their time trying to come to a lucrative deal. The competition between Van Druten and Bohn in the case of both *Daniel Deronda* and *Impressions of Theophrastus Such* is a good example of this shifting attitude.

George Eliot has left a lasting impression on Dutch readers, earning her after her death a slightly paradoxical place in the series *Mannen van beteekenis in onze dagen* [*Men of importance in our days*], in which the editor expresses his gratitude to Eliot for opening up a whole new world of intriguing characters.[14] This effect would not have spread so far had there been no translations. Most of Eliot's Dutch readers have the translators to thank for bringing George Eliot to them in an accessible language, as well as publishers like Van Druten & Bleeker, who offered these books at very reasonable prices.

Appendix:

Dutch translations of George Eliot

[*KUL= University Library of the Catholic University of Leuven; SBA= Stadsbibliotheek Antwerpen; Tresoar= Tresoar, Leeuwarden; UBL= Leiden University Library; UvA= Amsterdam University Library*]

01. Anna Dorothea Busken Huet-Van der Tholl, trans. *Adam Bede*. 3 vols. Haarlem: A.C. Kruseman, 1860.
Copy consulted: UvA, Kru 12:31-33
Bibliographical source: Baker and Ross A4.32, Werven, Brinkman

02. Conrad Busken Huet, trans. *Herders en schapen: drie novellen*. 2 vols. Haarlem: A.C. Kruseman, 1861.
Copy consulted: SBA, 658644
Bibliographical source: Baker and Ross A3.35, Werven, Brinkman

03. Jacoba van Westrheene-van Heijningen, trans. *De molen van Dorlcote*. 3 vols. Amsterdam: P.N. van Kampen, 1861.
Copy consulted: KUL, BIBC A24826
Bibliographical source: Baker and Ross A5.36, Werven, Brinkman

04. *Silas Marner*. Huis- en reisbibliotheek 18. Deventer: A. Ter Gunne, 1861.
Copy consulted: no copy found in a public collection
Bibliographical source: Baker and Ross A6.28, Werven, Brinkman

05. Jacoba van Westrheene, trans. *Silas Marner, de wever van Raveloe*. Amsterdam: P.N. van Kampen, 1861.
Copy consulted: UvA, UBM: P66-1950
Bibliographical source: Baker and Ross A6.28, Werven, Brinkman

06. Anna Dorothea Busken Huet-Van der Tholl, trans. *Adam Bede*. 3 vols. 2nd ed. Sneek: Van Druten & Bleeker, [1863].
Copy consulted: SBA, 658632
Bibliographical source: Baker and Ross A4.33, Werven, Brinkman

07. Julius Christiaan van Deventer, trans. *Romola*. 3 vols. Haarlem: A.C. Kruseman, 1864.
Copies consulted: UvA, Kru 12: 36-38; SBA, 658670
Bibliographical source: Baker and Ross A7.18, Werven, Brinkman

08. Jacoba van Westrheene-van Heijningen, trans. *Felix Holt, de radikaal: een verhaal*. 2 vols. Sneek: Van Druten & Bleeker, 1867.
Copy consulted: UvA, UBM: P67-4386, 4387
Bibliographical source: Baker and Ross A8.17, Werven, Brinkman

09. Jacoba van Westrheene-van Heijningen, trans. *Felix Holt, de radikaal. George Eliots Romantische Werken* V. Sneek: Van Druten & Bleeker, [1870].
Copy consulted: SBA, 658687
Bibliographical source: Baker and Ross E10, Werven, Brinkman

10. *George Eliot's Romantische Werken*, 5 vols. Sneek: Van Druten & Bleeker, [1870-1873].
Copy consulted: SBA, 658687
Bibliographical source: Baker and Ross E10, Werven, Brinkman

11. Anna Dorothea Busken Huet-Van der Tholl, trans. *Adam Bede*. 3rd ed. Sneek: J.F. van Druten, 1871.
Copy consulted: no copy found in a public collection
Bibliographical source: Brinkman

12. Jacoba van Westrheene-van Heijningen, trans. *Novellen. George Eliot's Romantische Werken* I. Sneek: Van Druten & Bleeker, [1871].
Copy consulted: SBA, 658687
Bibliographical source: Baker and Ross E10, Werven, Brinkman

13. Jacoba van Westrheene-van Heijningen, trans. *De molen van Dorlcote. George Eliot's Romantische Werken* III. Sneek: Van Druten & Bleeker, [1872].
Copy consulted: KUL, BIBC A30452
Bibliographical source: Baker and Ross A5.37, Werven, Brinkman

14. Julius Christiaan van Deventer, trans. *Romola. George Eliot's Romantische Werken* IV. Sneek: Van Druten & Bleeker, [ca. 1872].
Copy consulted: SBA, 658687
Bibliographical source: Baker and Ross E10, Werven, Brinkman

15. Marie Neve, trans. *Uit George Eliot.* Haarlem: A.C. Kruseman, 1872.
Copy consulted: SBA, 922549
Bibliographical source: Baker and Ross D29, Brinkman

16. Jacoba van Westrheene-van Heijningen, trans. *Middelmarch: een verhaal*. 4 vols. Sneek: Van Druten & Bleeker, [1872-1873].
Copy consulted: SBA, 658652
Bibliographical source: Baker and Ross A10.16, Werven, Brinkman

17. Jacoba van Westrheene-van Heijningen, trans. *Felix Holt, de radikaal*. Sneek: J.F. van Druten, 1873.
Copy consulted: No copy found in a public collection
Bibliographical source: Brinkman

18. Anna Dorothea Busken Huet-Van der Tholl, trans. *Adam Bede. George Eliot's Rmantische Werken* II. Sneek: Van Druten, [1873].
Copy consulted: UvA, UBM: Microfiche 150649
Bibliographical source: Baker and Ross E10, Werven, Brinkman

19. Jacoba van Westrheene-van Heijningen, trans. *Daniel Deronda*. 4 vols. Sneek: J.F. van Druten, 1876.
Copy consulted: UvA, UBM: Microfiche 146424
Bibliographical source: Baker and Ross A11.21, Werven, Brinkman

20. Jacoba Berendina Zwaardemaker-Visscher, trans. *De opgeheven sluier. Broeder Jacob*. Sneek: J.F. van Druten, 1878.
Copy consulted: UvA, OBM: Microfiche 146518
Bibliographical source: Baker and Ross B1.8, Brinkman

21. *Indrukken van Theophrastus Dinges*. Haarlem: Erven F. Bohn, 1879.
Copy consulted: SBA, 658647; UBL, GM, Bohn 1879:9
Bibliographical source: Baker and Ross A12.7, Werven, Brinkman

22. Anna Dorothea Busken Huet-Van der Tholl, trans. *Adam Bede*. 4th ed. Sneek: J.F. van Druten, 1885.
Copy consulted: UBL, MNL, 1040 G 37
Bibliographical source: Brinkman

23. C. van Kempe Valk, trans. *Dichterlijke verhalen: navolgingen van François Coppee, Louis de Ronchaud, George Eliot, John Keats*. Amsterdam: A. Rössing, 1888.
Copy consulted: UvA, UBM: Microfiche 110929
Bibliographical source: Baker and Ross B7.4, Brinkman

24. Anna Dorothea Busken Huet-Van der Tholl, trans. *Adam Bede.*
6th ed. Sneek: J.F. van Druten, [1891].
Copy consulted: SBA, 658633
Bibliographical source: Baker and Ross A4.34, Brinkman

25. Anna Dorothea Busken Huet-Van der Tholl, trans. *Adam Bede.*
5th ed. Sneek: J.F. van Druten, [1893].
Copy reported: Tresoar, B1661a (not seen)
Bibliographical source: Brinkman

26. *Adam Bede*. Beroemde romans 2. Amsterdam: Uitgeversmaatschappij 'Vivat', 1896.
Copy consulted: no copy found in a public collection
Bibliographical source: Brinkman

27. Anna Dorothea Busken Huet-Van der Tholl, trans. *Adam Bede.*
7th ed. Sneek: Van Druten, s.d.
Copy consulted: SBA, 658636
Bibliographical source: none

Bibliography

Baker, William and John C. Ross. *George Eliot: A Bibliographical History*. Delaware/ London: Oak Knoll Press/The British Library, 2002.

Brinkman's catalogus der boeken, plaat- en kaartwerken, die gedurende de jaren 1850-1882 in Nederland zijn uitgegeven of herdrukt. Amsterdam: Brinkman, [1883-1884].

De Schepper, Susanna. *A Publishing History (1860-1896) of George Eliot in the Netherlands with a Short History of the Van Druten Firm (Sneek)*. Diss. Leiden University, 2007.

Feather, John P. *A History of British Publishing*. London: Routledge, 1988.

Finkelstein, David. *The House of Blackwood: Author-Publisher Relations in the Victorian Era*. University Park: The Pennsylvania State University Press 2002.

Haight, Gordon Sherman. *George Eliot: a Biography*. Oxford: Oxford University Press, 1978.

Haight, Gordon Sherman, ed. *The George Eliot Letters*. 9 vols. New Haven: Yale University Press, 1954-1978.

Mannen van beteekenis in onze dagen: levensschetsen en portretten 12. Haarlem: Tjeenk Willink, 1881.

Molhuysen, P. C., P. J. Blok et al., eds. *Nieuw Nederlandsch Biografisch Woordenboek*. 10 vols. Leiden: Sijthoff, 1911-1937.

Nieuwsblad voor den boekhandel. 's Gravenhage: J.M. van 't Haaff, 1838-1950.

Sutherland, J. A. *Victorian Novelists and Publishers*. London: Athlone, 1976.

Universiteitsbibliotheek van Amsterdam (UvA), Bibliotheek van het Boekenvak (BB), BDr, letter (21 December 1872).

Universiteitsbibliotheek van Leiden (UL), Bohn Archive, BOH C3, fol. 254, letter from De Erven F. Bohn to George Eliot (9 October 1875).

——— Bohn Archive, BOH C3, fol. 261, letter from De Erven F. Bohn to Blackwood & Sons (19 October 1875).

——— Bohn Archive, BOH C5, fol. 356, letter from De Erven F. Bohn to Blackwood & Sons (9 May 1879).

Verheul, Clazien. "Ethisch realisme: de ontvangst van de romans van George Eliot in de periode 1860-1881." *Voortgang. Jaarboek voor de Neerlandistiek* 5 (1984): 130-164.

van der Weel, Adriaan. "Dutch Nineteenth-century Attitudes to International Copyright." *Publishing History* 47 (2000): 31-44.

———. "Nineteenth-Century Literary Translation from English in a Bookhistorical Context." *Textual Mobility and Cultural Transmission/Tekstmobiliteit en Culturele Overdracht* Eds. Martine de Clercq, Tom Toremans and Walter Verschueren. Leuven: Leuven University Press, 2006. 27-40.

van Werven, Diederik Lüch. *Dutch Readings of George Eliot 1856-1880.* Zutphen: Wöhrman, 2001.

Notes

[1] See Van der Weel's "Dutch Nineteenth-century Attitudes to International Copyright" (37-41) and his "Nineteenth-Century Literary Translation from English in a Bookhistorical Context" (31-33) for an analysis of the reasons underlying this belated event.

[2] Numbers between square brackets refer to specific editions listed in the appendix.

[3] "The Sad Fortunes of the Reverend Amos Barton", "Mr Gilfil's Love-Story" and "Janet's Repentance".

[4] This first volume, entitled "Novellen", was published in eleven duodecimo parts in 1870, and bound in one volume in 1871. Cfr. *Nieuwsblad*, 7 February 1871 for the bound edition, and *Nieuwsblad*, 9 March 1870 through 30 July 1870 for the installments.

[5] P. N. Van Kampen, 29 March 1861 (*Nieuwsblad*, 4 Apr 1861); A. C. Kruseman, 3 April and H. Nijgh 5 April (*Nieuwsblad*, 11 April 1861).

[6] He translated, amongst others, Trollope, Kingsley, Taine, and Wieland. (Molhuysen and Blok I: 715-716).

[7] Whether this was coincidence or an agreement between both publishers, I could not track down.

[8] This title was first sold in 48 parts of 3 sheets or 48 pages at f0,25 per part.

[9] Cf. *Nieuwsblad*, 9 March 1870 up to and including 24 December 1870.

[10] John Blackwood telegraphed Lewes about this on 3 October 1871 (Haight, *The George Eliot Letters* V: 223n.2). See also Blackwood's letter to Lewes 22 November 1872 (V: 330), Haight's *Biography* (438), and Baker and Ross (309).

[11] They obtained the rights on 3 January 1876 (*Nieuwsblad*, 7 Jan 1876).

[12] "Ik bericht U mits dezen, dat, ten gevolge van overeenkomst met de Engelsche Uitgevers, 1 Febr. e.k., TE GELIJK met de uitgaaf van het eerste deel van het oorspronkelijke werk, bij mij zal verschijnen het eerste gedeelte der Nederlandsche vertaling van: Daniel Deronda." (UvA, BB, BDr, 21 December 1872)

[13] See Eliot to William Blackwood 15 May: "I see the Dutchman Van Druten gave me £25 for the translation of Middlemarch but £40 for the translation of Deronda. Certainly £10 for the one volume of Theophrastus is *not* out of proportion to those prices" (Haight, *The George Eliot Letters* VII: 149). And Blackwood to Eliot 20 May, "I wrote yesterday to Herr Bohn at Haarlem accepting his offer £10 for right to translate it into Dutch" (VII: 150).

[14] "George Eliot has given us in Adam Bede, Dina Morris, Janet, Hetty Sorrel, Romola, Magie Tulliver and so many others, unforgettable friends and acquaintances." ["George Eliot heeft ons in Adam Bede, Dina Morris, Janet[,] Hetty Sorrel, Romola, Magie [sic] Tulliver en zoovele anderen, vrienden en kennissen geschonken, die we niet meer vergeten kunnen." (*Mannen van beteekenis* 132)]

PART 2

The Critical Reception and Translation of English Literature in Belgium

Lieven D'hulst (Katholieke Universiteit Leuven)

'English Literature in Belgium': Some Introductory Remarks

The terms used in the title refer to complex and changing realities and should therefore solicit further explanation: needless to say, 'English' may cover more than one literature in English (American, British, Irish, etc.), whereas 'Belgium' is both a changing geopolitical construct (at least between 1800 and 1830) and a network of institutional and discursive practices in more than one language (Dutch / Flemish / French / Walloon), each being carrier of literary repertoires. As a consequence, the study of Anglo-Belgian literary relations better renders explicit the different steps of a comparative analysis, while relating them to a corresponding frame of reference.

By way of an introduction to a subject that has remained largely unexplored,[1] I should like to trace back some of the theoretical and historical problems involved in such a study. Some of them will be tackled in more detail in the case studies of this section.

On relations

Literary texts enter into relation through numerous procedures of mediation (translation, quotation, allusion, adaptation, parody, etc.), with texts belonging to different discursive practices such as philosophy, criticism, history, as well as with other semiotic constructs, such as painting, sculpting, architecture, etc. These relations may take place within the same cultural system or 'polysystem'[2] or between different systems (e.g. two national literatures). To cut out from this dynamic network of relations one procedure, or one practice, is always an artificial move, even when it seems more obvious to study at first hand procedures (such as translations) that establish a high number of common features between products (source texts and target texts): the latter are therefore supposed to interact more closely than products that belong to different practices (such as the outcomes of intersemiotic adaptations). It is at least a convenient way to start a tentative reconstruction of the larger picture. One of the procedures of mediation that benefits from a more or less steady interest by researchers on interliterary relations is translation. But while it is the natural focus of research in translation studies, it does not seem to occupy a core position in other disciplines interested in interliterary relations (such as cultural studies or comparative literature).[3] Yet, since translations (understood in a broader sense) take place in most cultural practices (history, philosophy, the sciences), it is reasonable to see them as belonging to a network of translation relations, comparable to the general network of cultural practices they are part of. The question remains, once again, to what extent the study of translation between two specific literatures should take into account other translation relations and other cultural practices.

The latter question is probably more difficult to answer in the case of Anglo-Belgian literary relations, even when considered in one direction only (from A to B): in addition to the moves already mentioned, both as to procedures and practices, the study of Anglo-Belgian relations is not *a priori* coupled with, say, the study of German-Flemish and/or German-French and/or Flemish-French relations. But, more importantly, perhaps, the situation of literature in Belgium during the 19th century requires some additional comments.

On Belgium

In a century during which languages, literatures and ethnic identities tended to cluster more strongly than ever before, diglossic Belgium offers a complex picture. More than one language was a candidate to become the carrier of the national literature: French during the French period (till 1815), Dutch till 1830 (when it was called "la langue nationale" and even "la langue belgique"),[4] and from then on till the end of the century both languages in changing combinations on an axis between two extremes: a single literature in two languages and two national literatures in two languages. The dominant combination throughout has been: one national literature into French, but integrating a number of Flemish discursive items (topoi and stereotypes and formal devices, esp. in narrative prose and poetry) through the frequent use of procedures of mediation such as translation, borrowing, allusion or quotation.

As a consequence, the study of Anglo-Belgian interliterary relations, even limited to a single procedure, should take into account not only Flemish and French translations of English literature, but also the relations between the latter, along the hypothesis that the selection, treatment and reception of English texts in both languages are somehow mutually influenced.

Nevertheless, what follows is based on a small inquiry into the Francophone part of Belgian literature only,[5] covering the first three quarters of the century. But even this restriction in itself shows ample evidence of the necessity to cross the barriers of a single system: Anglo-Belgian literary relations are not *a priori* 'Belgian'.

A handful of hypotheses

In general terms, Anglo-Belgian literary relations, like most interliterary relations in 19th-century Belgium, have been strongly (over)determined by Anglo-French relations. This phenomenon of indirect contacts – i.e. contacts that are mediated by a different, more prestigious instance – is quite common in peripheral literatures. It had an overwhelming impact in Belgium, at least during the first half of the century, to the extent, for example, that whole French journals devoted to English literature and culture, such as the *Revue britannique*, were pirated in Belgium in the 1830s and 1840s.

Consequently, the recourse to the set of traditional hypotheses at our disposal when questioning literary relations becomes problematic: the selection and treatment of English cultural or literary items barely address a specifically 'Belgian' interest or literary programme. They appear much more to be the outcome of a larger cultural intake process, which is probably the dominant mode of Belgian culture production and consumption at that time. Import, even massive import, mainly from France, is the most efficient way to establish a literary (and cultural) system, in view of its recognition by the major surrounding cultures, esp. France. And this process includes the import of English-French literary and cultural relations.

This does not imply that English literature and culture as filtered through French literature and culture are not being discussed in Belgium, but these discussions precisely aim at developing a variety of adequate reading attitudes (or habitus) vis-à-vis foreign literatures and of adequate critical modes of writing about the latter. In other terms, if readers are aware of Byron, Wordsworth, Mrs Trollope, even Burns, these authors exert a limited direct modelling function on the emergent Belgian literature. Even byronism, quite a strong habitus in European Romantic writing, makes its way in Belgium through French translations first and even secondly through the effects these have on French writers and critics also read and commented in Belgium.

Recent bibliographical research on poetry (limited to volumes published in Belgium between 1830 and 1880[6]) shows that translations from English occupy the 4th position (14 volumes), after Dutch/Flemish (26 volumes), Latin (24) and German (15). Byron is most frequently translated; the 18th-century fabulist John Gay comes in second place; a smaller number of translations of individual poems are scattered in collective volumes. These figures are too small to show evidence of clear trends in the selection process. Yet, most translations are either retranslations by Belgian translators of texts already translated in French, or reeditions of French translations.[7]

In the domain of narrative and historical prose, one may see a larger amount of books translated from English (54 in total), with names such as Mayne-Reid, Charles White, Disraeli, John Halifax, Ainsworth, Wiseman, Washington Irving, Hawthorne, Dickens, James Grant, Thackeray. Some trends may be conjectured: there is a prevalence of translations of short popular prose (including children's literature); the works translated in case of major authors are either short prose or lesser known work; French reeditions (till 1850 in pirate versions) or Belgian retranslations dominate the translation market. In addition, imitations are the more frequent labels for short and popular literature, while translation applies to texts with higher prestige (history and to a lesser extent the novel).

It should not come as a surprise that Walter Scott has not been translated in Francophone Belgium, since the pirate versions of Defauconpret's translations circulated widely and rendered retranslations pointless. And yet, as elsewhere in Europe, these translations have played a major role in the construction of a proper national model of writing historical narrative. Let us give but one example. One may observe in contemporary novels or shorter narrative forms how the French translations shaped not only the development of techniques such as narration, description, portrayal, dialogue or chronotopes, but also the creation of an auctorial habitus. During the 1830s and 1840s, for instance, an I-narrator (clearly an instance of the author) tends to represent himself as a character in the incipit of a story, before the author changes his status in that of an extradiegetic narrator of another story based on a different chronotope (often a medieval one). Such techniques of embedding and embedded narration convincingly show the impact of the mediated Scottian model on the emergence of the genre novel as well as of an emerging Belgian authorship as such: an evolution that will free the author from the need for historical or social justification of the writing act.

Conclusions?

The apprehension of the roles played by translations in target literatures is often a missing link in historical research at large. But many more facets of translation in Belgium remain uncharted so far: translations in journals and magazines, theatre translations, translation criticism; translations into Flemish, and, as mentioned at the outset, the larger set of procedures that go hand in hand with translation as well as the relations between literature and other cultural systems like the arts, history or manners. There is ample material for generations to come. Let that be the conclusion of this introduction. In the following pages, three studies are devoted to the role played by Anglo-Belgian relations in journals of the end of the 19th and the beginning of the 20th century. They may serve as examples to be followed.

Bibliography

Busekist, Astrid von. *La Belgique. Politique des langues et construction de l'Etat, de 1780 à nos jours*. Paris-Bruxelles: Duculot, 1998.

Charlier, Gustave. *Le mouvement romantique en Belgique (1815-1850)*. Vol. 2. Bruxelles: Palais des Académies, 1959.

———. "Pour une histoire de la poésie belge antérieure à 1880." *Littératures en contact. Mélanges offerts à Vic Nachtergaele*. Eds. Jan Herman, Steven Engels & Alex Demeulenaere. Leuven: Presses universitaires de Louvain, 2003. 15-30.

D'hulst, Lieven. "Comparative Literature versus Translation Studies: Close Encounters of the Third Kind?" *The European Review* 15:1 (January 2007): 95-104.

Even-Zohar, Itamar. "Polysystem Theory (Revised)". *Papers in Culture Research*. Tel Aviv: The Porter Chair of Semiotics, Tel Aviv University, 2005. 38-49.

Gilsoul, Robert. *Les influences anglo-saxonnes sur les lettres françaises de Belgique de 1850 à 1880*. Bruxelles: Palais des Académies, 1953.

Notes

1 The book by Robert Gilsoul is one of the rare specialised studies on the subject.
2 See Even-Zohar's "Polysystem Theory (Revised)".
3 See D'hulst's "Comparative Literature versus Translation Studies".
4 See von Busekist's *La Belgique*.
5 The three case studies that follow taken also into account Anglo-Flemish relations.

[6] See D'hulst's "Pour une histoire de la poésie belge".

[7] It should be noted, in addition, that an important number of French translations of Flemish poetry are made and published in Holland. These translations equally apply the translation techniques prevalent in France at that time.

Francis Mus (Katholieke Universiteit Leuven)

The Image of English Literature in Belgian Avant-Garde Periodicals

Introduction: a privileged partner?

In the age of Internet and globalisation, it may seem inadequate to consider literary relations between two 'national literatures', both on a structural and on a more pragmatic level. An artificial demarcation of the object of study ('English literature') and, consequently, an impalpable corresponding reality, make that the initial research project seems doomed from the very beginning. However, these two objections necessitate a profound nuance regarding a fraction of the interbellum period in Belgium that will be the subject of this article.

First, the existing exchanges were much more streamlined and literally more 'channelled' than they are today: as regards public exchanges, the (literary) magazines constituted the privileged medium to strike up a dialogue.[1] Indeed, the initial function of the periodical was precisely to provide a kind of (passive) support and fulfil the role of vector, carrier of texts. Moreover, magazines can also acquire an active role when they become the nucleus in which ideas are born, developed, debated, etc.[2] If literary magazines are traditionally seen as more peripheral research objects, they nonetheless occupy a central position in histories of literature when they assume such a more active role.[3] This second function is often attributed to the so-called avant-garde periodicals, as by Paul Aron: "It is due to the periodicals that we owe the largest part of the international openness of our literature, their participation in the main flows of avant-garde, and even the mere existence of a scriptural activity in the country."[4]

Secondly, even if there is no exact referent responding to the signifier 'English literature' – and this goes in fact for every 'national' literature – there can nonetheless be an implicit consensus about what is meant, the projection of an 'imagined (literary) community' that can circulate and create effects.[5] Moreover, the more the contact with these foreign literatures is mediated, the more all kinds of clichés, commonplaces, and stereotypes surface and start to determine a more heterogeneous reality.[6] As Joep Leerssen argues in his essay on "The Rhetoric of National Character", these images, provoked by a geographical distance, obey to "structural patterns rather than case-specific patterns". He gives the example of the opposition north-south, "[that] can work in intranational, regional terms as well as between countries [...]" (275-276). An equivalent opposition can isolate the relations with 'English literature' from those with 'other literatures', according to the cliché that the Island, opposed to the Continent, is wallowing in its own 'splendid isolation'. Even if every 'other' is always already stereotyped in an eccentric way (the concrete manifestations then differ from nationality to nationality), the case of the Englishman is striking and is clearly illustrated in literary creations. For instance, in his short story "Thyl Uylenspieghel in Londen", published in the Flemish literary magazine *Het Roode Zeil* (Brussels, 1920), the author Herman Teirlinck accumulates stereotypes both about Flanders and England. When arriving in London, the main character Thyl "opened his eyes astonishedly", and comments on the English that "[t]hey are miaowing like cats", so that "he did his best to miaow with them".[7] A whiff of Englishness is suggested by typical objects (for example whisky (147)), linguistic interjections à la Blake & Mortimer ("all right" (148), "old fellow" (153)), and a homogenisation of the English people ("in the entire world, there is no people more comfortable than ourselves") that leads to an opposition with Flanders ("a medieval relic basket") and even to a comparison with their "continental" women (154).[8] Another example of this division between island and mainland is provided by André de Ridder, in a review article on the work of George Bernard Shaw published in *Vlaamsche Arbeid* in 1909. He ascribes the popularity of Shaw's work to its purely Anglo-Saxon character, which can't be grasped by "us mainlanders":

> This scarce popularity might be due to the pure Anglo-Saxon character of Shaw's work: the sober-minded and sly mentality of the British people cannot be sufficiently profoundly grasped by us mainlanders; the Englishman always finds principles to justify his interest and to give his brutal egoism the semblance of world-benefaction. Moreover, the strong practical spirit of this people still remains somewhat strange to us.[9]

In what follows, I will take into consideration a sample of both francophone and Dutch literary magazines produced in Belgium during the interwar period (*Le Disque Vert*, *Ruimte*, *Het Roode Zeil* and *Vlaamsche Arbeid*), so as to analyse more closely the image and function of English and, by extension, Anglophone literature. The magazines in question are traditionally associated with the so-called literary historical avant-garde.[10]

The Francophone sector: *Le Disque Vert*

With reference to the Francophone sector, the magazine *Le Disque Vert* occupies a central place.[11] This magazine was known under several names (*Signaux de France et de Belgique* (1921-1922), *Le Disque Vert* (1922, 1923-1925, 1941), *Ecrits du Nord* (1922-1923, 1935), *Au Disque Vert* (1934), and *Nord* (1929-1930)). From the perspective of interliterary contacts adopted in this article, *Le Disque Vert* offers some interesting insights. As Sophie Levie recalls, one of the main objectives of Franz Hellens, the driving force of the magazine, was to "redefine the place of the Belgian literature in contact with other literatures and in Belgium and safeguard its independence and its authenticity."[12] Moreover, the contacts with Anglophone literatures were most intensive during the years 1921-1925: within the span of four years, no less than 13 contributions were dedicated to English literature. The list is completed by a handful of more 'peripheral' texts, mainly reviews of English books translated in French, discussed by Franz Hellens.

Eleven articles, written by Herbert Read or Jethro Bithell, appeared within the regular features, whereas two contributions were written by occasional authors. It should be noted that, along with the English-speaking authors Read and Bithell, the translator Piet Heuvelmans had a permanent place within the feature. Heuvelmans was the director of the Dutch-speaking service of the summary report of the Belgian Senate and was member of a group of Flemish nationalists. At the beginning of the Second World War, he wrote a regular column ("Les lettres flamandes") in the collaborating *Nouveau Journal* (1940-1944). He translated almost every English article for *Le Disque Vert*.

Given that a literary magazine was one of the most important means of communication between literatures, staff members were able to exploit this apparently inherent characteristic of the magazine. In the case of the explicitly internationally oriented *Le Disque Vert*, this becomes all the more important. According to Hellens, not only the medium, but also its Belgian roots, explain the *inevitable* openness to other literatures:

> The Belgian finds himself in the position of a man standing on a balcony, and dominating the vastness surrounding him. It is impossible for him to look straight ahead without noticing the variety of countries surrounding him; he cannot completely realise his need for activity without crossing the balustrade in order to involve himself in the life that he sees taking place underneath him. At any price, he has to breach his small limits or renounce free movement.[13]

Within this framework of an almost intrinsic necessity of international contacts, it is not surprising that an "illusion of immediacy" (Geldof 7) regulates the discourse on other (in this case, Anglophone) literatures. This manoeuvre suggests that the articles are showing *linea recta,* without *décalage*, the 'truth' about a foreign literature. Hence, the illusion is created that the discourses of the critics could only be read *as they want them to be read.* Several discursive interventions contribute to the creation of this illusion. In the articles written by Herbert Read, four factors intervene:

(a) First, the status of the critic determines the way in which the text will be read. Contrary to other texts in *Le Disque Vert*, we are not dealing with a Belgian critic who comments on Anglophone literature, but with a correspondent *on the spot*. Because the critics of the regular features are British (Read) or Irish (Bithell), the discourse is imbued with a higher degree of credibility. The image and, accordingly, the posture of authority of the author affect the efficacy of what is said or written. Besides discursive tricks, the exterior authority ("l'ethos social"[14]) indeed plays an important role and is foregrounded (for example, several contributors hold a university chair).

(b) Concerning peritextual elements, the titles try to guide the interpretation of the text. English titles such as "Notes from England" offer a whiff of Englishness, while the text itself is written in French. The text-type, made explicit in the title, can also accentuate the immaculate status of the text, for example a confidential "lettre d'Angleterre" or even "une lettre inédite". However, the text that follows does not meet the created expectations: the so-called letter is written in a rather pedagogical style and is twice labelled by the author in the text as "cet essai" instead of "cette lettre".

(c) The major part of the articles written by Read or Bithell are translations. Indeed, it was a frequent technique to translate in magazines not only (primary) fictional texts (prose, poetry, theatre), but also (secondary) pieces of literary criticism. Translation, then, is mobilized to suggest authenticity and can function as a barometer to measure the openness towards other literatures. The literary quotations, inserted as illustrations in the critical texts, are also translated, without reference to the source-text. This can be taken as indicative of the *relative* international dimension of *Le Disque Vert*. The translations, then, hold the position of "boundary maintenance".[15] However, this rather modest openness should come as no surprise, given the interest taken by Hellens in the individuality of Belgian literature itself.

(d) The authenticity and veracity of the author's notes are even confirmed in an *explicit* way. In his first notes to the 1921 "Notes from England", for example, Read writes:

> In my opinion, he who sets himself the task of writing about the activity of a country for a foreign public has to limit himself to a descriptive critique of the positive aspects of the intellectual life, which, because of the merit of their originality and their significance, gain a value largely surpassing the boundaries of one language.[16]

The quotation also reveals an unequal relation between English and Belgian literature. According to Read, (modern) English literature can matter to the Belgian reader "as a factor of inspiration for a foreign intelligence" ["en tant que facteur d'inspiration pour une intelligence étrangère"], by which he implicitly revalues English literature almost as if to place it above Belgian literature. In a sense, Read confirms the separation between continental and Anglo-Saxon literature. Jethro Bithell, focussing on Irish literature, adopts the opposite viewpoint by stressing a definite resemblance with Belgian literature, in that both were oppressed by English and French literature, respectively. The specific attention paid to Irish literature should not come as a surprise: Ireland became officially independent in 1922, the year in which Bithell wrote several contributions for *Le Disque Vert*. Also articles in other magazines dealt with Irish literature and Ireland's political situation and often made a parallel with the Belgian case. For instance, in his critique on the book *Ierland en het Iersche volk* [*Ireland and the Irish*

People], published in the Flemish magazine *Vlaamsche Arbeid* in 1923, L.J. Callewaert stated: "And even if the Flemish struggle seems quite small next to the moving greatness of the Irish drama, still there remains much to be learned for us from this age long and sad adventure." At the end of the article, the author reformulates it in even stronger terms: "Father Callewaert intended this work for our people." [17]

The role of Jethro Bithell

The Irishman Jethro Bithell has become a rather obscure figure nowadays. Levie characterizes him as "a critic who, unlike Read and Erenburg, didn't leave a trace in the annals" ["un critique qui, contrairement à Read et à Erenburg, n'a pas laissé de trace dans les annales" (111)]. This marginal position is nuanced by David Roe, who, although recognising the fact he is no longer in the literary limelight, is not afraid to label him as «one of the most remarkable figures of the first half of the century in the teaching of European languages and literatures in Great Britain." ["l'une des figures les plus marquantes de la première moitié du siècle dans l'enseignement des langues et littératures européennes en Grande Bretagne." (212)] With respect to Anglo-Belgian relations, Bithell remains an interesting figure. His career as a literary critic and historian started in 1912, with the publication in Brussels of a small volume on W.B. Yeats, which was translated by Hellens.[18] In his introduction, Bithell presents Yeats as a founding father of the (future) Ireland and highlights a resemblance between his country and Belgium. Like Ireland, Belgium is "another equally famous country." ["un autre pays aussi célèbre."] The captatio benevolentiae indicates another condition that both countries share: they were both brought under the yoke of a literature that surpasses them. There can be little doubt that Bithell perceived affinities between the relations that existed between Ireland and England on the one hand, and Belgium and France, on the other. In 1915, he translated Stefan Zweig's monograph on Emile Verhaeren (Zweig 1915). His sympathy for Belgium also looms large in his 1915 survey of *Contemporary Belgian literature*, which was published in London during the war. David Roe considers the survey "the first serious study of Belgian literature – Francophone and Flemish – that was published in English." ["la première étude sérieuse de la littérature belge – francophone et flamande – à paraître en anglais." (212)] In the preface Bithell describes the literatures of Ireland, Switzerland and Belgium as relatively small:

> There is always the question whether "Belgian literature" exists at all... I have indicated in the course of the book that some eminent Belgian writers will not hear of such a thing. And after all, one never hears of Swiss literature... That may be, however, because there are so few Swiss writers of international reputation. Belgium, on the other hand, is not only rich in distinguished writers, but these writers have a marked Belgian individuality, and for these reasons we are surely justified in claiming a national literature (one of the most interesting in Europe to-day [sic]) for the little country over which the Germans have ridden rough-shod. To the living writers of Belgium this book would express a practical sympathy by calling attention to their work. They will need readers after the war; and they deserve them. (xiii-ix)

Bithell was not only a prominent intercultural figure, he was also given a very specific mission. In every contribution he dealt with Irish literature, which he wanted to revalue as a sovereign 'national' literature. To enforce this demarcation, Belgian literature could serve as a model. Several key features, then, are geared towards convincing his readership that Irish literature is in fact autonomous. The glorious past, for one, reads as a sort of etymological account for the nascence and individuality of Irish literature. The existence of a national history (albeit avant la lettre) may trigger off the self-awareness of a previously non-existent literature, as is and should be the case for Irish letters: "Ireland had to recover its Irish soul" ["l'Irlande devait retrouver son âme irlandaise" ("W.B. Yeats" 522)], Bithell refers to "the Irish atmosphere" ["l'atmosphère irlandaise" (524)] and "in Ireland, tradition makes law" ["en Irlande, c'est la tradition qui fait la loi" ("Synge" 6)]. Bithell's assumptions are essentialist in the sense that he discerns in both nation and literature an inherent, persistent core. Unlike the compound Belgian literature, Irish literature is yoked by its own language, gaelic, "one of the most beautiful languages of Europe" ["une des plus belles langues de l'Europe" ("La literature Irlandaise" 386)]. It goes without saying that language ties in with Bithell's emphasis on the Irish soul. Given the stance that Bithell adopts in his contributions, then, it comes as no great surprise that for him the translations of the literary quotations (and not of the entire translation of the review) affects the uniqueness of Irish literature. For instance, when he quotes George Russell in a French translation, he repeats the following commonplace about the role of the translator: "the 'traductore' (sic) has to satisfy himself with being a 'traditore', as the 'timbre' of the original voice is untranslatable." ["le 'traductore' [sic] doit se résoudre à n'être qu'un 'traditore', le 'timbre' de la voix originale étant intraduisible." ("A.E." 669)]

The univocal character of Bithell's 'mission' precludes subtle nuances in his discourse and is inherently reductive in its essentialist approach – little or no suggestion of any evolution, and a circular vocabulary that offers no analytic depth. For instance, what does the critical reader do with the characterization of Synge as a "*véritable* Anglais"? ("Synge" 4) If any literary *dialogue* takes place – and the perspective of an international framework was not an innocent question in *Le Disque Vert* – it is always in relation to its own (national) literature. In other words, as Levie reminds us (111) there is a tension between an open internationalism and the quest for one's own identity, although the former remains subordinated to the latter. The political situation exerts a definite influence on the literary sphere.

The Flemish sector

Unlike Francophone periodicals, Flemish literary magazines paid little attention to Anglo-Belgian relations.[19] In general, the Flemish cause and 'indigenous' literature were valued more highly. Explicitly avant-garde publications such as *De Stroom*, *Staatsgevaarlik*, *De Driehoek* or *Het Overzicht* hardly mention Anglophone literature. When it is mentioned, there is a clear difference with the Francophone periodicals. Whereas the latter give the floor to a correspondent 'on the spot' for the longer articles, this is not the case for the former. This is probably due to their less markedly international outlook and to the fact that the periodicals I mentioned were only short-lived, which made the elaboration of an international network much more difficult. Nonetheless, a certain continuity or even cross-references appear in the themes and authors mentioned. The small number of collected texts about Anglophone literature requires a more individual approach than the structural analysis of the first part.

In 1920, the magazine *Ruimte* (Antwerp, 1920-1921) published an article introducing the aforementioned critic Herbert Read. Three poems ("Vrees" [Fear], "De gelukkige krijger" [The Happy Warrior] and "Liedholz") from his volume *Naked Warriors* were published translations of Herman Bossier. Read is thus presented foremost as a poet, "one of the most outstanding collaborators to the magazine *Art and letters*" ["een van de meest vooraanstaande medewerkers van het tijdschrift *Art and letters*"], and not as a critic. The poems, associated with expressionism, are impregnated with the sense of despair and meaninglessness associated with the Great War. To broaden the magazine's outlook on foreign literatures, the editors also published other translations, for example an essay on Rupert Brooke[20] (including a translation of the poem "Retrospect"), *Das Himmlische Licht* (L. Rubiner), two poems by T. Daübler ("Madonna uit Zwabenland" and "Sneeuw") and even a presentation of Chinese lyrical poetry. In all, however, the attention paid to foreign literatures (especially English letters) was low. The statement of Eugène de Bock (1950:2) in a survey article, that "we also tried to follow (up) the English and the German literature" ["wij trachtten ook de Engelse en de Duitse literatuur te volgen"] was thus quite opportunistic.

G.B. Shaw as recognized cross-reference

In the same year, *Het Roode Zeil* (Antwerp-Brussels, 1920), the counterpart of *Ruimte* and the successor to *De Boomgaard*, published a contribution by Fabrice Polderman (1920: 42-46) on Bernard Shaw's *Heartbreak House* in the section *Engelsche letteren* [*English letters*]. Just like De Ridder, he denounces the pre-war situation of English literature, but recognizes an improvement in the figure of Shaw. Polderman, as Bithell, also had a special relation with the British Isles. At the outbreak of the Great War, he fulfilled the role of contact person and helped some painters of the first school of Latem (Valerius de Saedeleer, Edgar Gevaert, George Minne, GustaafVan de Woestijne) to find shelter in Wales. Polderman, a professor at the university of Ghent, arrived in Cardiff in 1914 and took part in the organisation of the life of Belgian artists 'in exile', who could thus continue their work and bring their talent to the Welsh people.[21] "The Belgian professor in Cardiff" (De Clerck 34) translated, wrote (among others, in *The Welsh Outlook*, a literary and political magazine) and also taught French at the university of Birmingham. Shaw, who was to receive the Nobel Prize for literature in 1925, appeared both Flemish and Francophone magazines.[22] In *Le Disque Vert,* Bithell (1921:385) characterizes him as an "expatrié" ["expatriate"] from an Irish (national) perspective, whereas Polderman quotes Shaw's description of his own book as an image of modern Europe. Read, for his part, also praises the author in an overview of modern English literature:

"Shaw, perhaps the most talented man of modern England. One has to recognize that Shaw is our best polemic prose-writer since Swift, who was our greatest".[23]

The minor position of foreign literature in Flemish avant-garde periodicals

The contributions on foreign literature in the (ephemeral) Flemish avant-garde periodicals were quite occasional, whereas those in more conservative magazines, such as *Vlaamsche Arbeid* (Antwerp, 1905-1914, 1919-1930), were more structural. André de Ridder, for instance, wrote several texts about English literature in the section on "Vreemde Arbeid" ["Foreign Labour", in opposition to "Flemish labour"]. In two successive articles published in 1906 ("De kunst voor de kunst" and "Drink en The Bondman"), he sketches, sometimes very ironically, a negative image of current English literature: "Contemporary English literature is essentially a folk literature and a literature of a people that is very poorly developed, very poorly refined, very little art-minded. [...] Don't I have the right, then, to speak of a period of paralysis, a time of crisis?"[24] However, nearly one year later, in his article on the occasion of Kipling's Nobel Prize, de Ridder strikes a different note with a panegyric on his novel *The Jungle Book*: "The Nobel Prize of 1907 rests in noble hands." ["De Nobelprijs van 1907 berust in nobele handen." (160)]

During its twenty five years of existence, the names of the columns in *Vlaamsche Arbeid* changed. In the beginning, there had been a simple distinction between "Vlaamsche Arbeid" and "Vreemde Arbeid", but gradually the "Vreemde Arbeid" began to diversify into "Amerikaansche letterkunde", "Engelsche letterkunde", "Duitsche letterkunde", "Fransche letterkunde", etc. It is interesting to note that the magazine evolved from a catholic-conservative periodical to a more modernist publication.[25] In this respect, the 1914 article on Newman, in which the latter is discussed within a catholic context, is significant and contrasts sharply with several articles published after the war dealing with "The New Direction in American Poetry" (as in the title of Van Roosbroeck 1920 contribution) or with a concealed critique of provincialism (as in Van Roosbroeck's 1922 contribution) with progressive statements as "the fight against provincialism has begun" ["de kamp tegen provincialism (sic) is begonnen" (1922:419)]. In general, however, here too, English literature was allocated a minor place, whereas French and especially German literature received more attention.

Conclusion

The analysis of this spot check of literary magazines shows that there was no or very little interaction between the Francophone and Flemish magazines. Due to their more ephemeral character and the intranational nature of their debates, Flemish periodicals couldn't develop a structural dialogue with foreign literatures. The existing contacts were tied with geographically contiguous partners such as French, German and Dutch literature. Moreover, they took a keener interest in a political and cultural debate that was not strictly literary, such as the "Flemish question". A more organised and explicit international magazine such as *Le Disque Vert* could more easily develop a network of literary relations that more or less included Anglophone literature. The tension between literature and nation in Anglophone literature described by Bithell and others was much more similar to the Francophone Belgian literature than to the Flemish literature.

Bibliography

[When referring to the articles published in *Vlaamsche Arbeid*, I mention only the year of publication and the page number of the volume (ascending within one year of publication). When referring to the articles published in *Le Disque Vert*, I use the Jacques Antoine reprint version (1978) mentioning the tome, followed by the original page number (if applicable), and the reprint page number between brackets. I always use the recovering title *Le Disque Vert* without differentiating between *Signaux de France et de Belgique*, *Nord*, *Ecrits du Nord*, etc.]

Adriaens-Pannier, Anne. "Tijd- en strijdschriften van de van de avant-garde in België 1917-1929." *Avant-garde in België, 1917-1929*. Eds. F. Leen and A. Adriaens-Pannier. Brussels: Gemeentekrediet, 1973.

Amossy, Ruth. "L'ethos au Carrefour des disciplines: rhétoriques, pragmatique, sociologie de champs." *Images de soi dans le discours*. Eds. Ruth Amossy. Lausanne : Delachaux et Niestlé. 1999. 127-154.

Anderson, Benedict. *Imagined Communities: Reflections on the Origin and Spread of Nationalism*. London : Verso, 1991.

Aron, Paul. "Les revues littéraires en Belgique francophone de 1914 à 1940." *La revue des revues* 11 (1991): 55-62.

——— "Les pastiches de la revue *Le Masque* (1910-1914).". *Lettres ou ne pas Lettres, Mélanges de littérature Française de Belgique offerts à Roland Beyen*. Eds. Jan Herman, Lieven Tack and Koenraad Geldof. Leuven : Leuven University Press, 2001. 573-584.

——— Lecture presented at the conference *L'étude de revues littéraires en Belgique : questions de méthode et perspectives*. Leuven, 2007 [at the press].

Bithell, Jethro. *W.B. Yeats*. Brussels : Edition du Masque, 1912.

——— *Contemporary Belgian Literature*. London: Fisher Unwin, 1915.

——— "La littérature irlandaise contemporaine." *Le Disque Vert* 8. (1921) : (384-391).

——— "W.B. Yeats et les symbolistes irlandais." *Le Disque Vert* 10. (1922) : (521-527).

——— "Synge et le drame irlandais." *Le Disque Vert* 11-12. (1922) : 3-5. (5-7).

——— "A.E." *Le Disque Vert* 11-12. (1922) : 667-669.

Callewaert, L.J. "Ierland en het Iersche Volk." *Vlaamsche Arbeid* (1923): 157-158.

Charlier, Gustave. *Les lettres françaises de Belgique*. Bruxelles : La renaissance du livre, 1938.

De Bock, Eugène. "Ruimte", *De Vlaamse Gids* 34 (1950): 1-10.

De Clerck, Karel. Prof. Fabrice Polderman. Ambitieus en mysterieus. Gent: Archive Ghent University, 2005.

De Geest, Dirk. *Literatuur als systeem, literatuur als vertoog: bouwstenen voor een functionalistische benadering van literaire verschijnselen*. Leuven : Peeters, 1996.

de Ridder, Andre. "Vreemde Arbeid. 'De kunst voor de kunst.' Beweging in Engeland." *Vlaamsche Arbeid* (1906): 155-159.

——— "Vreemde Arbeid. Iets over Engelsche literatuur. Drink en The Bondman." *Vlaamsche Arbeid* (1906-1907): 126-128.

——— "Vreemde Arbeid. Engelsche literatuur: het werk van Rudyard Kipling." *Vlaamsche Arbeid* (1907-1908): 157-160.

——— "Vreemde Arbeid. Vreemde letterkunde. Engelsche literatuur: George Bernard Shaw." *Vlaamsche Arbeid* (1909): 132-136.

Fairclough, Oliver. *Kunst in ballingschap: Vlaanderen, Wales en de Eerste Wereldoorlog*. Antwerpen : Pandora, 2002.

Geldof, Koenraad. *Kritische profielen*. Leuven: Peeters, 1999.

Hellens, Franz. "La Belgique, balcon sur l'Europe." *Le Disque Vert* 1 (1922) : 34 (204).

Herschberg-Pierrot, Anne & Ruth Amossy. *Stéréotypes et clichés : langue discours, société*. Paris : Colin, 2005.

Le Disque Vert. Brussels : Editions Jacques Antoine, 1921-1941 [repr. 1978].

Leerssen, Joep. "The Rhetoric of National Character: a Programmatic Survey." *Poetics Today* 21.2 (2000): 275-276.

Levie, Sophie. "Ouvert à tous, difficile cependant à ouvrir' – la revue belge Le Disque Vert, 1921-1941." Reviews, Zeitschriften, Revues. Die Fackel, Die Weltbühne, Musikblätter des Anbruch, Le Disque Vert, Mécano, Versty. Ed. Sophie Levie. Amsterdam and Atlanta : Rodopi 1994. 97-138.

Polderman, Fabrice. "Engelsche letteren. Bernard Shaw: Heartbreak House." Het Roode Zeil. 1. (1920): 42-46.

Pym, Anthony. "Cross-cultural networking: Translators in the French-German network of *petites revues* at the end of the nineteenth century" 9 june 2008. <http://www.tinet.org/~apym/on-line/translation/networks_jan.pdf>.

Read, Herbert. "Notes from England." *Le Disque Vert* 3 (1921): (136-138).

——— "Notes from England. " *Le Disque Vert* 9 (1922) : (492-495).

——— "Le grand courant de la littérature anglaise moderne. Lettre inédite." *Le Disque Vert* 3 (1923) : 134-140. (308-314).

Rodker, John. "Préface à la traduction anglaise des chants de Maldoror." *Le Disque Vert* numéro spécial 'Le cas lautréamont' (1925) : 77-79 (367-369).

Roe, David (2000). "Max Elskamp et son premier traducteur anglais." *Lettres romanes* 54 (2000): 211-231.

Teirlinck, Herman. "Thyl Uylenspieghel in Londen." *Het Roode Zeil*. 4 (1920):145-157.

Verhasselt, Veerle. "Kunsttijdschriften 1900-1930." *Vlaams expressionisme in Europese context* Ed. R. Houzee Gent: Snoeck-Ducaju & zoon, 1990.

Van Roosbroeck, Gust. “De nieuwe richting in de Amerikaansche poëzie.” *Vlaamsche Arbeid* (1920): 206-209.
Roosbroeck, Van, Gust. “De opstand tegen het stadje in de Amerikaansche literatuur.” *Vlaamsche Arbeid* (1922): 413-420.
Warmoes, Jean. *Cinquante ans d'avant-garde*. Brussels : Bibliothèque royale Albert 1er, 1983.

Notes

1 There is also a counterpart on a *private* level that offers an interesting insight in literary relations, namely the correspondence between authors, critics, editors, etc.
2 This division was further elaborated in Aron's 2007 lecture.
3 De Geest, for example, observes a growing attention for literary and cultural magazines in literary histories (11).
4 “[c]'est aux périodiques que l'on doit l'essentiel de l'ouverture internationale de nos lettres, leur participation aux courants de l'avant-garde et jusqu'à l'existence même d'une activité scripturale dans le pays.” (“Les revues littéraires en Belgique” 55)
5 See Anderson's *Imagined Communities*.
6 On the differences between the terms ‘cliché’, ‘commonplace’ and ‘stereotype’, see Herschberg-Pierrot & Amossy.
7 “stak verwonderd zijne oogen open”; “Ze miauwen als katten, [...] en hij deed zijn devooren om mee te miauwen [...]” (145).
8 “in de gansche wereld is er geen komfortabeler volk dan wij” (146); “een mediëvale relikwiekorf” (153).
The fragment in question continues stereotypically: “It exhibited in the bowels of civilisation the wonderful witnesses of its glorious past, its halls and belfries, its churches and town halls, its oaken rampart-gates and gilded corporation-fronts. It spread its quiet fields, its sweet villages as piles of poverty, its poor Breughel-farmers and its medieval faith.” [“Het vertoonde in den schoot der beschaving de wondere getuigen van zijn roemrijk verleden, zijne hallen en belforten, zijne kerken en stadhuizen, zijn eiken walpoorten en vergulde gildegevels. Het spreidde zijne rustige velden, zijne lieve dorpen als hoopjes schamelheid, zijne arme Breugelboeren en zijn middeleeuwsch geloof.”]
9 “Die schaarsche populariteit spruit misschien wel voort uit het zuiver anglosaksisch karakter van Shaw's werk: we kunnen, wij vastelanders, niet genoegzaam innig de zoo nuchtere en sluwe mentaliteit van het britsche volk begrijpen; de Engelschman vindt altijd principen om zijn belang te wettigen en om aan zijn brutaal egoïsme den schijn eener wereld-weldaad te lenen. De opper-practische geest van dat volk ook blijft ons nog altijd min of meer vreemd.” (132)

Another example can be found in John Rodker's 1925 discussion in *Le Disque Vert* of the English translation of *Les Chants de Maldoror*, a book that is impregnated with both “continental” and “English” influences.
10 See the overviews of literary and art magazines in Belgium by Adriaens-Pannier, Warmoes, Verhasselt and Aron (“Les revues littéraires en Belqique”). I will not consider in detail the more conservative sector of literary periodicals in which Anglophone literature was also mentioned, sometimes within another literary framework. For instance, the Belgian professor Paul de Reul is not mentioned within the avant-garde corpus, although he wrote several articles in *Le Flambeau*, translated two works of Robert Browning (*Sordello* in 1935 and *Pippa* in 1936), and was praised for his “importants travaux [...] sur la littérature anglaise” by Charlier (85).
11 For a complete overview of the articles published in *Le Disque Vert*, see: http://homepage.mac.com/emmapeel/ Disquevert/.

[12] "redéfinir la place de la littérature belge au contact des autres littératures et en Belgique même et de sauvegarder son indépendance et son authenticité." (97)

[13] "Le Belge est un peu dans la position d'un homme qui se trouverait debout sur un balcon et dominerait, de cet endroit, une large étendue. Il lui est impossible de regarder devant lui, sans apercevoir la variété des pays qui l'environnent; il ne peut réaliser totalement son besoin d'activité sans enjamber la balustrade pour se mêler à la vie qu'il voit se dérouler sous lui. Il lui faut, à tout prix, franchir ses limites étroites ou renoncer à se mouvoir librement. " (204)

[14] As opposed to "l'ethos discursif" – see Amossy.

[15] For other examples of "boundary maintenance", see Pym.

[16] "Celui qui s'impose la tâche d'écrire sur l'activité de son pays au profit d'un public étranger, doit, à mon sens, se borner à une critique descriptive des aspects positifs de la vie intellectuelle, lesquels par le mérite même de leur originalité et de leur signification, donnent à leur valeur une portée qui dépasse les frontières d'une langue." (136)

[17] "En al lijkt de Vlaamsche strijd wel wat klein nevens de ontroerende grootheid van het Iersche drama, toch is er voor ons veel te leeren uit dit eeuwenlang en droevig avontuur"; "Pater Callewaert heeft dit werk voor ons volk [the Flemish people] bestemd." (157)

[18] Note that *Le Masque* was primarily a literary review, published in Brussels from 1910 until 1914. In 1912 (no. 1: 2-16 and no. 2: 69-77), the review published Bithell's essay on Yeats in two articles, translated by Hellens. For more details, see also Aron's "Les pastiches de la revue *Le Masque*". It should be mentioned that Bithell already in 1911 published a volume of translations from French to English in his *Contemporary Belgian Poetry*. In order to get the fragments published, he needed the authorisation of the authors, which sometimes constituted the start of a correspondence. For a more complete bio-bibliographical sketch of Bithell, see Roe.

[19] See also the contribution of Karen Vandemeulebroucke in this volume.

[20] Note that *Vlaamsche Arbeid* (1923: 291-292) also published two poems by Brooke: "Waikiki. Tover." and "In 't blanke huis", both translated by Amaat Burssens. In 1930, Willy Koninckx provided a sketch of Brooke's life in a laudatory article "De dood van Rupert Brooke" (329-333).

[21] The role of Polderman is mentioned in Fairclough (45-47, 61-62, 196-197).

[22] De Ridder (1909), Polderman (42-46), Read (1922 and 1923) and Bithell (1921 and 1922).

[23] "Shaw, l'homme peut-être le mieux doué de l'Angleterre moderne. Shaw est, il faut l'admettre, le meilleur écrivain de prose polémique depuis Swift, notre plus grand" ("Le grand courant" 314).

[24] "De hedendaagsche Engelsche literatuur is essentieel eene volksliteratuur en eene literatuur van een volk dat zeer weinig ontwikkeld, zeer weinig verfijnd, zeer weinig kunstminnend is. (...) Heb ik dan niet het recht om te spreken van eene periode van verlamming, een crisistijdperk?" ("Drink en The Bondman" 156-157)

[25] In fact, after 1923 the periodical again exhibited a more conservative character. See Adriaens-Pannier (169-170).

Karen Vandemeulebroucke (Katholieke Universiteit Leuven)

Presence and Treatment of English Poetry in 19th-Century Belgian Literary Periodicals

Any literary 'province' is forced to be conscious of the presence and representation of other literatures. This also goes for 19th-century Belgian literature, which had to cope not only with the literary influences of prestigious neighbouring countries (France in particular), but also with intra-national linguistic diversity. From that perspective, even though a large number of 19th-century Belgian literary periodicals advocated the development of a truly Belgian literary identity, reality appeared to be far more complex. As such, any literary periodical defining itself as a mere "Belgian" mouthpiece should be considered a dual entity, a crossing of intra-national (Flemish-Francophone) and inter-national (Belgian-French-German, but also English and other) borders.

The present contribution focuses on how English poetry[1] is presented and treated within 19th-century Belgian literary periodicals. After an introductory historiographical overview of the production of poetry in Belgium during the 19th century and a brief discussion of the ways in which literary periodicals can act as a (trans-)national space,[2] I will deal more extensively with the presence of English poetry in two periodicals. The first periodical is *La Jeune Belgique* (1881-1897), a Francophone periodical and the voice of a new generation of Belgian poets who were actively involved in the struggle for international recognition for literary Belgium; the second one is *Van Nu en Straks* (1893-1901), a fin-de-siècle periodical by Flemish youngsters who were trying to give new impulses to Flemish literature. I will both examine the critical reception of English poetry and the publication of English poems, be it in English or translation, in these periodicals.

19th-century Belgian poetry and the periodical as a (trans)-national space

At a time when Belgium is occupied with affirming its political identity, literary periodicals reflect what seems to be not only a national, but also a trans-national viewpoint of identity. This (trans-)national viewpoint also goes for the production of 19th-century poetry in Belgium as a whole.

At the beginning of the 1830s one could barely speak of a truly Belgian "literary system": there were hardly any editors or authors, and critics as well as readers focused their attention on France. French literature, which had been a role model for more than two centuries, remained as vigorous as ever. Even when it comes to the 19th century as a whole, the definition of a "Belgian literature" is an illusion;[3] it was characterized by pirated editions and translations. And yet, literary historians have conceived of this literature in different ways and divided it up into different periods. Usually, a distinction is made between two periods: the first one includes the years 1830-1880, with a peak around 1830,[4] the second one starts with a turning point in 1880, associated with the founding of the periodical *La Jeune Belgique* in 1881, and extends to the end of the 19th century. In 1893, at a time when *La Jeune Belgique* was declining as a consequence of internal aesthetic discussions, August Vermeylen launched a Dutch-language periodical, *Van Nu en Straks*. Yet, the Flemish authors of *Van Nu en Straks* remain tributary to their Francophone colleagues: the lay-out of the periodical corresponds to that of *L'Art Moderne* and the title is an adaptation of *La Littérature de tout à l'heure*, a French periodical by Charles Morice (Nachtergaele 372).

By condensing the history of Belgian poetry into two phases, we necessarily fail to entirely grasp the complexity of the interplay of trends and tendencies during the 19th century. From this angle, the periodical acts as a witness providing a more subtle overview of the complexity of the literary landscape. Whereas, on a meta-discursive level, literary historiographies have focused on the tendency of the periodical to promote nationalism,[5] the purely discursive level reveals a more hybrid viewpoint. Indeed, paradoxically, the plea in favour of a Belgian identity appears to have been partly supported by the presence of foreign literatures.

In my opinion, 'foreign literature'[6] is the presence of non-Belgian literature (e.g. French or English literature) in the periodicals: critical texts with respect to 'foreign literature', but also translated texts, as well as non-translated texts in a foreign language. Even by merely using statistics, one can objectively show that this literature formed a substantial part of the periodicals that called themselves 'Belgian'. It is, however, more interesting to study the representational side of the issue, by tracing the presence of 'the Other'[7] in the discourse of the literary periodical.

In order to examine how English poetry is presented and treated within Belgian 19th-century literary periodicals, we shall first concentrate on *La Jeune Belgique* (1881-1897) before turning to *Van Nu en Straks* (1893-1901).

The presence and place of English literature in *La Jeune Belgique* (1881-1897)

National and non-national literature in La Jeune Belgique

The programmatic text of *La Jeune Belgique* states the following:

> *La Jeune Belgique* will ascribe to no school whatsoever. We consider that all genres are good if they remain moderate and if they have real talents to interpret them. [...] We are inviting the young, that is to say, those who are vigorous and loyal, to help us in our work. Let them show that there is a Jeune Belgique as there is a Jeune France, and let them follow our advice: *Let's be ourselves*.[8]

Paradoxically, the poets want to be "themselves" ("Soyons-nous") and to belong to no school whatsoever, by following the example of the French periodical *La Jeune France*.[9] From the viewpoint of a national literature, the collaborators' dream was to gain a greater autonomy for literature. In this respect, *La Jeune Belgique* was trying to create a new Belgian poetry, one that no longer served the nation. However, they also wanted to come up with a poetry different from the poetry produced in the neighbouring countries. In other words, while looking for a certain singularity, they also tried to distinguish themselves. This is reflected, for instance, in the fact that, from various points of view, they tried to produce a more hybrid poetry. Belgian, and Flemish authors in particular, often 'embellished' their works by the introduction of elements referring to the 'Northern myth' and the emphasis on their so-called 'Nordic soul'.[10] Apart from that, authors writing in Flemish are barely present in *La Jeune Belgique*. Hence, literature in Flemish was here not seen as a part of the national literature. On the contrary, it was regarded as non-national, as the *Other*, since it was not Francophone.

International (non-national) literature was also substantially present in *La Jeune Belgique*. French authors functioned as models of *habitus*, which can be derived from several observations. In the first place, many critical texts dealt with French authors. For instance, several chapters were dedicated to Baudelaire, or the *Jeune Belgique* poets dedicated their poems to French authors. Second, poems by French authors were published directly without any paratextual environment. The French were seen as 'the Other', but the *Jeune Belgique* poets tried to associate themselves with these French poets, hoping that this mimetic tactic would in the long run add to the legitimacy of their own work.

Other foreign authors have a special yet limited place in *La Jeune Belgique*.[11] In general, the presence of English literature in *La Jeune Belgique* is rather restricted. Whereas the whole first series of the periodical counts more than 5.000 records, only 16 of them concern English literature. We count 12 translations of English texts into French. Ten of these are poems: one by Tennyson (trans. Charles Gros); one by Swinburne (trans. Georges Destrée); one by Edgar A. Poe (trans. Iwan Gilkin); one by Coleridge (trans. Maurice Desombiaux); four by Dante Gabriel Rossetti (trans. Georges Destrée); and two by Keats (trans. Georges Destrée and Paul Tiberghien). One English prose text, a series of three Japanese stories, was translated from English into French by Jules Destrée who tried, as mentioned in a footnote, to respect the "familiar and naïve" form of the original texts as much as possible (*LJB* 8.2 (1889): 57). Also, a translation by Paul Tiberghien of Swinburne's play *Atalanta in Calydon* appeared serialized in *La Jeune Belgique*. Four critical texts are dedicated to English authors: two announcements in the section *Memento* (both of them devoted to Swinburne), and two book reviews (one dealing with a translation of a collection of poems by Gabriel Rossetti, the other dealing with a poem of Herbert P. Horne). Furthermore, one text is dedicated to Swinburne and two texts contain an epigraph written by this poet.

Table 1:
English literature in *La Jeune Belgique*

Translations (12)

Poems (10)

Tennyson, Lord Alfred. "La fin du Luth". ["All in All"]. Trans. Charles Gros. *LJB* 1.9 (1881): 130.

Swinburne, Algernon Charles. "Sapphiques". ["Sapphics"]. Trans. Georges Destrée. *LJB* 7.6 (1886): 195-198.

Poe, Edgar Allan. "Israfel". ["Israfel"]. Trans. Iwan Gilkin. *LJB* 7.11 (1888): 350-351.

Coleridge, Samuel Taylor. "La Ballade de l'Ancien Marin". ["The Rime of the Ancient Mariner"]. Trans. Maurice Desombiaux. *LJB* 9.2 (1890): 119-122.

Rossetti, Dante Gabriel. "Le sommeil de ma sœur". ["My Sister's Sleep"]. Trans. Georges Destrée. *LJB* 10.10 (1891): 379-380.

Rossetti, Dante Gabriel. "Sœur Hélène". ["Sister Helen"]. Trans. Georges Destrée. *LJB* 10.11 (1891): 406-411.

Rossetti, Dante Gabriel. "Trois ombres". ["Three Shadows"]. Trans. Georges Destrée. *LJB* 11.11 (1892): 69-70.

Rossetti, Dante Gabriel. "Ave". ["Ave"]. Trans. Paul Tiberghien. *LJB* 13.7/8 (1894): 319-321.

Keats, John. "La Belle Dame sans Mercy". ["La Belle Dame Sans Mercy"]. Trans. Georges Destrée. *LJB* 11.3 (1892): 153-155.

Keats, John. "La cigale et le grillon" ["The Cicada and the Ant"]. Trans. Paul Tiberghien. *LJB* 13.7/8 (1894): 321.

Prose texts (1)

An. "Trois Contes Populaires Japonais". ["Japanese Fairy Tales"]. Trans. Jules Destrée. *LJB* 8.2 (1889): 57-63.

Plays (1)

Swinburne, Algernon Charles. "Atalante à Calydon". ["Atalanta in Calydon"]. Trans. Paul Tiberghien. *LJB* 12.3 (1892): 143-150 (first appearance).

Critical texts (4)

Announcements (section "Memento") (2)

Reference to Algernon Charles Swinburne's "Anactoria". *LJB* 7.6 (1888): 209.

Reference to Algernon Charles Swinburne's "Au Tombeau de Banville". *LJB* 10.5 (1891): 228.

Book reviews (2)

Rossetti, Dante Gabriel. "La Maison de Vie". ["The House of Life"]. Trans. Clémence-H. Couve. Reviewer Joséphin Péladan. *LJB* 6.8 (1887): 269-270.

Horne, Herbert Percy. "Diversi Colores". Reviewer Joséphin Péladan. *LJB* 10.11 (1892): 412-413.

Epigraphs (3)

Destrée, Georges. "Vénus Aphrodite", text dedicated to "Monsieur A.C. Swinburne". *LJB* 10.7 (1891): 264-266.
Fontainas, André. "Fleurs de serre. Poème"; epigraph by Swinburne: "With insatiable eyes that kindle / And insatiable mouth that feeds". *LJB* 8.1 (1889): 14-22.
Anon. "L'inconnue"; epigraph by Swinburne: "A pallid and poisonous queen...". (Dolorès). *LJB* 8.7/8/9 (1888): 262-264.

When it comes to the presence of English literature in *La Jeune Belgique*, poetry is by far the most popular genre. Although this is supposedly due to the periodical's general preference for poetry, one should keep in mind that English classic poets were held in high esteem in those times. From the above, Swinburne (1837-1909) also emerges as one of the most popular English poets in *La Jeune Belgique*. This might have to do with the fact that this Pre-Raphaelite poet was profoundly influenced by French symbolism: he read French literature, lived in Paris for a long time and admired Gautier, Baudelaire and Hugo. He even wrote poems in French, like "Le tombeau de Gautier" or "Au Tombeau de Banville", a sonnet he wrote after the death of this French poet and which was published in the section *Memento* in *La Jeune Belgique* in 1891 (10.5: 228).

English poetry in critical texts

The question then arises as to *how* literary critics negotiated issues of English literature in general and English poetry in particular? A good example is provided by Olivier-Georges Destrée's review of *Diversi colores* (*LJB* 10.11 (1892): 412-413), a collection of poetry written by Herbert-P(ercy) Horne. This review appeared under the heading "Littérature anglaise". The reviewer expresses his admiration for the pre-Raphaelites like Dante-Gabriel Rossetti or William Morris, but also for Herbert Horne, who where poets as well as painters:[12]

> This combination of skilfulness in painting and poetry can also be found in some artists of the new generation and a striking example of such an artist is Mr Herbert Horne. [13]

Furthermore, the reviewer thinks highly of the classical (more precisely Greek) influence on English poets:

> [Herbert. P. Horne] evokes the images and the forms of the divine Attic beauty in the same powerful way as Keats' odes and Algernon-Charles Swinburne's beautiful verses of the *Atalanta*. This love and cult of perfect beauty make Mr Horne a classic poet in heart and soul, precisely in the very magnificent poem entitled: *A Song from an unfinished drama*. This poem is of a purely Greek inspiration, which is almost natural to these English poets.[14]

We can deduce from this excerpt that the reviewer admires both the Romantic Keats (1795-1821) and the Victorian Swinburne (1837-1909) as English models. Both are synchronised on the basis of a common poetical ("Parnassian") programme. However, for Destrée French hexagonal literature remains the model par excellence for universal literary quality, as we read in the following passage:

> The love poems of the collection [*Diversi colores*] are, in our opinion, closer to the exquisite and always young verses of the delicious Charles d'Orléans, and sometimes even to Pierre de Ronsard's admirable sonnets.[15]

The reviewer feels the necessity to refer to the poets who are well-known to the Belgian (Francophone) public, i.e. the French poets, in this case Charles d'Orléans and Pierre de Ronsard. Belgian poetry, then, is included in the (pseudo-contemporaneous) synchrony of Keats and Swinburne on the one hand, but also in a universal (trans-historical) position represented by the French model, on the other.

English poetry in translation

A first example of English poetry in translation, is Olivier-Georges Destrée's "literal translation" (this is explicitly mentioned: 7.6 (1886): 199) of Swinburne's ballad "Sapphics" (7.6 (1886): 195-199).

ALL the night sleep came not upon my eyelids,
Shed not dew, nor shook nor unclosed a feather,
Yet with lips shut close and with eyes of iron
Stood and beheld me.

Then to me so lying awake a vision
Came without sleep over the seas and touched me,
Softly touched mine eyelids and lips; and I too,
Full of the vision,

Saw the white implacable Aphrodite,
Saw the hair unbound and the feet unsandalled
Shine as fire of sunset on western waters;
Saw the reluctant

(…)

SAPPHIQUES

Toute la nuit, le sommeil ne vint pas sur mes paupières,
Ne répandit point de rosée, ne secoua et n'ouvrit pas une plume,
Mais les lèvres silencieuses fermées, et avec des yeux de fer
Se tint debout en me contemplant.

Alors que j'étais ainsi couché surgit une vision.
Elle vint sans sommeil par-dessus les murs et me toucha
Doucement toucha mes paupières et mes lèvres ; et moi aussi,
Rempli de la vision,

Je vis la blanche implacable Aphrodite
Je vis ses cheveux dénoués et ses pieds sans chaussures
Briller comme le feu des soleils couchants sur les eaux occidentales ;
Je vis ses pieds

(…)
ALGERNON CHARLES SWINBURNE. – *Poèmes et ballades.*
(Traduction littérale).
GEORGES DESTRÉE

It is immediately clear that we are dealing with a translation: Swinburne's name is mentioned (though in small font size), as well as the name of the translator (in large font size, as he is a regular collaborator of *La Jeune Belgique*). Destrée refers to the collection of poems in which "Sapphiques" was originally published, yet instead of mentioning the original title ("Poems and Ballads") he uses the French translation ("Poèmes et ballades"). Moreover, as is almost always the case in *La Jeune Belgique*, the original poem is not printed. Nonetheless, this translated poem is given a special place within a series of poems written by Valère Gille and Adolphe Frères, who frequently collaborated in *La Jeune Belgique*.

Furthermore, the original poem is composed of 20 stanzas of four verses each. Swinburne does not use rhyme, but applies regular pentameters of two trochees, one dactyl, and two trochees. The last verse of each stanza consists of one dactyl and one trochee. The combination of these three hendecasyllabic lines and the concluding line (known as the 'Adonic line') constitutes the 'Sapphic stanza', named after the classical Greek poet Sappho, who made regular use of this metrical form.

Destrée retains the number of quatrains and follows the original structure of the English poem (he does not even relocate parts of sentences from one verse into another). He also retains the punctuation marks and the concluding 'Adonic line' in each stanza. At the same time, however, Destrée does not adopt the English poetical alteration of stressed and unstressed syllables, nor does he opt for the French syllabic system (in which meter dominates over rhyme and the syllables have to be counted). Instead, he produces a 'literal translation' in which the content (and not the metrical pattern) of the poem is primordial – this, it might be noted, in contradiction to the general poetic strand of *La Jeune Belgique*. Destrée's translation can be considered as an example of 'vers-librisme' (or 'blank verse'). From this perspective, it is remarkable that Destrée still entitles his translation "Sapphiques".

Markedly different from Destrée's 'literal translation' is Iwan Gilkin's 'partial imitation' of Edgar Allan Poe's "Israfel":

ISRAFEL (1)

A Georges Destrée

In Heaven a spirit doth dwell
"Whose heart-strings are a lute";
None sing so wildly well
As the angel Israfel,
And the giddy stars (so legends tell),
Ceasing their hymns, attend the spell

Of his voice, all mute.
Tottering above
In her highest noon,
The enamoured moon
Blushes with love,
While, to listen, the red Levin
(With the rapid Pleiads, even,
Which were seven,)
Pauses in Heaven.
(…)

Dans les hauts palais d'ambre et d'ébène du ciel,
Aux parcs de roses d'or, qu'ombrent des violettes,
- La plus parfaite des créatures parfaites ! -
Chante en glissant dans la brise l'ange Israfel.

Les fibres de son cœur font les cordes d'un luth
Qui rhythme les accords des splendeurs éternelles
Quand le battement doux du velours de ses ailes
Baise le cœur en feu des étoiles du Sud.

Les astres frissonnants taisent leur vaste chœur,
La lune enamourée empourpre son visage
Lorsqu'aux sons lumineux de son léger passage
Se meurt au ciel en pleurs la langueur de son cœur.
(…)

Iwan Gilkin

(1) Imité partiellement d'Edgar Poë [sic]

Although Gilkin dedicates this poem to Georges Destrée, the former opts for a French (Parnassian) form in which he adapts the English tonic system to the French syllabic system (or to a versification system in which the syllables have to be counted). Gilkin thus chooses for the classic alexandrine with 12 syllables. In addition, he opts for alternate rhyme (ABBA) and for a constant alternation between masculine and feminine rhyme. In short, Gilkin's translation should be seen as a clear concession to the conventions of French poetry of the contemporary Parnassian tradition.

The presence and place of English literature in *Van Nu en Straks* (1893-1901)

National and non-national literature in Van Nu en Straks

Van Nu en Straks (1893-1894 and 1896-1901) was a fin-de-siècle periodical gathering Flemish youngsters such as Cyriel Buysse, Emmanuel De Bom, Prosper Van Langendonck and August Vermeylen (in the first series[16]), and, among others, Karel van de Woestijne, Herman Teirlinck and Stijn

Streuvels (in the second series). It aspired to provide an alternative to the typical provincialism of that era and championed a more international view on literature, as we can read in its programmatic text:

> '**Van Nu & Straks**' has a double purpose.
> Above all, it is the periodical of youngsters from the Southern Netherlands, an expression of the desires and thoughts of those who have come last, – without aesthetic dogmas, without school-tendency – a free vanguard organ devoted to the art of Now, curious about the art-that-is-still-developing – that art of Later – here and abroad.[17]

In the first place, *Van Nu en Straks* tried to give a Flemish response to the Dutch claim for individualism and 'l'art pour l'art' (represented, for instance, by Willem Kloos and the collaborators of *De Nieuwe Gids*). This response was based in the idea of an art that could serve the whole community. This did not imply, however, that Dutch authors did not play an important role in this periodical, especially in the first series.

Furthermore, the collaborators of *Van Nu en Straks* were very much oriented towards Belgian Francophone artistic movements such as *Les XX*[18] and *La Libre Esthétique*, as can be read in the following letters by Vincent van Gogh, published in French in *Van Nu en Straks*:

> It reminded me very much of contemporary Belgian painters when you told me that Maus had gone to see my paintings. Then I was overwhelmed by memories, which deluged me like an avalanche, & I searched how to reconstruct this school of modern Flemish artists for myself, until I suffered from home sickness, like a Swiss.[19]

Another example of this connection to Belgian Francophone literature is August Vermeylen's review of Maurice Maeterlinck's *La sagesse et la destinée* (*VNS,* new series, 4 (1900): 97). And also French authors took up a substantial part; Albert Verwey, for example, wrote a portrait of Verlaine (*VNS,* 2 (1992): 1).

Finally, the *Van Nu en Straks* youngsters were very much inspired by new anarchistic ideas imported from abroad. Two examples: the periodical published a review of Kropotkin's "Memoirs of a Revolutionist" (*VNS,* new series 4 (1900): 182-193) and Ferdinand Domela Nieuwenhuis, the frontman of the Dutch revolutionary socialists, wrote several socio-critical articles, e.g., on an international congress in London.

English literature in Van Nu en Straks

In the two series of *Van Nu en Straks*, British authors seem to be absent. The periodical did, however, publish a long critical article on the American poet Walt Whitman by a certain Dr. Karl Federn. The reviewer sees Whitman as one of the greatest American poets of his time, although he is not always appreciated by the American people:

> And it only proves how badly the clear view of America's educated people has tarnished by the alienation of the literary circles from people's lives, by the air of salons and libraries that they are used to breathing, by the critical and historical formulas in which they have wrapped themselves, when they are still refusing to recognize Walt Withman [sic] as their most perfect, most original, most wonderful poet.[20]

In the same article, the reviewer translates short abstracts from Whitman's work, without referring to the original poems. Consider, for example, the following passage taken from "Song of Myself" (*VNS,* new series 2 (1897): 198):

[I am he that walks with the tender and growing night,
I call to the earth and sea half-held by the night.
Press close bare-bosom'd night--press close magnetic nourishing night!
Night of south winds--night of the large few stars!
Still nodding night--mad naked summer night.]

Ik ben die, die wandelt met den teederen groeienden nacht,
Ik roep tot de aarde en de zee half-gehouden door den nacht.
Druk dichter bloot-boez'mige nacht - druk dichter magnetische voedende nacht!
Nacht van zuidwinden - nacht van de groote weinige starren!
Stil knikkende nacht - dolle naakte zomernacht.

The translator reproduces all the original poetical characteristics – even matrix-like structures such as syntactic groups that are rendered word by word – and all this is presented as new poetry. It would be interesting to examine how this relates to contemporary Flemish poetry, for instance to Van de Woestijne's complex epithet constructions.

Later, *Van Nu en Straks* also published a translation of Whitman's "Blue Ontario's Shore, 14" ["Vervalt achter mij"] (*VNS,* new series, 4 (1900): 198-199). This time, the translator is not mentioned.

How is it to be explained that, except for Walt Whitman, no other Anglophone authors appeared in *Van Nu en Straks*? Certainly, the periodical's first aim was to give new impulses to a literature in Flemish, which automatically created links with Dutch authors. More importantly, however, literature in 19th-century Belgium, whether it was Francophone or Flemish, still seemed to be very much controlled by the French centre.

Concluding remarks

We have observed that, in comparison with other 'foreign literatures', the space contributed to English literature remains rather limited in *La Jeune Belgique* and *Van Nu en Straks*. Translations of English poetry are in most cases literal translations, but sometimes the translators adapt English poems to the French syllabic versification system. Also, the original texts are not always given next to the translations. This weakening effect towards the English texts indicates that the collaborators of these periodicals emphasized their own literature (Belgian Francophone or Flemish) and that, at the time, French literature did not at all seem to have lost its status of model at all.[21]

Bibliography

Ashcroft, Bill, Gareth Griffiths and Helen Tiffin. *Post-Colonial Studies. The Key Concepts*. London and New York: Routledge, 2003.

Couttenier, Piet. "Nationale Beelden in De Vlaamse Literatuur Van De Negentiende Eeuw." *Nationalisme in België. Identiteiten in beweging 1780-2000.* Eds. Kas Deprez and Louis Vos. Antwerpen: Baarn, 1999. 60-69.

Delsemme, Françoise. *Les littératures étrangères dans les revues littéraires belges de langue française publiées entre 1885 et 1899: contribution bibliographique à l'étude du cosmopolitisme littéraire en Belgique*. Bruxelles: Commission belge de bibliographie, 1973.

Delsemme, Paul. "Le style coruscant, mouture belge de l'écriture artiste des Goncourt." *Revue littéraire en ligne* 11 (November 2004). 2 July 2008. <www.bon-a-tirer.com>.

Jauss, Hans-Robert. *Alterität Und Modernität Der Mittelaterlichen Literatur.* München: Fink, 1977.

Klinkenberg, Jean-Marie. "La génération de 1880 et la Flandre." *Les Avant-gardes littéraires en Belgique. Au confluent des arts et des langues (1880-1850).* Ed. Jean Weisgerber. Bruxelles: Éditions Labor, 1991. 101-10.

———. "Introduction. L'analyse institutionnelle de la littérature en Belgique francophone: où en est-on?" *Textyles* 15 (1999): 7-11.

Meylaerts, Reine. *L'aventure flamande de la Revue Belge. Langues, littératures et cultures dans l'entre-deux-guerres*. Bruxelles: Peter Lang, 2004.

Nachtergaele, Vic. "D'une littérature deux autres. " *Revue de littérature comparée* 3:299 (2001): 363-77.

Nautet, Francis. *Histoires des lettres belges d'expression française*. Vols. 1 and 2. Bruxelles: Charles Rozez, 1892.

Robyns, Clem. "Translation and Discursive Identity." *Poetics Today* 15:3 (1994): 405-28.

Sartre, Jean-Paul. *Being and Nothingness: An Essay on Phenomenological Ontology*. Trans. Hazel E. Barnes. London: Methuen, 1957.

Trousson, Raymond. "La Jeune Belgique et les lettres russes." *Lettres ou ne pas lettres. Mélanges de littérature française de Belgique offerts à Roland Beyen*. Eds. Jan Herman, Lieven Tack and Koenraad Geldof. Louvain: Presses Universitaires de Louvain, 2001. 555-64.

Vandemeulebroucke, Karen. "Les Lettres parisiennes de Georges Rodenbach: contestation ou confirmation du mythe nordique." *Cahiers du 19e siècle*, [forthcoming].

———. "The Periodical As a (Trans)-National Space: 19th Century Literary Periodicals in Belgium." *World Literature and World Culture: History, Theory, Analysis*. Eds. Karen-Margrethe Simonsen and Jakob Stougaard-Nielsen. Aarhus: University Press, 2008, 116-32.

Wauters, Karel. "De Vlaamse Literatuur Van De Negentiende Eeuw: Een Literair-Historisch Probleemgebied Doorgelicht." *Colloquium over de beeldvorming rond de 19de eeuw in Vlaanderen. Balans en perspectief 1791-1991*. Ed. F. A. Snellaert. Gent: 1991. 37-49.

Notes

1 The denomination 'English' literature(s) is somewhat problematic: does it refer to literature written in English, or written by British, Irish and/or American authors? In this paper, 'English' literature or poetry has to be understood in the second sense.

2 See also my article on "The Periodical As a (Trans)-National Space".

3 See Klinkenberg's "Introduction".

4 In the first decades of the Belgian nation, both Francophone and Flemish literature had a very Belgian character (see Wauters, Couttenier and Nachtergaele). It is only from 1840 onwards that a specifically Flemish literature starts to develop its own subnational identity within the context of the Belgian nation state (Couttenier 60).

5 See, amongst others, Nautet.

6 See also Delsemme's *Les littératures étrangères*.

7 Generally speaking, "the 'other' is anyone who is separate from one's self. The existence of others is crucial in defining what is 'normal' and in locating one's own place in the world" (Ashcroft, Griffiths and Tiffin 169). In existential philosophy (for example in Sartre's *Being and Nothingness*) this concept is frequently used to define the relations between Self and Other in order to create self-awareness and feelings of identity. In post-colonial theory, then, the definition of the Other can be related to the formation of subjectivity, for instance as described in the psychoanalytic work of Lacan (Ashcroft, Griffiths and Tiffin 169-173). Clem Robyns, on the other hand, argues that the Other is a discursive construction that is historically and sociologically determined. It is a relational concept that can only be understood with reference to a 'Self', a 'We'. This discursive 'We' defines itself *in relation with* or *in opposite to* other discourses. Moreover, as Meylaerts (55) points out, the discursive construction of the Other is also one of the privileged ways of a nation's identity construction. From this point of view, the Other transcends the hermeneutic category of "Alterität" which Jauss defines as a mere aesthetic concept based on the text. The Other is not one specific category, or one specific foreign influence (such as that of French literature).

In this regard, the influence of the Other as a discursive construction can be retraced in the genre of poetry: thus we can look for traces of the Other (French poetry, German poetry, Flemish poetry, ...) in Belgian Francophone poetry at different levels (linguistic, thematic, prosodic level). However, we are dealing here with a very abstract notion: what is understood as (the) "other" can differ from one situation to another – for instance, from one periodical to another or from one decade to another (as such, "Flemish" poetry can be seen as the Self, as a part of Belgian poetry, or as the Other, as a poetry opposed to the "own" Belgian Francophone poetry).

[8] "*La Jeune Belgique* ne sera d'aucune école. Nous estimons que tous les genres sont bons s'ils restent dans la modération nécessaire et s'ils ont de réels talents pour les interpréter. [...] Nous invitons les jeunes, c'est-à-dire les vigoureux et les fidèles, à nous aider dans notre œuvre. Qu'ils montrent qu'il y a une Jeune Belgique comme il y a une Jeune France, et qu'avec nous ils prennent pour devise: *Soyons nous.*" (*LJB* 1.1 (1881): 1)

[9] According to Paul Delsemme, "Soyons nous" did not mean "Soyons belges, soyons de chez nous". On the contrary, the motto served to convince the author to develop his personality without worrying about literary dogmas and extra-literary taboos. As such, it implied waving aside the older generation, its privileges and its opinions. This motto also suggested that one should refuse to subscribe to literary doctrines, coming from abroad. Finally, Delsemme claims, "soyons nous" asks collaborators to dispose of their own language in full freedom.

[10] The 'North' was seen as the contribution of Flemish culture to Francophone literature: the Germanic as opposed to the Latin "genius". The main characteristics of the "North" were the expression of a profound malaise, disillusionment, isolation and coldness of the soul. The landscape that was described was characterized by a certain heaviness, humidity, humility, effort, mist, the sea and the plains, small houses and high belfries. It also put in to words an atmosphere of tempestuousness, dejection and violent activity, sensuality and mysticism. See also Klinkenberg (105-108) and my "Les Lettres Parisiennes de Georges Rodenbach" (116-132).

[11] For Russian literature in *La Jeune Belgique*, for example, see Trousson.

[12] Pictorial poetry is said to be typical of Flemish poets also and was highly admired by the *Jeune Belgique* poets. This could (partly) explain the reviewer's admiration for the pre-Raphaelites.

[13] "Ces dons combinés de poète et de peintre se rencontrent à nouveau chez quelques artistes de la nouvelle génération et d'une façon tout à fait remarquable chez M. Herbert Horne." (*LJB* 10.11 (1892): 412)

[14] "[Herbert P. Horne] évoque les images et les formes de la divine beauté attique aussi puissamment que les odes de Keats et les beaux vers de l'*Atalanta* d'Algernon-Charles Swinburne. Cet amour et ce culte de la beauté parfaite qui font de M. Horne un artiste absolument classique, se retrouvent poussés aussi loin que possible notamment dans le très beau poème intitulé: *A Song from an unfinished drama*, d'une inspiration purement grecque, et comme naturelle à ces poètes anglais." (*LJB* 10.11 (1892): 413)

[15] "Les poèmes amoureux du volume [*Diversi colores*] se rapprochent plutôt pour nous des vers exquis et toujours jeunes du délicieux Charles d'Orléans et parfois même des admirables sonnets de Pierre de Ronsard." (*LJB* 10.11 (1892): 413)

[16] The first series was devoted to literature as well as to plastic arts (we find illustrations by Henry van de Velde, James Ensor, Georges Minne and Jan Toorop).

[17] "'Van Nu & Straks' heeft een tweevoudig doel. Het is vooral: het tijdschrift der jongeren uit Zuid-Nederland, eene uiting van het willen & denken der laatstgekomenen, – zonder aesthetische dogmata, zonder school-strekking – een vrij voorhoede-orgaan gewijd aan de kunst van Nu, nieuwsgierig naar de kunst-nog-in-wording – die van Straks – hier en in 't buitenland." (*VNS, "Woord Vooraf"*, 1 (1893): 1)

[18] *Les XX* was a group of 20 Belgian painters, designers and sculptors, formed in 1883 by Octave Maus (a Brussels lawyer and publisher). For ten years, these 'vingtistes' organized an annual exposition in collaboration with 20 international artists (such as Claude Monet, Paul Gauguin, Paul Cézanne and Vincent van Gogh). From 1892 onwards, the society of *Les XX* was transformed into *La Libre Esthétique*.
[19] "Cela m'a fait beaucoup penser à des peintres belges de ces jours-ci, quand tu m'as dit que Maus avait été voir mes toiles. Alors des souvenirs me viennent, comme une avalanche, & je cherche à me reconstruire toute cette école d'artistes modernes flamands, jusqu'à en avoir le mal du pays, comme un Suisse." (*VNS, Brieven en platen van Vincent van Gogh*, 3 (1893): 31)
[20] "En het bewijst alleen hoe zeer het klare zien bij de ontwikkelden in Amerika verdoft is geworden door de verwijdering der literaire kringen van het leven des volks, door de salon- en bibliotheeklucht, die zij gewend zijn in te ademen, door de kritisch-historische formules waarin zij zich gewikkeld hebben, wanneer zij nog altijd weigeren, in Walt Withman [sic] hunnen volmaaktsten, oorspronkelijksten, heerlijksten dichter te erkennen." (*VNS* new series, 2 (1897): 191)
[21] Even though I examined two leading Belgian periodicals of the second half of the 19th century, these results do, of course, not necessarily count for all the Belgian periodicals, or for the field of poetry as a whole, as a lot of choices can be due to a different position-taking within periodicals. These results should thus be supplemented with those taken from other periodicals (prominent periodicals as well as more peripheral ones).

Liselotte Vandenbussche (Hogeschool Gent/Universiteit Gent)

The Import of English Literature by Women Translators in Flanders, 1870-1914. A Comparative Survey

In December 1913, Dina Logeman-Van der Willigen (1864-1925), a Dutch translator living in the Belgian city of Ghent, wrote to her friend Marie Elisabeth Belpaire (1853-1948): "I never translate works from English because it *does not pay*. Everyone in Holland is able to translate from English [and] publishers are flooded by young girls who want to translate a *whole* book for *5* or *10* guilders!!"[1] Instead of choosing British authors, Logeman-Van der Willigen opted for writers from the smaller Danish, Norwegian and Swedish communities, such as Johannes Jørgensen, Georg Brandes, Ellen Key and Herman Bang.[2] By selecting these authors for her Dutch translations, she was not only able to supply a demand for highbrow literature from the then popular Scandinavian countries, but also managed to earn a living thanks to her translations, which might have been impossible when focussing on English or French literature.

In what follows, I will first give a short sketch of the (small) import of English literature by women translators between 1870-1914, and compare it to the import of literature from other countries and language areas. This analysis will not include a quantitative comparison of the production of translations, since that would need to cover translations by male authors as well and would largely exceed the scope of this article. I will rather focus on some of the motives of women writers to opt for translations in general and choose specific authors and source literatures.[3] In the final part of this article, I will supplement this material with some background information on the secondary schooling and higher education of women in Flanders and other elements that have played a role in the translation market. It will result in a qualitative micro-study that does not regard translations from a publisher's point of view,[4] but approaches the work from the perspective of the translators themselves.

Translations from English

During the late 19th and early 20th century, only a small number of translations from English were made by women living in Flanders. All of these women were writers who produced one or more translations as a sort of side-project to their own creative work. They include Maria Van Ackere-Doolaeghe (1803-1884), Siska Van Daelen (1879-1944), Hélène Swarth (1859-1943) and Anna Germonprez (1866-1957). The British and Irish authors whose works were translated, are Henry Wadsworth Longfellow, Lord Byron, John Henry Mackay, Elizabeth Barrett Browning, Oscar Wilde and Ian Maclaren (John Watson). The origins of these translations can be documented by means of the translators' correspondences.

In 1878, Maria Van Ackere-Doolaeghe asked Eugène van Oye (1840-1926), a poet who had published translations of Longfellow and William C. Bryant, if he wanted to revise her translation of a poem by Lord Byron.[5] Given that she did not have English at her command, Van Ackere-Doolaeghe confessed, she had asked a friend to make a translation into French, which she had, in turn, translated into Dutch. As was often the case in France, translation had been a joint effort here (Wilfert 36-37). Because her friend could not read Dutch and was therefore unable to pronounce a judgment on the Dutch translation, she asked Van Oye to revise her work. Thanking him for his translation of the poem that she would use as an aid to rewrite her work, she added her translation creed, borrowed from abbé Delettre: "The most essential duty of a translator, which implies everything else, is to try to make the same effort as the author in every part of the work."[6]

Anna Germonprez, a teacher and writer, was asked to translate a literary work of the Scottish writer Ian Maclaren (John Watson) by Marie Elisabeth Belpaire, the founder and editor of the Catholic literary and cultural journal *Dietsche Warande & Belfort*. Belpaire had published a study on Maclaren in May 1900 and wanted to provide her readers with a translation of his work as well (Reymenants 113, Belpaire "Het landleven in de letterkunde"). Germonprez, who had shown a fondness of the Flemish traditions and knowledge of the Flemish national character in her novels, seemed to be tailor-made for the job and agreed at first. She liked *The Days of Auld Langsyne*: "so tolerant, uplifting, stimulating the good".[7] However, the translation did not turn out to be that easy. The religious situation in the novel was typically Scottish and, according to Germonprez, difficult to explain to 'our nation'. Moreover, the Scottish dialect of the peasants would not be convincing when translated in her own dialect.[8] When a partial translation of the work was finally published in *Dietsche Warande & Belfort*, Germonprez used the typical strategy of the 'humble servant', displaying her discomfort and almost apologizing to a colleague who had offered some remarks: she emphasized that the translation was made at the insistence of Belpaire and that translating was not one of her best qualities.[9]

Van Ackere-Doolaeghe, Van Daelen, Swarth and Germonprez published their work alongside translations from other languages, such as French, German or Romanian. English literature did not occupy a dominant position in the charts of translations by women in Flanders, although it is difficult to make general statements on the basis of these, after all, small-scale activities.

Other source literatures

When looking at the source literatures women chose to translate, some tendencies become clearly visible. A quick overview of the translated works by women during the late 19th and early 20th century in Flanders shows us that they mainly chose authors from German, Danish, Norwegian and Swedish literary systems on the one hand, and some works from Russia, Estonia and Greece, on the other.

Almost no works from French-speaking authors in Belgium or writers in France, Italy or Spain were translated. Exceptions to this rule were Van Ackere-Doolaeghe, who translated a French poem by the Belgian Minister of State Rogier in 1872 ("De tehuiskomst"), and Swarth, who in 1888 translated work from Charles Fuster ("Een doode") and, after her move to the Netherlands in 1894, work from Johannes Allarda, Alfred de Musset and Rachilde (Marguerite Vallette-Eymery). The reasons for this omission can be manifold. A first and obvious reason is that the intellectual elite and most of the literate people spoke and read French in Belgium and therefore did not need translations from French. It also points to the centrality of French literature in the cultural world-system (Heilbron 43). A second reason, however, might be that, in Flanders, French literature was regarded as dandyish and perverted for a long time, to which a sound and healthy literature had to be put in contrast (Klinkenberg 519). The critic Frans de Potter (1834-1904) for instance, was clearly delighted with

Rosalie Loveling's (1834-1875) 1864 translation of a novel by the German writer Klaus Groth (1819-1899) and placed the work in sharp contrast with the products of the "light literature" of the South (Simons 336).

Russia, Romania, Estonia and Greece sporadically functioned as source systems for women translators in Flanders, but in most of these translations the original authors were omitted and difficult to identify. Only Laura Hiel's (1859-1945) 1895 translation of Turgeniev and Swarth's 1909 translation of Hélène Vacaresco explicitly mentioned the original authors. Other translations were published without a reference to the author, which suggests that they were not directly translated from the original. Mina Sleeckx's (1851-1939) Slavonic fairytales, for example, were translated from Marmier's *Contes populaires de différents pays*. Also in the case of translations of folktales from Turkish and Hebrew, no source was mentioned, and it seems unlikely that they would have been translated from the original sources.

German literature functioned for most women translators as a source system. The sisters Paula and Mina Sleeckx, Rosalie and Virginie Loveling (1836-1923), Laura Hiel, Esther Stinissen, Siska van Daelen and Hélène Swarth published work from authors such as Victor Blüthgen, Paul Heyse, Eugenie Marlitt, the Austrian writer Emil(e) Mario Vacano, Klaus Groth, Heinrich Heine, August von Platen, the unknown Katharina Koch and Emil Schattke, as well as the Romanian princess Carmen Sylva (Elisabeth Pauline Ottilie Luise zu Wied).

However, when looking at the number of translations, works from the smaller Danish, Norwegian and Swedish communities clearly outnumber all other source systems. This is mainly due to the most prolific and professional woman translator in Flanders, Dina Logeman-Van der Willigen, who published more than a hundred translated novels by the Danish Jørgensen, Brandes and Bang, or the Swedish author Key.[10] Apart from Logeman-Van der Willigen, also the Catholic writer Marie Elisabeth Belpaire translated some of Jørgensen's works. In addition, the unknown Mathilde van Engelen adapted a Scandinavian fairy tale, and Virginie Loveling translated a poem by Knut Hamsun, which was published in a review of modern Norwegian literature by Logeman-Van der Willigen in 1908.[11]

Kinds of import

Using Blaise Wilfert's continuum of practices (35-36), we can observe that the most prestigious forms of literary import, such as prefaces, conferences, chronicles and criticism, were not widely used by these women translators. Only Logeman-Van der Willigen and Marie Elisabeth Belpaire seemed to use their participation in literary journals as a conscious means to stimulate interest in their translations. Loveling looked for a position as a chronicler during the early eighties, but never succeeded to achieve such a position. She wrote one review on Groth (1881) in which she stressed his excellent qualities, yet never explicitly presented him as a promise or the future for literature in Flanders. Van Ackere-Doolaeghe wrote a foreword to the translation of Rogier's poem, and Swarth published some reviews and prefaces in which she included her views on authors she had translated. Most of the other women merely published the translations as such, without any secondary activities such as commentaries, essays or literary criticism in journals.

Prose translations were by far the most prominent. Hiel, Loveling, Lava, Sleeckx and Germonprez mainly published short stories and novellas. Fairy tales were translated or adapted by Mina Sleeckx and Mathilda van Engelen. Poetry was mainly translated by women who wrote poetry themselves, such as Van Ackere-Doolaeghe, Hiel, Swarth and Van Daelen. Their publications appeared both in cultural magazines and literary journals and in separate volumes. The journals in which they participated were fairly traditional and conservative institutions, although the translated authors sometimes counted as progressive writers in their homeland, such as the decadent writer Herman Bang in Denmark. They did not include *petites revues* in which experimentation was encouraged. Logeman-Van der Willigen and Swarth also published their translations in book form. Some of the translations mentioned were pre-published in journals and also separately distributed, such as the work of Loveling and Germonprez.

Linguistic proficiency and educational resources

Most of these women translators excelled in several languages. Their family resources came in handy, since they often could not count on secondary resources such as schooling. Secondary schools for girls, that offered a high-quality education in Dutch, were rare in Flanders before the last quarter of the 19th century. Besides Catholic institutes and private institutions that offered only a limited curriculum (catechism, reading, sometimes writing and arithmetic, French, housekeeping, but most of all embroidering, sewing, dancing and painting), the first municipal secondary school for girls was only founded in 1864 in Brussels by the feminist Isabelle Gatti de Gamond (1839-1905) (Verbeke 5). It aimed at higher standards in education and offered natural sciences instead of religion (Verbeke 24).

Besides 25 municipal initiatives inspired by Gatti de Gamond's example (Verbeke 56), one had to wait until 1881, when a law was enacted that provided for 50 lower secondary schools for 11 to 15-year-old girls. These measures contrasted heavily with the hundred secondary schools for boys, supplementing the state initiatives taken since the 1850s, where higher class boys received six to seven years of schooling, with four to two hours of English in the last four to five years (Brants 25-26). In theory, girls received the same school timetable as boys in the lower secondary schools (Brants 53), but in practice, they received fewer classes in Dutch, French and German, and, remarkably, more classes in English (Verbeke 47). This did not take long: in 1888, the three hours of German and English in the lower secondary schools became optional (Brants 54, Verbeke 49-50). In 1897, girls received two hours of English (and German) in the second and third year of a commercial training (Brants 61). In the more general education, English and German did not become compulsory again.

In the Netherlands, the situation was different. High-quality secondary state education in Dutch was provided much earlier to boys and girls, and offered girls more opportunities to study languages (Brants 106-107). Moreover, the final exam of secondary schools contained for instance translations of prose or elementary poetry from French, German or English (Brants 103-105). This might explain Logeman-Van der Willigen's complaint that the proficiency of English was so widespread that translating English works was not lucrative for her.

Finally, there were also Teachers' Training Colleges in Belgium. In 1849 10 state institutions instructed future schoolmistresses for primary schools (Verbeke 23); in 1879 and 1880 colleges were founded in Liège and Brussels to train secondary school teachers for the newly established state institutions (Verbeke 26). These schools offered the sole higher education available to 15-year-old girls and comprised two years. They contained a scientific and a literary department, where English and German were optional, and a modern languages department, where four languages were compulsory. At the end of 1912, the course of study was prolonged to three years (Alliet and Deridder 46). In the primary Teachers' Colleges, English or German were taught as an optional third language (*Programmes de l'enseignement* 40-43). Some of the above-mentioned women followed this training, others were teaching there themselves. Mina Sleeckx taught Dutch, English and German in a state college for women teachers in Liège and Paula Sleeckx was head of a similar college in Bruges. Anna Germonprez, Fanny Delvaux and Laura Hiel taught in primary education. Germonprez also spent some years of study in Great-Britain and Germany: she lived more than two years in Herne-Bay (Kent) and eighteen months in Hof (Bavaria) (Rijckaerts 1950: 14 & 239).

The other women did not follow secondary school or a teacher training and had to count on their own family resources and travel experiences. The Loveling sisters' father was a German who knew the main European languages and read many authors in their original languages.[12] He taught his daughters German at an early age (Van Elslander 19-20), in addition to the French and Dutch they spoke at home. Using their father's grammars and dictionaries after his death, the sisters taught themselves English, Italian, Spanish, and even Danish and Swedish. In her diary Virginie Loveling writes that they spoke a different language every day from morning till noon. She made some trips to friends in Britain and Australia and must have had a good command of English.

Hélène Swarth was raised in Brussels and learnt French in a boarding-school.[13] Her father taught her German and she taught herself English: she read and understood the latter almost perfectly, but was not capable to speak it very fluently. She wrote her debut in French, but switched to Dutch in the early eighties.

Logeman-Van der Willigen went to Denmark and learnt Danish afterwards to be able to read Andersen's fairytales; she also learnt Norwegian and Swedish, and translated Finnish works using Swedish intertexts (Broomans 50). Her husband, Henri Logeman (1862-1936), was a professor in Dutch linguistics, who later founded the Scandinavian Department at Ghent University and joined his wife on her many journeys to the North.

Fanny Lava (1858-1938), also known as Florence MacLeod-Maertens, was a friend of Peter and Sophie Kropotkin. She translated non-fictional works by Kropotkin into English in 1904 and 1907, for which she was highly praised (Hamelius 486), but could also have been motivated to learn Russian by their correspondence. The network of international or Russian authors could unfortunately not be traced. Lava probably lived by her husband's income, which gave her enough time to invest in language acquisition, such as Russian. In the university library of Uppsala, many letters from and to her Russian friends are kept.

Money as a motive

The reasons why these women started to translate were often prosaic. Many of them mentioned in their letters that they mainly translated to earn some (extra) money. Logeman-Van der Willigen, for whom translating was an important source of income since her husband was often ill,[14] even let money decide what kind of literatures she rejected to translate. The fierce competition from the many young girls who were able to translate from English and who were apparently willing to do it at very low rates, made her opt for more "exotic" and unfamiliar Scandinavian languages.

Virginie Loveling did not get paid for the translations of German, English and Swedish texts that she published before 1870. She did not seem to mind because she considered it a nice occupation and a good exercise.[15] Yet, when she moved to Ghent to live on her own, money became an important drive to publish. In 1880, she wanted a job that would yield both intellectual satisfaction and a regular income. She longed to earn some money as a correspondent for a journal abroad by providing translations and summaries, or by joining the editorial board of a periodical.[16] She preferred to translate non-fictional work and stated: "If it is not a work of imagination, what is really difficult to render into a foreign language, it goes very well".[17] In a letter to her nephew Paul Fredericq, she wrote: "I'd prefer to make summaries for the *Athenaeum belge*. *That*, and translations, I consider – but that's between you and me – as my specialty".[18] Still, she held ambivalent feelings towards translating prose. She wrote, again to her cousin and counsellor: "For the moment, I am working on a translation of 'Witen Kross' by Klaus Groth. Very difficult, but I extremely like it. It is – so to say – only *main d'oeuvre*".[19] In 1882, she wrote again to Fredericq: "I cannot always write original work and I am looking for an occupation: if you could show me something to translate or review, I would be most grateful".[20] However, the difficulties and small profits of translating fiction and non-fiction finally made her count on her own children's stories, folklore, literary reports and, of course, novels to earn a decent living. The poem by Knut Hamsun in 1908 is her last translation, probably made at the insistence of Logeman-Van der Willigen.

Hélène Swarth also held an ambivalent view on translating. Since she could not live decently from the money she earned by publishing poetry, she felt obliged to turn to prose, children's literature and translations, which she often regarded as drudgery. In 1882, she asked a Dutch publisher for permission to translate a work by the British writer Ouida.[21] In 1887, she wrote to her colleague Pol de Mont (1857-1931): "Just a word to ask if you know a publisher who pays rather well for translations. I made some efforts now and then to get a book to translate, but I never succeeded".[22] However, she would not accept anything. Some years before, she had refused to translate a drama by Betsy Perk in French verse because she did not consider its quality high enough.[23] It took her a long time before she got the authorization to translate some works and even then she wrote to De Mont: "Translating is repugnant to me, it takes too much time and it is very badly paid".[24] Nevertheless, the translations she made, especially after 1910, are generally regarded as work of high quality work (Brouwers 130). The authors she chose were both male and female writers to whom she definitely felt connected.

Mina Sleeckx published her first translation as a separate volume (*Geoffroy en Garcinde*) and later published her translations and adaptations in *De Toekomst* (1857-1898), a pedagogical journal edited by her father and brother, where money was tight. Almost none of the contributions in this journal were remunerated. Except for Logeman-Van der Willigen, there were no professional women translators in Flanders, who used their translations as their main source of income. Most of them were writers or teachers who looked for some extra money, although not all translations were remunerated and some were mainly published for content-based and ideological reasons, which will be elaborated in the next section.

Ideology and canon formation

Besides the (small) remunerative aspects of translating, some of these translators also had a particular mission. I will single out some content-based motives and some motives with regard to canon formation. In line with Rakefet Sela-Sheffy's argument in "Canon Formation Revisited", two strategies can be discerned in the latter respect: consolidating and supporting an existing repertoire on the one hand, and prefiguring a future repertoire, on the other. Content-based motives could further be divided into two strands: politically motivated translations and didactic genres.

Some translators, such as Loveling, Swarth, Belpaire and Logeman-Van der Willigen, acted as ambassadors for other styles or cultures and introduced new repertoires, be it by their translations themselves or by their other critical activities. Loveling translated the novels by the Low German writer Klaus Groth, whom she had personally met on his tour through Flanders (Simons 334).[25] She was introduced to the author and his work by Constant Jacob Hansen (1833-1910), a Groth fan who fancied her sister Rosalie, which supports Wilfert's view that coincidence plays an important role in the reception of an author (Wilfert 37). Groth's work was a revelation at the time, both in Germany and in Flanders, because it dealt with the common themes of patriotism, nature, domestic happiness or the loved mother tongue in an innovative and realistic fashion. His concise, analytic and moderately pompous style, his psychological insight and his striking details received praise, in contrast with the perverted style of the French novels and the more didactic literature of earlier authors as Conscience and Ledeganck (Simons 338-343). In her 1881 critical article in *l'Athenaeum belge*, Loveling praised Groth's moderate and exact language and psychological feeling and thus prefigured a future canon. By translating Groth, as an author from the peripheral Low Germany, she took part in a larger movement supported by other authors such as Guido Gezelle (1830-1899), Jan van Droogenbroeck (1835-1902) and de Mont, which both praised this author for his strong realism and defended his sound and healthy style against French literary influences.

Logeman-Van der Willigen functioned as a real ambassador for modern Danish, Swedish and Norwegian authors, introducing and commenting upon recently appeared work in numerous critical articles in journals as *Scandia* (1904), *Scandinavia-Nederland* (1905-1906), of which she was also an editor, *De Vlaamsche Gids* (1905-1914)[26] and *De Week* (1909-1912).[27] She knew a lot of authors personally, which led to an almost inexhaustible supply of new works and an enormous enthusiasm to persuade publishers and editors to distribute or publish her translations. She was one of the rare women translators who actively took the initiative to import specific authors and works.[28] To Max Rooses, the editor of *De Vlaamsche Gids*, she wrote: "Herman Bang offers me his 'Personal

Memories of Hendrik Ibsen' that appear in Denmark today. Could that be of interest for your review? If so, I'll translate them immediately so that you can publish them at once, otherwise it is too late to be of any use. I beg you for a quick reply, if not, I'll offer them elsewhere."[29] Besides using the social capital these authors passed on, she also tried to consolidate authors and prefigure a new literary generation. Additionally, it was also her view that smaller countries had to support each other in their struggle against the political and cultural ascendancy of bigger nations like France, Germany or Russia (Broomans 59).

Other writers, such as Van Ackere-Doolaeghe, Belpaire, Van Daelen and Germonprez were led by religious or politically inspired motives. Belpaire was fond of the Catholic writer Jørgensen and wanted to spread his word in Flanders. Van Ackere-Doolaeghe and Germonprez served a nationalist goal with their publications, aiming at a defence of the Flemish culture and language. Van Ackere-Doolaeghe used her achieved symbolic capital to defend the former liberal Minister of State, Rogier, against the claims that he bore ill-will to the Dutch language in Flanders. In translating a French poem into Dutch, Van Ackere-Doolaeghe wanted to honour his literary talent and his often neglected support of Dutch literature. Her other translation of a poem by Longfellow was not politically inspired, but probably consolidated an existing repertoire. The sad and melancholic tone probably determined her choice in this case. Fanny Delvaux, who was not renowned when she published two translated poems by Heinrich Heine and John Henry Mackay, mainly used her translations to give voice to their (and her) anarchist creed. Heine's poem cursed God, king and country who did not relieve in any way the burden of the poor, and Mackay's poem defended the tenets of anarchism.

Some writers did not mention the authors of the translated works. Their motives were clearly content-based and either diverting or didactic. Fanny Lava considered translating to be both very pleasant and particularly instructive: not so much because of the knowledge displayed in the work itself, but because she learnt to write and entered the world of letters.[30] She wrote to her son that she would be really pleased if he would find as much pleasure in translating as she did before.[31] In a letter to professor Thiery, a colleague of her husband, she wrote that she really loved Gogol's works. She called *Dead Souls* perplexing for a Western human being but typically old-Russian and regretted the low quality of most German translations.[32]

Like most of Paula and Mina Sleeckx' translations and Mathilda van Engelen's work, some of Lava's translated stories had a hidden but after all clear message. The translated folktales mainly dealt with the burden of life and the destiny and luck of poor people, who realized that property was not all. The pedagogical value of the fairytales was probably the reason to translate and publish them. Except for Victor Blüthgen and Hans Christian Andersen, none of the original authors were mentioned. The stories dealt with faraway places but the images and characters were most familiar: efforts are rewarded, the burden of life is heavy, curiosity is punished, and everything ends happily when one is modest, generous and helpful. These translations fitted in with the didactic goals of many Flemish reviews and did not have any aspiration to influence the literary field of their time. They are consolidating an existing repertoire, without defending the canonization of particular authors.

Symbolic capital?

Making oneself known or entering the field did not seem to be a major motive to translate. Loveling and Lava considered it a good exercise to translate, but Loveling was already publishing for a couple of years and Lava never started a literary career. Still, translating Groth's novels might have influenced Loveling's switch from poetry to prose (Simons 347). Germonprez and Swarth mainly considered translating as an activity that did not contribute to their literary careers. But then again, Loveling did not merely introduce Groth's work by translating it, her choice also suggested that she had common literary grounds with him and other realist European writers, which could have influenced future views on her own literary production. Groth's work showed the same choice of themes and style as the strategic options that seemed available to Loveling. She thus gained some symbolic capital, which, however, she would lose again when a new literary generation appeared.

Apparently, none of the other women writers consciously opted for translating as a means to enhance their prestige. None of the women explicitly claimed that she wanted to revive the canonized forms of expression. Although they did open up the local culture and enriched the language and domestic forms of expression, none of them took a radical stance in setting a new trend (Sela-Sheffy, "How to Be a (Recognized) Translator" 8). In contrast to France, where in the middle of the 19th century two groups (the Symbolists and the academics) were competing for legitimacy in an autonomous field, no such clear antagonism was present in the (not yet autonomous) literary field in Flanders. For the greater part of the 19th century, Flemish writers were still bound by political ties and wrote partly to meet the needs of the public. As we have seen above, there was an opposition between nationalist, patriotic and pedagogical translators, such as Van Ackere-Doolaeghe or Germonprez, and translators such as Loveling and Logeman-Van der Willigen, who were interested in more recent literature. However, the struggle to occupy certain positions in a stratified space with particular gains and losses, was not fully present yet.

The group of female translators in Flanders consisted of a rather invisible, semi-professional group whose occupation was auxiliary (Sela-Sheffy, "How to Be a (Recognized) Translator" 9). They were mostly individual names who could not benefit from a sort of group dignity and who were mainly not renowned because of their translational activities. Antagonism, heresy or liberation of the established repertoire did not explicitly come into view as main motives. The opposition between gatekeepers or cultural custodians, on the one hand, and trendsetters or cultural importers, on the other, was therefore not clearly marked yet. Consequently, there was neither a clear distinction between a restricted elite of well-known translators and a wide circle of underprivileged anonymous agents (21). Implicit status contests and a hidden struggle for symbolic capital were gradually becoming visible in the Flemish literary field, but did not yet infect translation as a socially organized activity.

Coda

Besides these micro-stories and particular motives, and of course the available educational resources, one also has to bear in mind the larger picture. During the 19th century, Flanders was a highly Gallicized area in which the intellectual elite spoke and read French (Klinkenberg 517). The middle and lower classes, on the other hand, opted for Dutch, but were not always able to spend money on (highbrow) literature. Hence the publication of original and translated literature was by no means a straightforwardly profitable business. Only a small public was interested in Dutch translations – which made Loveling and Swarth consider to translate into French – and there was also an underdeveloped publishing trade, in which booksellers and printers still filled the positions of editors.

Logeman-Van der Willigen and Swarth published the largest part of their oeuvre in the Netherlands, where, then again, competition from other translators was heavier. Without choosing rare languages (a proficiency evidently not acquired at school), or combining translation work with another profession, it was hard to earn a decent living by means of translating. Even in cultural and literary magazines, contributions were not always remunerated, and translations mostly yielded an additional profit only. Both Loveling and Swarth complained of the difficulties in finding interested editors or publishers who wanted to pay for their translated work.

Reading these writers' correspondences, the translations made in Flanders between 1870 and 1914 seemed to be a matter of coincidence, linguistic proficiency, and rare contacts with particular editors and authors. It was not a practice chosen to enhance their own prestige or make oneself known as a writer in a field in the making. Nevertheless, ideological motives with regard to politics or education, and motives concerning canon formation, whether this meant importing new authors or consolidation an existing repertoire, did play a (albeit modest) part.

Bibliography

Alliet, I. and Deridder, I. *Geschiedenis van de wetgeving in verband met het middelbaar onderwijs voor meisjes (1894-1962). Casus middelbare normaalschool Onze-Lieve-Vrouw-ten-Doorn Eeklo.* Master's thesis, Ghent University, 2005.

Belpaire, M.E. *De jongste dag*. Antwerpen: Opdebeek, 1900.

———. *Levensleugen en levenswaarheid*. Gent: A. Siffer, 1900.

———. "Het landleven in de letterkunde." *Dietsche Warande & Belfort* 1.5 (1900): 234-261.

———. *Sinnoeve Solbakken*. Maldeghem: Delille, 1902.

———. *Klokke Roland*. Bussum: Brand, 1916.

Brants, M. *De hervorming van het middelbaar onderwijs*. Gent: A. Siffer, 1906.

Broomans, P. "'Vertalingen waar haast bij is, boeken die gerecenseerd moeten worden'. Dien Logeman-Van der Willigen." *De overzet: een bundel over vertalen.* Ed. I. Desmidt. *Spieghel Historiael* 42 (2002): 47-66.

Germonprez, A. "Drumsheugh's Liefdesgeschiedenis [Ian Maclaren]." *Dietsche Warande & Belfort* 2.11/12 (1901): 455-477, 584-596.

———. *Jeronimo. Verzamelde novellen met voorrede en levensschets van de schrijfster door: Edgard Rijckaerts*. Antwerpen: De Vlijt, 1950.

Hamelius, P. "Boekbeoordeling." *Vlaanderen* 2 (1904): 478-486.

Heilbron, J. "Het wereldvertaalstelsel." *Filter* 7.4 (2000): 38-44.

Hiel, L. "Grieksch Liefdeverhaal. Uit de Grieksche Volksverhalen." *Vlaamsch & Vrij* 1 (1893): 7.

———. "*Jehova* van Carmen Sylva. Vrij naar het Duitsch." *Vlaamsch & Vrij* 2 (1894): 675, 712, 751.

———. "Wat waren die rozen toch frisch en schoon (naar een prozastukje van Tourguenef)." *Vlaamsch & Vrij* 3 (1895): 633.
Klinkenberg, J.-M. "De Franse literatuur in Vlaanderen." *Van Arm Vlaanderen tot De voorstad groeit.* Eds. M. Rutten and J. Weisgerber. Antwerpen: Standaard Uitgeverij, 1988.
Logeman-Van der Willigen, Dina. *De paradijsvogel* [Otto Rung]. Antwerpen: De Magneet, s.d.
———. "Scandinavische Kroniek." *De Vlaamsche Gids* 2 (1906): 274-281.
———. "Persoonlijke herinneringen aan Henrik Ibsen van Herman Bang." *De Vlaamsche Gids* 2 (1906): 475-488.
———. "Jongere krachten in de moderne Noorsche literatuur." *De Vlaamsche Gids* 4 (1908): 77-93.
———. "Gustaf Siösteen: 'Det moderna Belgien'. Iakttagelser och Studier." *De Vlaamsche Gids* 4 (1908): 94-96.
———. "Holger Drachmann." *De Vlaamsche Gids* 4 (1908): 187-192.
———. "Scandinavische Kroniek." *De Vlaamsche Gids* 5 (1909): 279-288.
———. "Uit Noorwegen." *De Vlaamsche Gids* 6 (1910): 320-327.
———. "Fridthjof Nansen." *De Week* 2 (1910): 8-9.
———. "Een dag te Trondhjem." *De Week* 2 (1911): 1-3.
———. *De vluchtelingen* [Johannes Linnankoski]. Antwerpen: Kompas, s.d. [1914].
Loveling, R. "Trina." *Het Letterkundig Zondagsblad* 7 (1864): 11-24.
Loveling, V. "Detel. Naar het Platduitsch van Klaus Groth [translation of *Detelf*]." *Het Nederduitsch Tijdschrift* 4 (1866): 27-64.
———. "Antoon (van Quickborn). Naar het Platduitsch van Klaus Groth [translation of *De Waterbörs*]." *Het Nederduitsch Tijdschrift* 4 (1866): 47-85.
———. "Een Holsteinsche jongen. Naar het Platduitsch van Klaus Groth [a revised version of *Detelf*]." *Nederlandsch Museum* 7 (1880): 174-268.
———. "Drei plattdeutsche Erzählungen zum Theil Erlebtes und Erinnerungen von 1848 aus Schleswig-Holstein, von Klaus Groth." *Athenaeum belge* 5 (1881): 51-52.
———. "Witen Slachters. Nog een vertelling uit mijn jongheidsparadijs. Naar het Platduitsch van Klaus Groth." *Nederlandsch Museum* 9 (1882): 316-348.
MacLeod-Maertens, F. [Fanny Lava] "Mengeling. Een handvol aarde (Oostersche vertelling)." *Het Vaderland* 11 mei 1894.
———. "Mengeling. De last (translated from the Russian journal *Niwa*)." *Het Vaderland* 8 juni 1894.
———. "Vier Dagen. Uit het Russisch vertaald." *Gazette van Gent* (1894): 3-4.
———. *Wederkeerig dienstbetoon, een factor der evolutie*. Amsterdam: Van Looy, 1904.
———. *Idealen en werkelijkheid in de Russische literatuur*. Amsterdam: Van Looy, 1907.
Programmes de l'enseignement à donner dans les écoles normales et les sections normales primaires de l'état. Gent: A. Siffer, 1892.
Reymenants, G. *Vrouweninvloed in het literaire veld. De medewerking van vrouwen aan katholieke Vlaamse tijdschriften, weekbladen en kranten*. Dissertation Ghent University, Ghent, 2005.
Sela-Sheffy, R. "Canon Formation Revisited: Canon and Cultural Production." *Neohelicon* 29.2 (2002): 141-159.
———. "How to Be a (Recognized) Translator. Rethinking Habitus, Norms, and the Field of Translation." *Target* 17.1 (2005): 1-26.
Simons, L. *Vlaamse en Nederduitse literatuur in de 19de eeuw. II. Vertalingen, receptie, beïnvloeding.* Gent: Koninklijke Academie voor Nederlandse taal- en letterkunde, 1985.
Sleeckx, M. *De Twaalf Apostelen* [Eugenie Marlitt]. Antwerpen: De Vos, s.d.
———. *Het geheim van den ouden kaemer* [Emile Mario Vacano]. Antwerpen: De Vos, s.d.

———. *Geoffroy en Garcinde* [Paul Heyse]. 's Gravenhage:Bibliotheek voor alle Standen/ Volksuitgaaf van Romantische Verhalen, 1873.

———. "Marten. Een Hoogduitsch sprookje." *De Toekomst* 21 (1877): 97-101.

———. "De Padde. Een sprookje uit Esthland." *De Toekomst* 22 (1878): 119-124.

———. "Paascheieren." *De Toekomst* 23 (1879): 311-315.

———. "De Pochhans. [Victor Blüthgen]." *De Toekomst* 25 (1881): 306-312.

———. "Twee Slavische sprookjes. I. De taal der dieren; II. Het wijze vonnis." *De Toekomst* 26 (1882): 455-467.

Sleeckx, P. "Dragen en verdragen (naar Katharina Koch)." *De Toekomst* 20 (1876): 206.

Stinissen, E. "Iets over Pestalozzi (vrij naar eenen reisbrief van Emil Schattke)." *De Toekomst* 41 (1895-1896): 529-535.

Swarth, H. *Portugeesche sonnetten* [Elizabeth Barrett Browning]. Amsterdam: Maatschappij voor Goede en Goedkoope Lectuur, s.d.

———. *La paix durable* [Johannes Allarda]. Bussum: Van Dishoeck, s.d.

———. "Lied van A. von Platen. Sonnet XLIV van A. von Platen." *Nederlandsche Dicht- en Kunsthalle* 8 (1886): 525-526.

———. "Een Doode: Théodore Aubanel, door Charles Fuster." *Nederlandsche Dicht- en Kunsthalle* 11 (1888): 339-342.

———. *Roemeensche volksliederen en balladen* [Hélène Vacaresco]. Amsterdam: Maatschappij voor Goede en Goedkoope Lectuur, 1909.

———. "Gedichten in proza [Oscar Wilde]." *Europa. Maandschrift voor Nederlandsche en vreemde letteren* (1910). [no copies of this issue have survived].

———. *De nachten, metrisch overgezet en ingeleid door Hélène Swarth* [Alfred de Musset]. Amsterdam: Wereldbibliotheek, 1912.

———. *Haar lente* [Rachilde]. Amsterdam: Van Holkema & Warendorff, 1913.

———. *Hélène Swarth. Brieven aan Pol de Mont.* Gent: Sekretariaat van de Koninklijke Vlaamse Academie voor Taal- en Letterkunde, 1964.

Van Ackere-Doolaeghe, M. "De tehuiskomst. Naar 'Le Retour à la maison' van M. Ch. Rogier, Minister van Staat." *De Vlaamsche Kunstbode* 2 (1872): 112-117.

———. "De laatste zang van Lord Byron. In Griekenland." *Nederlandsche Dicht- en Kunsthalle* 5.4 (1882): 161-162.

———. "Het open venster. Naar het Engelsch van Longfellow." *De Toekomst* 27 (1883): 253.

Van Daelen, S. "Liedjes van Opstand. De Wevers (van Heinrich Heine)." *Ontwaking* 8 (1907): 270.

———. "Liedjes van Opstand. Anarchie (John Henry Mackay)." *Ontwaking* 8 (1907): 271.

Van der Weel, A. "Nineteenth-Century Literary Translations from English from a Book Historical Context." *Textual Mobility and Cultural Transmission/Tekstmobiliteit en Culturele Overdracht.* Eds. M. De Clercq, T. Toremans and W. Verschueren. Leuven: Leuven University Press, 2006. 27-40.

Vandenbussche, Liselotte. *Het veld der Verbeelding. Vrijzinnige vrouwen in Vlaamse literaire en algemeen-culturele tijdschriften (1870-1914.* Gent: Koninklijke Academie voor Nederlandse Taal- en Letterkunde, 2008.

Van Elslander, A. and Musschoot, A.M. "Correspondentie van de Gezusters Loveling. Brieven van en aan Paul Fredericq II." *Mededelingen van het Cyriel Buysse Genootschap* 10 (1994): 31-156.

Van Engelen, M. "De Huisduiveltjes. Een sprookje uit Scandinavië." *De Toekomst* 23 (1879): 16-20.

Verbeke, M. *Rijksmiddelbaar onderwijs voor meisjes: 100 jaar geleden een werkelijkheid.* Gent: Centrum voor de Studie van de Historische Pedagogiek, 1982.

Wilfert, B. "Cosmopolis et l'homme invisible. Les importateurs de littérature étrangère en France, 1885-1914." *Actes de la recherche en sciences sociales* 144.2 (2002): 33-46.

Notes

[1] "Ik vertaal nooit uit het Eng. omdat het zich niet betaalt. Iedereen in Holland kan uit het Eng. vertalen + de uitgevers worden overstroomd door jonge meisjes die voor 5 of 10 gulden een heel boek willen vertalen!!", Dina Logeman-Van der Willigen to Marie Elisabeth Belpaire, December 1913, AMVC-Letterenhuis, B417/B2, no 166169/2442.
[2] See Broomans.
[3] The results are partly based on my PhD research on the participation of liberal women writers to cultural magazines and literary journals between 1870 and 1914: *Het veld der verbeelding. Het aandeel en de receptie van niet-confessionele publicistes in Vlaamse, literaire en algemeen-culturele tijdschriften, 1870-1914*. By digging up their contributions and analyzing their correspondences, I obtained a fairly detailed view of the women writers who translated poetry and prose. To that information, I added some data from secondary sources, library catalogues and the Dutch database WomenWriters.nl, which, unfortunately, does not provide much information on Flemish women translators.
[4] For an example of such an approach, see Van der Weel.
[5] Maria Van Ackere-Doolaeghe to Eugeen Van Oye, 2 January 1875, University Library Ghent, Hs 3375, no 165.
[6] "Le devoir le plus essentiel du traducteur, celui qui les renferme tous, c'est de chercher à produire dans chaque morceau le même effort que son auteur."
[7] "zoo verdraagzaam, verheffend, tot zedelijk groote zaken opwekkend'; Anna Germonprez to Marie Elisabeth Belpaire, 15 June 1900, AMVC, B417/B2, no 80751/10. See also Reymenants (114).
[8] Anna Germonprez to Marie Elisabeth Belpaire, 30 April, 1900, AMVC, B417/B2, no 80751/14, and 15 June, 1900, B417/B2, no 80751/7.
[9] Anna Germonprez to Alfons de Cock, 10 January 1902, AMVC, G314/B1, no 13394/401.
[10] Logeman-Van der Willigen published translations from the following authors: Hans Aanrud, Herman Bang, Jenny Blicher-Clausen, Johan Bojer, Walter Christmas, Elsa Dovlette-Lindberg, Carl Ewald, Evy Fogelberg, Christian Gierloeff, Per Hallström, Rakel Harbitz, Verner von Heidenstam, Frank Heller, Adolf Johansson, Johannes Jørgensen, Aho Juhani, Ellen Key, Bernt Lie, Johannes Linnankoski, Sophus Michaëlis, Avilde Prydz, Barbra Ring, Ingeborg Maria Sick, Werner Söderhjelm, R. Steffen, Marieke Stjernstedt, Sigrid Undset. They were almost all published by Dutch editors. Belgian editors published only a few translations. See the bibliography for further details.
[11] Loveling's translation of Knut Hamsun's poem "Munken Vendt" is published on pages 81-82 of the review.
[12] Virginie Loveling to Paul Fredericq, 8 May 1914, University Library Ghent, Hs III 69:148. (University Library Ghent, Hs III 69, p. 178).
[13] Hélène Swarth to Lode Scheltjens, 29 June 1938, AMVC S995/B, no 19754/5.
[14] Dina Logeman-Van der Willigen to Marie Elisabeth Belpaire, 16 October 1912, AMVC-Letterenhuis, B417/B2, no 166196/2438a-c, 2439.
[15] Virginie Loveling to Maurits Basse, s.d., University Library Ghent, Nalatenschap Maurits Basse, Hs III 69: 350-351.
[16] Virginie Loveling to Paul and Leon Fredericq, February 4, 1880 (Van Elslander and Musschoot: 41-42).
[17] Ibidem.
[18] "Liefst zou ik résumés voor het Ath. B. maken, *dat* en vertalingen aanzie ik, onder ons gezeid, voor mijne specialiteit."; Virginie Loveling to Paul Fredericq, 24 October 1880 (Van Elslander and Musschoot 58).
[19] "Thans werk ik aan eene vertaling van 'Witen Kross' van Klaus Groth. Zeer moeilijk, doch dat doe ik buitengewoon gaarne, het is toch om zoo te zeggen maar main d'oeuvre."; Virginie Loveling to Paul Fredericq, 19 January 1881 (Van Elslander and Musschoot 68).

[20] "Ik kan niet altijd oorspronkelijke stukken schrijven en zoek bezigheid, indien gij mij iets te vertalen of te critikeeren kondet aanduiden, zoudt ge mij zeer verplichten."; Virginie Loveling to Paul Fredericq, 6 January 1882 (Van Elslander and Musschoot 86).

[21] Hélène Swarth to the Erven Bohn, 23 June 1882, University Library Leiden, BOH C82. In 1884, she also asked the Belgian publisher De Seyn whether he was interested in a translation of Ouida's *Strathmore* (July 1884, AMVC, Album De Seyn, 25716/8bis), but this translation was apparently made by a Dutch friend of her (3 July 1884, AMVC Album De Seyn, 25730/5).

[22] "Een woordje om u te vragen of gij ook een uitgever weet, die vertaalwerk niet te slecht betaalt. Ik deed nu en dan veel moeite om een boek te vertalen te krijgen, doch het mocht mij nooit gelukken"; Hélène Swarth to Pol de Mont, 14 September 1887 (*Hélène Swarth. Brieven aan Pol de Mont* 122). On 19 November she wrote to de Mont that none of the recommended publishers had answered her plea (131). On 15 July she repeated that she had done a lot of effort to receive source texts without any results (141).

[23] Hélène Swarth to Pol de Mont, 13 December 1884 (*Hélène Swarth. Brieven aan Pol de Mont* 82).

[24] "Vertalen staat mij tegen, neemt zeer veel tijd en wordt zeer slecht betaald"; Hélène Swarth to Pol de Mont, 10 July 1891 (*Hélène Swarth. Brieven aan Pol de Mont* 222).

[25] The Loveling sisters met Klaus Groth in August 1861, when he travelled through Belgium.

[26] Besides the articles published in 1908, they were published in 1906, 1909 and 1910.

[27] In *De Week* they appeared in 1910 and 1911.

[28] Wilfert (2002: 37) states that most translators who take the initiative themselves, are 'les traducteurs les plus artistes et les plus 'fidèles' à un auteur'. This does not hold true in the case of Logeman-Van der Willigen.

[29] "*Herman Bang* biedt me zijn 'Persoonlijke Herinneringen over Hendrik Ibsen' aan, die heden in Denem. verschijnen. Zou dit niet iets zijn voor Uw blad? Ik vertaal ze dan dadelijk zodat U 't direct kunt plaatsen, anders is 't mosterd na de maaltijd! Verzoeke spoedig antwoord – daar ik ze anders elders geef."; Dina Logeman-Van der Willigen to Max Rooses, 22 June 1906, AMVC L 706/B2, no 166169/2442.

[30] Fanny MacLeod-Maertens to Andries MacLeod, 30 May 1917, University Library Uppsala.

[31] Fanny MacLeod-Maertens to Andries MacLeod, 6 June 1917, University Library Uppsala.

[32] Fanny MacLeod-Maertens to Michel Thiery, 3 December 1919, AMVC D128/B3, no 177317/441.

PART 3

Women's Writing in Dutch Translation

Suzan van Dijk (Universiteit Utrecht)

Researching Women's Place in the Literary Field: Anglophone Authors in the Netherlands

What about the reception of British or American women authors in the Netherlands? This question is discussed in the following four articles, which were prepared in the context of an international collaborative project dedicated to studying women's place in the European literary field before 1900. Entitled "New Approaches to European Women's Writing" (NEWW),[1] the project is particularly concerned with these authors' works being received: that is, bought, lent, read, commented on, translated or otherwise rewritten, by male as well as female readers more or less contemporary to publication. Women's place in the public sphere is to be traced, using a range of early reception documents as starting point. Indeed, post-canonization discourse on the subject is by definition incomplete, while selection criteria are unclear to us now. Even the study of *one* woman's literary fate, her commercial success or *échec* and possibly her international influence, needs, in our view, to be situated in its female context – in order for us to be aware of the degree of exceptionality or representativeness of her case. It has long been a general tendency in historiography to present as exceptions those rare female writers who survived canonization: their number and proportion is indeed small. Thanks to book history, however, the number and proportion of women who wrote and had their works published gradually appears to have been, in some countries and during certain periods, considerable. It might be necessary to write women back into history – possibly some of them into literary history and the whole of women's writing and publishing activities into women's history and cultural history.

The field is large and it is therefore necessary to envision the possibility of collective and collaborative work. To this end, the NEWW network was established, as a locally based national and cross-national environment where researchers and students are working together, each of them on a subject or domain of their own, but in close connection with each other, thanks to the online *WomenWriters* database (www.databasewomenwriters.nl). This database gathers and stocks research material, making it available for further analysis.

It is important to first specify briefly the objective of this *Women Writers* database and its current content. It was created as a means of ordering and storing evidence of the international reception of European women authors before 1900. The database structure and its present content (which will be extended further, but cannot ever be expected to be complete due to the nature of the subject) facilitate the quantitative as well as the qualitative study of women's place and role in the literary field. At present, the database contains over 13,500 pieces of information about the reception of women authors (Dutch and other[2]) in the Netherlands. Most of these have been entered on the basis of the perusal of large-scale sources: periodicals, inventories of translations, private correspondences, library catalogues. Data entry is continuing, and – needless to say – the present state of the database content will be evolving further. In particular, projects are being prepared for international collaboration across Europe.[3]

Therefore, all figures provided in the following articles are *provisional* and subject to change – just as, of course, the interpretation of data. However, for the moment they do furnish starting points and contexts, and they are here presented as such. These articles are meant to illustrate the potential of this undertaking by presenting four cases focusing on the relationship between female writings in English and the responses provided by the Dutch reading public.

Notes

1 International networking project funded by the Netherlands Organisation for Scientific Research (NWO) from 2007 to 2010. See www.womenwriters.nl: *Women Writers' Networks*, website of the NEWW project.

2 English and Irish authors: 3200 records; American authors: 400 records.

3 For the moment, next to Dutch reception, reception of French women's literature abroad is relatively well documented (5200 records). Note that it is not always the information itself that is entered into the records of the database, but rather *references* to them, and also hyperlinks to online versions. More details about the sources consulted up to now can be found in the "Sources" section of www.womenwriters.nl.

Suzan van Dijk (Universiteit Utrecht)

Was Jane Austen Read in the 19th-Century Netherlands?

The question as to whether Jane Austen was or was not being read in the Netherlands was recently addressed in one of the contributions to the volume *The Reception of Jane Austen in Europe*. It seems to me, however, that this question was only partially answered. In a sense, such incompleteness is characteristic of any research on the reception of literary works, and should, in general, not be considered a major obstacle to our appreciation of such efforts. Nevertheless, the book, and in particular the article by Maximiliaan van Woudenberg entitled "Going Dutch: The Reception of Jane Austen in the Low Countries", gives rise to certain observations about the particular problems which emerge in research concerning the reception of female authors.

Jane Austen in Europe

Jane Austen in Europe presents the two centuries of international Austen reception. The 20th century proves by far the most productive, even before the first film adaptations of the novels began to appear. On the whole, the book tends to demonstrate that "Jane Austen's presence on the continent during the 19th century was relatively restricted" (4): during this period, translations of her works appeared in only four languages, French (in Switzerland and France), German, Danish, and Swedish. Explanations for this limited presence are not always offered. In some cases it is attributed to circumstances in the receiving country, in others to characteristics of Austen's writing. It is thought in particular that the limited society depicted in her novels represents social classes non-existent in other countries, and therefore insufficiently recognisable to potential readers. Other prohibitive factors might have been the wit and irony contained in her narrative voices. What is more, the early appreciation of Austen's work in her home country – besides Walter Scott's much quoted article on *Emma* published in 1816 – was not immediate either: her fame only began in the 1830s, with the publication of new editions (Richard Bentley's Standard Novels).[1]

"Going Dutch" also claims a limited presence of Austen in the Netherlands.

Van Woudenberg distinguishes three periods: "neglect (1815-1922), appreciation (1922-80) and popularity (1980 onwards)" (75). In fact he is focusing on the latter two – not without stating that probably "a limited readership for Austen in French did exist in the Netherlands" during the 19th century. Indeed, two French-language copies of Austen-novels had been traced, dated 1816 and 1876 (77) The absence of instant recognition in the Netherlands, for the now universally acknowledged author, had also been noted by Dutch literary historian Riet Schenkeveld-van der Dussen, who studied 19th-century Dutch women writers and looked for connections with colleagues abroad.[2] When writing on Elisabeth Hasebroek, she expressed her regrets about the fact that Jane Austen "play[ed] hardly any role" ("Elisabeth Johanna Hasebroek" 20) for this novelist and translator of English novels.[3] Some years before, Hanna Stouten had tried to establish the missing link between Jane Austen and Dutch women authors: she emphasised the parallels to be found between Austen's novels and those of her Dutch/Swiss contemporary Belle van Zuylen (Isabelle de Charrière). The use of irony by both authors to some extent justifies this take, but there is a total lack of evidence regarding any influence or mutual reading, and in fact, the European overview shows this to be well in line with the situation in most countries.

Still, it is valid to wonder whether this estimate is conclusive. As the introduction to *Jane Austen in Europe* suggests, the outcome of this first large overview should be treated as provisional and in fact as an *incentive* to look more closely into Austen's destiny in the Netherlands (as well as abroad): the book "presents a point of departure for future and more extended evaluations of the reception of Jane Austen in Europe" (11). One thing to dwell on, for instance, is the issue as to whether truly all possible sources of information have been considered. And, even if Austen's absence from the Netherlands is to be confirmed, some questions still remain. In particular, a better understanding of the context of this 'refusal' could be gained. One of the complementary questions – raised indeed explicitly in some of the other chapters in *Jane Austen in Europe*[4] – concerns the role of gender: if Austen was not translated, who of her 'sister authors' was?[5] And how did Dutch readers comment on the works of these women?

In what follows I shall first provide a 'female' context to Austen's absence in the Netherlands, by showing that quite a lot of her female colleagues *did* occupy a position in the Dutch literary field. Indeed, van Woudenberg's argument that "given the economic recession in the Netherlands [...] there would have been little demand for mass translations of foreign authors" (78) does not hold. Next, I shall argue that there is more to be said about Austen's reception in the Low Countries. The database of the project "New approaches to European Women's Writing", as described in the introductory essay to this section, has provided some new data indeed. Although these data do not constitute a massive reception of Austen's works, they are indicative of a certain perceptiveness of 19th-century readers – both male and female. On a meta-level, they allow for a discussion of particular problems related to research into women authors' reception.

English women writers in the Netherlands

In order to broadly sketch the context of what is presented in *Jane Austen in Europe* as something like a 'non-reception' of Austen in the Netherlands (and elsewhere), I concentrate on the years between 1800 and 1829. This is the period in which 'immediate reception' would have taken place, as it did indeed in Switzerland and France: seven French translations of Austen's novels were published between 1815 and 1824. It is also the period covered by the *British Fiction* website and by the overview of Garside, Raven and Schöwering, which will allow for some comparisons. Garside et al. demonstrate that, for part of this period (between 1800 and 1820), there was a dominance of women novelists in England (2: 73-75). For the Netherlands, this was not really the case but given the relatively small number of novelists during this period,[6] the proportion of women authors is honourable: 11 out of 32.[7]

For the period 1800-1829, the *WomenWriters* database contains 274 records relating to the reception of British women writers (not only novelists) in the Netherlands.[8] This very broad quantitative approach indicates that the writings of British (and Irish) women authors were certainly very much a feature of Dutch literary life at the time, more important than French and German women's writing.

Table 1:
Reception of foreign and Dutch women writers referenced in the *WomenWriters* database (July 2008)

	Published translations[9]	Press comments
Works by British/Irish women	74	98
Works by French/Swiss women	62	86
Works by German/Austrian women	37	46
Works (non-translated) by Dutch women	185	217

Eleven Dutch women authors[10] were publishing narrative fiction during this period, while novels by 33 women from Britain and Ireland found their way to the Netherlands (as opposed to works by 22 French/Swiss and 18 German/Austrian female novelists[11]). The traditional French dominance in this domain[12] had clearly given way to a British one. The lesser presence of German literature in this table is also striking, considering that literary historians hold that the Dutch early 19th century was under the influence of German authors, especially when it came to novels.[13] These figures reflect the late start of German women's participation in the literary field, which only began at the end of the 18th century.

For a selection of the 33 British women novelists whose work was 'imported' into the Netherlands, a provisional comparison[14] has been made with numbers of translations into French. The period covered is roughly the same, and the comparison gives some insight into apparent preferences and dislikes of the Dutch reading public.

Table 2:
Comparison of numbers of Dutch and French translations of British women novelists

	Dutch translations	French translations
Austen, Jane (1775-1817)	–	7 (1815-24)
Bennett, Agnes Maria (1750-1808)	2 (1789-1816)	7 (1788-1822)
Burney, Fanny (1752-1850)	3 (1780-1790)	5 (1779-1815)
Burney, Sarah Harriet (1772-1844)	2 (1816-20)	5 (1816-25)
Edgeworth, Maria (1767-1849)	7 (1810-20)	26 (1801-29)
Hays, Mary (1759-1843)	–	1 (1810)
Hofland, Barbara (1770-1844)	3 (1819-29)	6 (1817-29)
Kelty, Mary Ann (1789-1873)	–	3 (1823-24)
More, Hannah (1745-1833)	12 (1801-26)	4 (1817-19)
Opie, Amelia (1769-1853)	3 (1809-19)	10 (1806-26)
Owenson, Sydney (1775-1859)	8 (1812-22)	13 (1812-29)
Radcliffe, Ann (1764-1823)	4 (1815-23)	13 (1794-1829)
Robinson, Mary (1758-1800)	3 (1793-1800)	–
Roche, Regina (1764-1845)	2 (1802-18)	9 (1797-1825)
Sandham, Elisabeth (c.1770- c.1840)	2 (1817-28)	–
West, Jane (1758-1852)	2 (1810)	3 (1799-1820)
Wollstonecraft, Mary (1759-1797)	3 (1796-1801)[15]	3 (1792-99)

This is of course no more than a point of departure for further comparative analysis. The number of translations per author is clearly larger in France than in the Netherlands, which may correspond to the recession (mentioned by van Woudenberg) and the general depression experienced by the Dutch book trade at the time.[16] Nevertheless, these figures disclose some striking information, confirming not only the Dutch absence vs. French presence of Jane Austen, but also calling attention to the much greater French enthusiasm for gothic novelist Ann Radcliffe and her epigone Regina Maria Roche, as opposed to Dutch preference for the ‘evangelical’ writer Hannah More, principal representative of the “Moral-Domestic fiction” of the time.[17]

In order to further document these Dutch preferences, it is worthwhile to turn to the periodical press for explicit comments on the choices made by translators and publishers. Until now, my research has mainly concentrated on review articles published in one literary review, *Vaderlandsche Letteroefeningen*, which was published for over a century (1760-1876) and was the leading periodical during the period concerned.[18] Other periodicals have been examined by sample years. Like the figures provided above, this inventory of opinions and judgments gathered from reviews offers a *provisional* impression of the general attitude at the time towards British women's writing in the Netherlands. Accordingly, the differences between the various periodicals are for the moment considered less relevant.

A closer look at the review articles in the Dutch press of the period[19] suggests that, in general, the Dutch appreciated most of those British novels that entered the country, be it with some reserve:

> The fare of [the British] nation tends to be somewhat heavier on the stomach than that of our continental neighbours to the left and right. Yet we hope that the aromatic dishes served up by earlier writers of real British taste and wit have not yet been banished from memory by German hartshorn or French ragouts, to the extent that readers aren't eager for a new tasting.[20] [about Edgeworth]

In particular *De Recensent* regularly repeats that "the English manner is somewhat boring in the long run, lessening the lust of reading" [about Sarah Burney's *Wanderer*].[21]

As for the phenomenon of the woman author, critics had evidently not quite grown accustomed to it: "A 'Miss' as writer! This may well surprise some, attract a few, and put others off or deter them" [about Edgeworth].[22] Does this explain selections that were made? In all, British women authors of the period produced a literary output of great variety, which is indeed less pronounced in its Dutch reception than in their home country and, at first glance, in France. Authors who apparently did not correspond to the dominant Dutch taste of this period, like the radical Mary Hays, gothic novelists Ann Radcliffe and Regina Roche, or Jane Austen and the 'post-Austenian' Mary-Ann Kelty, were not or not widely translated into Dutch, and if they were, they received unfavourable reviews. Disapproval of Radcliffe's novels was the strongest, because they were "full of chivalric love and loyalty, full of war and rape, full of ghosts and miracles […]. It would be regrettable indeed if such means proved necessary to keep world history alive, at least to some degree, among the frequent readers of today".[23] However, clearly Radcliffe's growing international reputation helped in overcoming these negative tendencies, even in the Netherlands.

The demand – at least among critics – was for moral lessons. They were shocked about Mary Robinson's *Julia St Lawrence*: "How can the majority [of] characters be described? Vices, mostly of the lowest and most despicable nature, and betraying a contemptible and undignified heart".[24] Jane West's *William Beaumont*, on the contrary, provided pleasure because of "the clear and deterring light in which vices are displayed and the abhorrence and rebuke they cannot fail to cause in anyone in possession of a modicum of virtue and morality".[25] Likewise, "the excellent morality of [Opie's *New Tales*] makes us recommend this work wholeheartedly" and the "high moral import" of her work is regarded as "positively improving human happiness".[26] The critics were most satisfied when, as in Elisabeth Sandham's *Twin Sisters*, moral lessons were combined with religious ones. This explains the vast enthusiasm for Hannah More. The wish is expressed that her work may be read "to teach people self-knowledge and make them recur from pride and self-esteem, in order to walk meekly with God while practising true Christianity".[27] In another instance, the critic "most heartily recommend[s] [*Coelebs in Search of a Wife*] for its excellent depiction of Religion and Christianity".[28] Barbara Hofland's novels were much praised for the same reason: "We have here a well-made and highly instructive story, which strongly evokes our sense of, and trust in, the Fatherly guidance of divine Providence and does so in a noble and truly religious fashion".[29]

These women were considered to be addressing the female part of the reading public in particular. Critics in fact sketched a women's circle or subsystem where these works were to play a role in the education of girls. Therefore, the reviewer of Jane West's *The Advantages of Education, or the History of Maria Williams* "particularly [recommended] it to our Dutch Mothers, wishing to draw their attention to the example of the amiable Miss Williams, who was raised by a wise mother to possess many silent and graceful qualities of soul and virtues".[30] Amelia Opie's "capable writer's hand" ["bekwame schrijfstershand"] was extolled as "the hand of your Friend, my dear young Lady!" ["de hand van uwe Vriendin, lieve Jongedochter!"] (*Vaderlandsche Letteroefeningen* (1810) 139). It seems that more frequently than in the case of reviewing novels written by men, the hope was expressed that these young female readers would "emulate" ["zich zullen spiegelen aan"] the (female) protagonists (*Vaderlandsche Letteroefeningen* (1820) 358 [about Edgeworth]).

The importance of these novels to the assumed – and possibly really existing – female readership was in the warnings they provided. Opie's novels, for example, were thought to show their young female readers "the abominable consequences of a single *faux pas*, so that they may be warned against frivolity and overconfidence".[31] As we know, this image of the woman as a *warner* of young girls is perfectly mocked by Jane Austen herself. In one of her earliest writings, for example, a mother addresses her "Girls" about their "Introduction into Life":

> My dear Girls the moment is now arrived when I am to reap the rewards of all my Anxieties and Labours towards you during your Education. You are this Evening to enter a World in which you will meet with many wonderfull Things; Yet let me warn you against suffering yourselves to be meanly swayed by the Follies and Vices of others, for believe me my beloved Children that if you do – I shall be very sorry for it.

Both girls succeed in comforting their mother:

> they were prepared to find a World full of things to amaze and shock them: but [...] they trusted their behaviour would never give me reason to repent the Watchful Care with which I had presided over their infancy and formed their Minds. ("A Collection of Letters" [1791] 82. *Love and Friendship and other early works*. The Women's Press, 1978. 82.)

Given this mocking tone and attitude regarding certain supposedly important features of the genre, I tend to believe that Austen might also have been more or less consciously *left aside* by Dutch intermediaries for not conforming to the received image (current in the male press) of the woman author – just as had been the case in Sweden.[32]

Some Dutch exceptions appreciating Jane Austen?

The 'being left aside'-hypothesis is based on the fact that there has indeed been traced at least one early Dutch reaction to Jane Austen: in 1817 *De Recensent* presented *Emma*, as being written by a "wom[a]n who ha[s] already made a fine reputation for [herself] by [..] earlier Works: [..] *Sense and Sensibility, Pride and Prejudice*", and stating it contained "well-painted scenes from family life that at present English readers are beginning to prefer to stories of extraordinary and usually unbelievable events.[33] It is interesting to note that the two earlier novels seem to be presented as being familiar to the public, and also that the reviewer was conscious of the particularity and novelty of Jane Austen, as different from Radcliffe, Roche, and others. The article, however, was in fact a translation of an article in the German *Jenaïsche Allgemeine Literatur-Zeitung*, published in June 1816. This, in turn, was probably itself a reflection of Walter Scott's famous review of *Emma* in the *Quarterly Review* of March of the same year.[34] The announcement in *De Recensent* does not seem to have provoked any Dutch response. Does this fact endorse my hypothesis that Austen's absence from the Dutch literary field in this period is the result of a more conscious refusal? Anyhow, it is notable that the Dutch version of the article insists upon the appropriateness of Austen's novels for a changing *English* taste.

The situation in the Netherlands, finally, would not seem to have been fundamentally different from that in France and Switzerland. Although French versions of Austen's novels admittedly *did* appear, it was not the 'real Jane Austen' but adapted versions of her texts that were admired and read: rewritings by the Swiss novelist Isabelle de Montolieu.[35] According to Valérie Cossy, she "deliberately manipulate[d]" (23) Austen's novels, reducing them "to a vehicle for moral and good sentiments." (25) What these translators and publishers appreciated in novels was – just as with the Dutch critics appreciating Hannah More – "their value as moral examples," which if not enough present in the original text could of course be added in the translation. And so, as Cossy states,

> however complimentary such patronage was meant to be, especially under the pen of critics with a Swiss Protestant background, the nineteenth-century reception of Austen's work in French suffered from being so firmly entrenched in this niche of "feminine" and moral literature. [...] Thus Austen's novels were translated into a generic recipient that differed widely from her own conception of the genre. (33-34)

The Dutch 'non-acceptance' of Jane Austen during the whole of the century is not only put into perspective by this comparison to the reception elsewhere. As far as it can be traced to 'official' intermediaries, probably most of them male, non-acceptance can also be *counter-balanced* by considering the opinions of 'ordinary readers', male and female. Some of them – not many[36] – may have been familiar with the English language. Up to now, we have not found any records or traces of such readings. But there are also less explicit testimonies, such as catalogues of circulating libraries. Van der Hoek's in Leiden is interesting in this respect: it mentions a copy of *Sense and Sensibility* in English, acquired in 1865. Given the fact that this circulating library was a commercial enterprise, clients must be supposed to have *asked* for this work, probably a little before 1865.

There is another possibility for counter-balancing, by focusing on *female* readers. We found an announcement in a late 19th-century feminist journal, entitled *Ons Streven*, headed by the words "A New Novel by Miss Austen". It announced the publication in England of *Lady Susan*, saying that "this *well-known* authoress" ["deze *welbekende schrijfster*", emph. added] had left the manuscript after her death and that it had now been published, together with some other short works (*Ons Streven* (15 February 1871) 27). The announcement suggests, again, that Austen was known in the second half of the century – but since when and among which readers? Just as the 1817 article, it may have come to us from Germany: *Ons Streven* and its editor Reinoudina de Goeije[37] had close contacts with German women's periodicals and the announcement may have simply been copied from Louise Otto-Peters's *Neue Bahnen*, for example. But she may also have been influenced by James-Edward Austen-Leigh's *Memoir of Jane* Austen (1870), also mentioned by Van Woudenberg, and which has influenced Léon Boucher's article in the *Revue des Deux Mondes*, which was widely read in the Netherlands, and possibly responsible for another appearance of an Austen-novel, *Emma* (the original version) in the Van der Hoek catalogue for 1878. This 'Austen-wave' may have continued: the "Damesleesmuseum" ["Ladies' Reading Museum"] in The Hague also bought a copy of *Pride and Prejudice* in 1896.[38]

So, the Dutch may seem to have become more ready to accept Jane Austen during the second half of the century, when the insistence on the Moral-Domestic had diminished, and a certain feminism was emerging, even in the Netherlands. The changing taste in (women's) novels is – in a modest but clear way – illustrated by the series of Van der Hoek catalogues, which started in 1859. The only earlier English women novelists who survived right to the end of the century were Radcliffe (four titles) and Roche (three), with only Owenson (one) and Edgeworth (two) following suit. Of Hannah More – not a trace[39].

Further research

Clearly many questions remain to be answered, and the recent findings about Jane Austen in the 19th-century Netherlands can perhaps be dismissed for not being really 'massive'. Nevertheless, part of this recent evidence has international connections and is an illustration of the fact that it is difficult to study the reception of an author in another country *without* taking context into account. Given the large international diffusion of 19th-century French, German, and English periodical press, this context is international. German reception has demonstrably played some part, since Dutch reception documents refer to it. Comparisons with other countries also prove helpful for explanation or confirmation.

The necessity of such an international approach applies to women authors in particular, whose reception is liable to be under-researched. Their work has often been visibly judged less interesting by male intermediaries who have dismissed it by insisting upon women addressing merely a female audience. Supposing that this prevailing image of the woman writer and her women readers is not completely false, one cannot assume that for female authors reception has been sufficiently covered when most of the sources consulted are male. A number of sources are at our disposal for the second half of the 19th century, when women's press and female journalism were developing. Many of the women concerned were connected to wider international 'networks', as the feminist reaction concerning *Lady Susan*, probably rooted in Germany, also tended to illustrate. These periodicals are presently being described and increasingly better understood,[40] so that they can be used as an interesting context for the study of Jane Austen's place in Europe. It is not at all certain that Jane Austen had a completely feminine reading public in mind – as those authors she was mocking –, but given her position on clichés about women, it is essential that gender aspects be included when studying her reception.

It is also important to state that Jane Austen was in a way 'ahead of her time', just as Isabelle de Charrière was. The above-mentioned comparison between both authors by Hanna Stouten is fairly just:[41] it may well be true for both women that their conception of the novel and their use of irony, which were completely misunderstood by contemporaries, are quite attractive to a modern reader, thus allowing us to rediscover them at the end of the 20th century. However it is not less important to recognize the perspicacity of those 19th-century readers who were early appreciators.

Translated by Brenda Mudde.

Bibliography

Claesson Pipping, Git and Eleanor Wikborg. "Jane Austen's Reception in Sweden: Irony as Criticism and Literary Value." *The Reception of Jane Austen in Europe*. Eds. Anthony Mandal and Brian Southam. London/New York: Continuum, 2007. 152-168.

Cohen, Margaret. *The Sentimental Education of the Novel*. Princeton: Princeton University Press, 1999.

Cossy, Valérie. *Jane Austen in Switzerland. A Study of the Early French Translations*. Genève: Slatkine, 2006.

Garside, Peter, James Raven and Rainer Schöwerling, eds. *The English Novel 1770-1829. A Bibliographical Survey of Prose Fiction Published in the British Isles*. Oxford: Oxford University Press, 2000.

Howard, Rachel. "Domesticating the novel. Moral-Domestic Fiction, 1820-1834." *Cardiff Corvey Articles* 13.3. 26 October 2007 <http://www.cf.ac.uk/encap/corvey/articles/cc13_n03.html>.

Janssen, F.A. "1725-1830 – Domestic orientation." *A Concise History of the Printed Book in the Netherlands. Bibliopolis*. 5 July 2008 <www.bibliopolis.nl>.

Jensen, Lotte. "*Bij uitsluiting voor de vrouwelijke sekse geschikt.*" *Vrouwentijdschriften en journalistes in Nederland in de achttiende en negentiende eeuw*. Hilversum: Verloren, 2001.

Kelly, Gary. *English Fiction of the Romantic Period 1789-1830*. London: Longman, 1989.

Kloek, Joost. *Een begrensd vaderland. De roman rond 1800 tussen nationaal karakter en internationale markt*. Amsterdam: Koninklijke Nederlandse Akademie van Wetenschappen, 1997.

Krol, Ellen. *De smaak der natie. Opvattingen over huiselijkheid in de Noord-Nederlandsche poëzie van 1800 tot 1840*. Hilversum: Verloren, 1997.

Mandal, Anthony and Brian Southam, eds. *The Reception of Jane Austen in Europe*. London/New York: Continuum, 2007.

Montoya, Alicia C. "French and English women writers in Dutch library (auction) catalogues, 1700-1800. Some methodological considerations and preliminary results." *"I Have Heard About You." Foreign Women's Writing Crossing the Dutch Border: From Sappho to Selma Lagerlöf*. Eds. Suzan van Dijk, et al. Hilversum: Verloren, 2004. 182-216.

NEWW project (New approaches to European Women's Writing, dir. Suzan van Dijk). *Women Writers' Networks*. Utrecht: Igitur Utrecht Publishing & Archiving. <http://www.womenwriters.nl>.

Saalmink, Louis G. *Nederlandse bibliografie 1801-1832*. Houten: Bohn Stafleu Van Loghum, 1993.

Schenkeveld-van der Dussen, Riet. "*Met en zonder lauwerkrans* in an International Perspective." *Writing the History of Women's Writing. Toward an International Approach*. Eds. Suzan van Dijk, Lia van Gemert and Sheila Ottway. Amsterdam: Koninklijke Nederlandse Akademie van Wetenschappen, 2001. 239-250.

——— "Elisabeth Johanna Hasebroek: vertaalster om godswil." *Filter. Tijdschrift over vertalen* 13.3 (2006): 13-20.

Schenkeveld-van der Dussen, Riet, et al., eds. *Met en zonder lauwerkrans. Schrijvende vrouwen uit de vroegmoderne tijd 1550-1850, van Anna Bijns tot Elise van Calcar.* Amsterdam: Amsterdam University Press, 1997.

Stouten, Hanna. "Verloren voor het Nederlands. Isabella Agneta Elisabeth van Tuyll van Serooskerken (Belle van Zuylen)." *Met en zonder lauwerkrans. Schrijvende vrouwen uit de vroegmoderne tijd 1550-1850, van Anna Bijns tot Elise van Calcar.* Eds. Riet Schenkeveld-van der Dussen et al. 649-652.

van Woudenberg, Maximiliaan. "Going Dutch: The Reception of Jane Austen in the Low Countries." *The Reception of Jane Austen in Europe*. Eds. Anthony Mandal and Brian Southam. London/New York: Continuum, 2007. 74-92.

Wilhelm, Frans. *English in the Netherlands: a History of Foreign LanguageTeaching 1800-1920*. Utrecht: Gopher, 2005.

Notes

[1] See Kelly's *English Fiction* (111).

[2] Schenkeveld-van der Dussen was co-editor of *Met en zonder lauwerkrans*; see also her "*Met en zonder lauwerkrans* in an International Perspective".

[3] During the 1850s, Hasebroek translated novels by Margaret Maria Brewster, Charlotte Elizabeth, and Elizabeth Charles-Rundle.

[4] For example those about Norway and Sweden.

[5] Jane Austen, *Northanger Abbey* [1818] (Hammondsworth: Penguin Books, 1972): "The advantages of natural folly in a beautiful girl have been already set forth by the capital pen of a sister author" (125). Austen is referring to Fanny Burney and her *Camilla* (1796).

[6] Joost Kloek provides explanations in his *Een begrensd vaderland* (16-22).

[7] According to figures derived from Saalmink's *Nederlandse bibliografie* (3: 162-166). For France, Margaret Cohen demonstrated that there is also an important proportion of women authors, practicing the so-called "sentimental novel".

[8] This figure (July 2008) includes critical reception, but also the presence in library catalogues, mentions in private correspondences, etc. For further details, see the "reading side" section on www.womenwriters.nl, where references are provided to the database. Note that data entry is in progress, so that figures are not "stable".

[9] In the near future, these figures are to be compared to those concerning male literary production and their reception.

[10] The authors in question are A.C. Brinkman, A. Deken, C.M. Dóll-Egges, J.J. van Haren-Beaumont, A. Kleyn-Ockerse, F. Mastenbroek, A.B. van Meerten-Schilperoort, P. Moens, M.J. de Neufville, K.W. Schweickhardt, B. Wolff.

[11] The most important of them being Stéphanie-Félicité de Genlis (France) and Karoline Pichler (Austria).

[12] For an extensive comment on this dominance in the 18th century, see Montoya's "French and English women writers".

[13] See Kloek (12-15).

[14] The selected authors have at least two novels translated into Dutch, in particular during the period 1800-1829. Quantities of Dutch translations on the basis of their being mentioned in the database *WomenWriters* (July 2008). Details are to be found on www.womenwriters.nl. For French translations I have used the Catalogue of the Bibliothèque nationale de France; this information will be included in the database *WomenWriters* as soon as possible.

[15] Translations are not always directly from the English, as Laura Kirkley shows for the *Vindication*; see her contribution in this volume.

[16] See *Bibliopolis* (www.bibliopolis.nl) "1725-1830 – Domestic orientation".

[17] See Howard's "Domesticating the novel".

[18] The journal is currently being digitalized online on the Virtual Workplace for Social Sciences and the Humanities (www.e-laborate.nl).
[19] A total of 87 articles concerning the authors mentioned in table 2; for the list and references, see the "reading side" section on www.womenwriters.nl.
[20] "[...] de kost dezer natie valt, over het geheel, wat zwaarder, dan die onzer linksche en regtsche vastelandsgeburen. Doch wij hopen, dat de geurige geregten der vroegere schrijvers van echt Britsche luim en scherpzinnigheid door Duitsche vliegop en Fransche ragouts nog niet zoo geheel uit het geheugen zullen verdrongen zijn, of men is wel begeerig naar een nieuw proefje." (*Vaderlandsche Letteroefeningen* (1816): 225)
[21] "de Engelsche manier op den langen weg iets vervelends heeft, en de leeslust doet kwijnen" ((1819) 1: 97). Such judgments need of course be compared with comments concerning male English authors.
[22] "Eene Miss Schrijfster! Dit zal welligt sommigen bevreemden, eenigen aanlokken, anderen terugstooten en afschrikken" (*De Recensent* (1811) 281).
[23] "[...] vol riddertrouw en ridderliefde, vol oorlog en maagdenroof, vol spoken en wonderen [...]. Het zou jammer zijn, indien het noodzaak ware, op die wijze de wereldgeschiedenis, ten minste eenigermate, bekend te doen blijven bij het thans levend en veel lezend publiek" (*Vaderlandsche Letteroefeningen* (1818) 411).
[24] "[...] wat kenmerkt het meerendeel [der] personen? Ondeugden, meestal van de laagste en verachtelijkste soort, die [...] slegts een verachtlijk en onedel hart verraden" (*Vaderlandsche Bibliotheek* (1801) 269).
[25] "[...] het heldere en afschrikkende licht, waarin de [...] ondeugden worden ten toon gesteld, en de tegenzin en verfoeiing van dezelve, welke zij, bij eenen ieder, die eenig gevoel voor deugd en zedelijkheid bezit, niet kunnen nalaten in te boezemen" (*Vaderlandsche Bibliotheek* (1811) 160).
[26] "De voortreffelijke zedelijke strekking van [Opie's *New Tales*] doet ons dit werk met alle vrijmoedigheid aanprijzen" (*Vaderlandsche Letteroefeningen* (1820) 650); "Eene goede zedelijke strekking [wordt gezien als] het menschengeluk inderdaad bevorderend" (*Vaderlandsche Letteroefeningen* (1821) 709).
[27] "[...] om de menschen zelfkennis te leeren, van den hoogmoed en zelfsverbeelding terug te brengen, om in de beoefening van een waar Christendom ootmoedig met GOD te wandelen" (*Vaderlandsche Bibliotheek* (1805) 400).
[28] "[...] allerbijzonderst mogen wij dit werk aanprijzen, vanwege de treffelijke voorstelling van Godsdienst en Christendom" (*Vaderlandsche Letteroefeningen* (1821) 263).
[29] "Wij hebben hier een welbewerkt en waarlijk leerzaam verhaal, hetwelk, op eene edele, regt hartelijk godsdienstige wijze, het gevoel van, en het vertrouwen op eene ons leidende vaderlijke voorzienigheid Gods krachtig opwekt" (*Vaderlandsche Letteroefeningen* (1821) 358). This Dutch preference for the Moral-Domestic and for what Rachel Howard terms the "Conversion novel" is to be related to the then prevalent idea that domesticity or "homeliness" was a characteristic of the Dutch national character. See also Ellen Krol's *De smaak der natie* (103, 131-135). Krol only discusses poetry, and the interesting thing – in our context – is the fact that "female poets were virtually inactive in this field" (378).
[30] "[Recensent beveelt] inzonderheid de lezing aan aan onze Vaderlandsche Moeders, haar wijzende op het voorbeeld der beminnelijke Miss Williams, door eene verstandige Moeder opgekweekt tot die stille en bevallige zielshoedanigheden en deugden" (*Vaderlandsche Letteroefeningen* (1811) 257).
[31] "[...] de ijsselijke gevolgen van eenen enkelen misstap, om [hen] tegen ligtzinnigheid en zelfvertrouwen (in eenen kwaden zin) te waarschuwen" (*Vaderlandsche Letteroefeningen* (1810) 139).
[32] See Mandal's "Introduction": "Austen's ironic perspective did not accord with Swedish perceptions of novels by 'English lady novelists': this in a country that saw two of her novels translated by mid-century" (6). See also Claesson Pipping and Wikborg's "Jane Austen's reception in Sweden".

[33] "Er zijn ook eenige Romans in het licht verschenen, welke niet slechts de Kunstregters voldoen, maar ook door het algemeen met groot genoegen gelezen worden. Twee derzelve zijn van vrouwen, die zich reeds door vroegere Werken gunstig bekend gemaakt hadden. *Emma, a Novel*, by the author of *Sense and Sensibility*, *Pride and Prejudice*, 3 deelen, in 8vo., behelst goed bewerkte familietafereelen, in dewelke men thans in Engeland meer smaak begint te krijgen, dan in verhalen van buitengewone en veelal ongeloofelijke voorvallen" (*De Recensent* (1817) 201).

[34] Which apparently had also been imported into Russia, see Mandal and Southam (335).

[35] Montolieu's work was also translated into Dutch (four translations between 1788 and 1820), and positively commented in the press.

[36] Unfortunately, as also stated by Van Woudenberg, in the beginning of the 19th century, they were not numerous. See also Frans Wilhelm's *English in the Netherlands*.

[37] Reinoudina de Goeije (1833-1893) was the daughter of a protestant. She published under the pseudonym of Agatha and was herself a translator (e.g. of *Robinson Crusoe*).

[38] About this Ladies' Reading Museum, see Lizet Duyvendak's contribution to this volume.

[39] The series of catalogues (1859-1887) contains 685 works (translated or not, including double copies) by English/Irish women; most importantly by Braddon, Eliot, Fullerton, Gaskell, Kavanagh, Linton, Marryat, Mulock, Oliphant, Ouida, Wood, Yonge.

[40] See, for example, Jensen.

[41] Another interesting resemblance between them concerns their lack of disposition to be impressed by the female celebrities of the time: Mme de Genlis and Mme de Staël.

Lizet Duyvendak (Open Universiteit Nederland)

English Reading in a Dutch Library for Women (1894-1900)

In 1894 a group of young gentlewomen from The Hague founded a library: the Damesleesmuseum ["Ladies' Reading Museum"]. In the second half of the 19th century, the fact that existing reading societies rarely admitted female members led to the foundation of reading societies and study clubs especially for women in Europe and the United States of America. The reading society was one of many women's organisations that developed in the first wave of feminism. It answered the need felt by upper-middle-class women for meaningful recreation and enhanced women's opportunities to learn a vocation. The founders' aim was to create a place which enabled its members to read recent periodicals, brochures and books. There were books in Dutch, English, French and German. Until 1964, the library also bought books in Italian and the Scandinavian languages.

The Damesleesmuseum started with 140 members; its largest membership (1478 members) was achieved in 1929, when it increasingly became a Women's Club, offering not only a large collection of books and periodicals, but also the opportunity to play bridge, take lunch and attend talks and courses. During the Second World War, the library was closed by the Germans. After the War it restarted with 350 members, and grew to 1125 by 1952. Subsequently, membership numbers fell to about 300 in 1985, but in the 1990s rose again to about 600 (including 60 male members). Nowadays this library still exists, with a collection containing some 40.000 volumes – and a reputation of old-fashioned aristocracy. This article, however, highlights the fact that at the end of the 19th century these women were in fact taking part in what Kate Flint outlined as a "reading community", centred around what used to be called the "New Woman". Although the public face of the Damesleesmuseum's executive committee was one of neutrality, many members were associated with the organisation of the National Exhibition of Women's Labour ["Nationale Tentoonstelling van Vrouwenarbeid"], which was held in The Hague in 1898 as one of the highlights of the first feminist wave.

The collection of the Damesleesmuseum

Before a book was actually bought, it was assessed by the so-called 'reading committee', which consisted of about 15 members of the Damesleesmuseum. A book was read by two committee members, who had to agree whether or not a book should be bought. In the event of disagreement, a third reader also read the book and made a final decision.[1] The Damesleesmuseum always did its best to maintain a broadly-based collection and the committee made its own choices independently of current literary criticism. Its recommendations were rarely objected to by the members: the archives contain only a few complaints, which mainly concerned the political tendency of a book or periodical, or overly explicit erotic passages. In 1902, for example, some members were of the opinion that the periodical *Graphic* was too politically outspoken ('Jingo') in the South-African Boer War.

Relatively few translations were included in the library, which was the result of the Damesleesmuseum's key principle that a book should be read in the original language as much as possible. As Andringa has noted (91-92), two main factors underlie this principle: apart from the conviction that women could practise their languages by reading the originals (reading as an utilitarian practice), there was also the widespread opinion that it was always better to read the original than the translation.

Importantly, English occupied an atypical position in the collection of the Damesleesmuseum. As Van der Weel has argued in his article on "Nineteenth-Century Literary Translation" (28-29), for most of the 19th century the position of English as a source language was very different than that of French (and German). French was widely spoken and read in the Netherlands (especially in educated circles), and, consequently, the need for translations was greater in the case of English texts. But this is not the case for the Damesleesmuseum: members of this specific group were able to read both foreign languages, and the English collection was even larger than the French collection. Only a few English books were also bought in translation, such a Radclyffe Hall's *The Well of Loneliness* (1929). Moreover, some members translated themselves, mostly from English and Scandinavian languages into Dutch. The best-known among them were Margaretha Meyboom and Claudine Bienfait. Meyboom, for example, translated works by Selma Lagerlöf, Henrik Ibsen and Bj. Björnson. Bienfait translated English children's books (of May Baldwin, for instance) and Gunnar Gunnarson, Nexo Anderson, Marie Hamsun and also Bj. Björnson.

Apart from a large number of realist and naturalist titles (by authors such as Louis Couperus, Frederik van Eeden, Lodewijk van Deyssel, Emile Zola, Leo Tolstoy and Henrik Ibsen), English novels were of particular interest to the members of the Damesleesmuseum. This contradicts the conventionally held ideas regarding the reception of naturalism in the Netherlands, as well as the idea concerning the quality of literature read by women of the leisured classes: according to literary historians, the average reader had little interest in naturalism and relatively affluent women only read French novels of dubious quality (Duyvendak 171-174).

The following figures give a more detailed picture of these observations. **Table 1** shows the number of books bought in the years 1894-1900.

Table 1:
Books purchased, 1894-1900

Dutch	English	French	German	Italian	Brochures[2]
455	350	206	139	12	120

In the first catalogue, published in 1896, only 4 titles out of 133 Dutch books were translations from English, 3 of which were written by women. The second catalogue (of 1900) mentions 28 translations (out of 322), of which 10 by women writers.

Table 2:
English and translated books, 1894-1900

Catalogue	Translations from English	Translations from English works by women writers	English books by women writers
1896	4 (out of 133)	3	65 (out of 196)
1900	28 (out of 322)	10	57 (out of 154)

A list of the translations included in the first two library catalogues can be found in Appendix I. In the beginning, canonical books such as the works of Dickens and Shakespeare were acquired. In addition, the library also included “light reading”, such as novels by Mrs Oliphant, Anna Sewell and Marie Corelli. Works of best-selling authors such as Jan Maclaren and E.N. Wescott were also purchased in translation. The translated non-fiction books either deal with social questions and/or the position of women (as is the case, for example with the works of Elisabeth Barnett and John Stuart Mill).

In the English collection, one can find similar categories: canonical works (Eliot, the Brontë sisters), non-fiction books with social themes and about women’s work, bestsellers (Marie Corelli, Rhoda Broughton, Wilkie Collins, Thomas Hardy) and many titles written by nowadays mostly unknown women writers. Appendix II lists the works by women writers bought between 1894-1900. Appendix III contains the *periodicals* which could be read in the DLM reading room. These periodicals dealt with literature, politics, art and feminism.

New Woman novels

Assumptions about gender attributes and differences were crucial components of the English literature of the 19th century. Victorian women in particular were saturated with prescriptive literature with instructions on the social duties and proper feminine behaviour. Educational tracks and advice books sanctified a belief in separate spheres and the resulting duties of women in the maintenance of a tranquil home and the ministering oversight of husband and children. The sources of weakness and fragility were located within the female body. Women were warned of the consequences of not respecting these phenomena as natural (Frawley 481).

But in English novels and periodicals in the 1890s a new female figure emerged in literature: the New Woman . The label ‘New Woman’ applied to many types of power-seeking females, ranging from women who pursued their own careers, to women who desired sexual liberation. These New Woman novels, debunking romantic expectations and emphasizing, among other things, prevalant double standards in respect to sexual behaviour and purity, were heavily disputed in the press. In “The Regeneration of Two”, for example, George Egerton wrote about a spoiled widow who starts a new life. Spurning social properties, she starts a co-operative in her country-home, composed of all the fallen women of the area, working together in love and harmony:

> I was sorry for myself, resentful because I had been reared in ignorance, because of my soul-hunger, but I had found myself all the same, and I said: From this out I belong body and soul to myself; I will live as I choose, seek joy as I choose, carve the way of my life as I will… Woman has cheapened herself body and soul through ignorant innocence, she must learn to worthen herself by all-seeying knowledge. (Egerton 241-242)

The critic of *Blackwood's Magazine* wrote in 1895 about the New Woman writers:

> Their chief delight seems to be in making their characters discuss matters which would not have been tolerated in the novels a decade ago. Emancipated woman in particular loves to show her independence by dealing freely with the relations of the sexes. (Vicinus vii)

The New Women (and the novels in which they figured) were clearly seen as a threat for the Second Fall of Man, because they did not comply to the conventional career of marriage and motherhood. In literary criticism these novels were characterized as a literary sub-cultural backwater, rank with hysterical feminist fervour. Commercially, they were a success, bought and read both by female and male readers. According Ann Ardis's *New Women*, between 1880-1920 more than 100 were published. They were written by both popular and literary, male and female authors like Thomas Hardy, Ouida, Grant Allen and Rhoda Broughton.

The New Woman was not only known and negatively discussed in English-speaking countries. Already in 1896 in the Dutch periodical *De Gids*, the reviewer Charles van Deventer wrote about "the nauseating theme of the New Woman".[3] From its inception, however, the Damesleesmuseum purchased many books by female authors, even if they had not known a favourable critical reception. Many of the New Woman books were in the Damesleesmuseum, some in translation but mostly in English; for instance the books of Grant Allen, Rhoda Broughton, Mona Caird, George Egerton, Sara Grand, Beatrice Harradan, Olive Schreiner and Humphrey Ward.

What explanation can be given for the popularity of the New Woman novel in the Damesleesmuseum? In the collection of the circulating library of Van der Hoek in Leiden, for example, these New Woman writers are absent.[4] The popularity of the New Woman novel in the Damesleesmuseum appears to be the result of a set of characteristics and ideals that were shared by the New Woman and the Damesleesmuseum-member. Firstly, the ideal of adequate education, which is reflected in the founding of the library and in the reading of works in their original language. Secondly, the desire to participate in political discussions. And thirdly, the conviction that a woman should be able to decide herself if, when and whom she wants to marry. The independent book selection reflects these ideals. Assumptions about proper feminine behaviour were deconstructed both by founding a women's library and by choosing a literature of their own.

If Kate Flint stated that the New Woman-fiction created a "community of women readers", this community included not only English, but also Dutch (and possibly European) readers. These New Woman-novels "served as a confirmation of the fact that [...] women readers were not without others who thought and felt along the same lines" (Flint 327-329). Further research should be done in this field, partly in the context of the further development of the *WomenWriters* database. The influence of the New Woman concept can also be seen in the most famous Dutch first wave feminist novel, *Hilda van Suylenburg* (1897), written by Cecile Goekoop-de Jong van Beek en Donk, member of the Damesleesmuseum and chair of the National Exhibition of Women's Labour in 1898, where the term "New Woman" is used (first edition, part 2: 101-102).

Conclusion

As can be derived from this overview of English books in the library of the Damesleesmuseum, the roles accorded to female readers in literary and social history must be critically examined. If the linguistic competences go the first members of the Damesleesmuseum were perhaps not typical for many readers in this decade, this should warn us about any claim concerning "THE woman reader" in the 1890s. A critical examination of what this group of women of the leisured classes actually read in translation or in the original languages, shows a more heterogeneous picture, and consigns cliches to where they belong. Therefore it is very important to assemble reception data as much as possible from readers all over Europe, to eliminate the cliches produced by reviewers and literary historians, and to see in which parts of the world the New Woman literature was actually read.

Appendix I:

Translations purchased between 1894-1896 (male en female writers)

[This appendix includes bibliographic references and the names of the translators. Unfortunately, the four translated books of the 1896 catalogue are no longer in the library of the Damesleesmuseum, and also the English title of some translated titles of the 1900 catalogue could not be found. In the 1900 catalogue it was not possible to retrieve neither the English title nor bibliographic references of the specific edition of the Oscar Wilde-title.]

1896 catalogue (female writers underlined)

Dickens, Charles	*Maarten Chuzzlewit* [*Martin Chuzzlewit*]
Keary, A.	*Een kasteel in Ierland* [*Castle Daily*]
Ouida	*Poussette* [*Poussette*]
Sewell, Anna	*Edelzwart* [*Black Beauty*]

1900 catalogue: translations purchased between 1896-1900 (female writers underlined)

Allen, Grant	*Een vrouw die den moed had* [*The Woman Who Did*] Amsterdam: De Roode Bibliotheek, 1898. Translator: unknown. *De hertogin van Powysland* [*The Duchess of Powysland*]. Amsterdam: Holdert, [s.d]. Translator: H.
Alexander, Mrs.	*Een strijd met het lot* [*A Fight with Fate*] Amsterdam: Holdert & Co, 1897. Translator: C. Baarslag.
Barnett, Edith A.	*Hoe bezorgen wij onze meisjes een gelukkige toekomst* [*The Training of Girls for Work*]. Almelo: Hilarius, 1895. Translator: Henriëtte.
Bellamy, Edward	*Gelijkheid voor allen* [*Equality*]. Den Haag: A. Abrahams. Translator: A.C.B.
Braddon, M.E.	*Die man zijt gij* [*Thou Art The Man*]. Amsterdam: Holdert, 1896. Translator: C.A. La Bastide & C. Baarslag.
Clodd, Edward	*De geschiedenis van den oorspronkelijken mensch* [*The Story of 'Primitive' Man*]. Zutphen: W.J. Thieme & Cie, 1897. Translator: unknown

Henry, George	*Vooruitgang en armoede* [*Progress and Poverty*]. Haarlem: Tjeenk Willink, 1885. Translator: J.W. Straatman.
Hickson, Sydney	*Het Leven der Zeeën* [*The Story of Life in the Seas*]. Zutphen: [s.n.], 1899. Translator: H.C. Redeke.
Kidd, Benjamin	*Sociale Evolutie* [*Social Evolution*]. Haarlem: H.D. Tjeenk Willink, 1897. Translator: L.v.B.
Kingsford, Anna	*De ware voeding* [*The Perfect Way in Diet. A treatise advocating a return to the natural and ancient food of our race*]. Amsterdam: Van Looy, 1895. Translator: F. Nordanus.
Kipling, Rudyard	*Het licht dat verdween* [*The Light that Failed*]. Amsterdam: [s.n.], 1892. Translator: unknown. *Drie soldaten* [*Soldiers Three*]. Amsterdam: S.L. van Looy en Gerlings, 1893. Translator: Guillette de Lange-Willumier. *Uit de Bergen* [*Plain Tales from the Hills*]. Amsterdam: S.L. van Looy en Gerlings, 1892. Translator: Guillette de Lange-Willumier.
Maclaren, Ian	*Harten van goud* [English title unknown]. Rotterdam: Bredée, 1896. Translator: W. van Nes. *Zielenadel* [English title unknown]. Rotterdam: Bredée, 1899. Translator: W. van Nes.
Martineau, Harriet	*In de Fjords* [*Feats on the Fiord*]. Amsterdam: Versluys, 1889. Translator: M. Reddingius-Wiarda.
Mulock, Miss	*Een kloeke vrouw* [*A Brave Lady*].
Oliphant, Mrs.	*De rijke erfgename* [*The Greatest Heiress in England*]. Haarlem: Erven Loosjes, 1882. Translator: A.A. Deenik MLZ.
Putman, Ruth	*Willem de Zwijger* [*William the Silent, Prince of Orange: the moderate man of the 16th century: the story of his life as told from his own letters, from those of his friends and enemies and from official documents*]. Den Haag: Loman & Funke, 1897. Translator: D.C. Nijhoff.
Shakespeare, W.	*De werken van -* [*Collected Works*]. Leiden: E.J. Brill, 1886-1888. Translator dr. L.A.J. Burgersdijk.
Stanton Coit, Sr.	*Buurtvereenigingen* [*Neighbourhood Guilds: An Instrument of Social Reform*]. Rotterdam: [s.n.], 1896. Translator: M.G. Kramers.
Stuart Mill, John	*De slavernij der vrouw* [*The Subjection of Women*]. Amsterdam: Van Looy, 1898. Translator: M. Elizabeth Noest.
Wescott, E.N.	*David Harum* [*David Harum: a Story of American Life*]. Haarlem: Loosjes, 1899. Translator: J. de Hoop Scheffer.
Wilde, Oscar	*Fantasieën* [English title unknown].

Translated Brochures

Barnett, Mrs. Samuel A.	*Onze woning* [*The Making of a Home: a reading-book of domestic economy*]. Amsterdam: Versluys, 1891. Translator: G.J. Bakker Korff-Hoogeboom.
Besant, Annie	*Theosophie en materialisme. Een lezing* [English title unknown]. Arnhem: De Muinck, 1894. Translator: unknown.

Appendix II:

English literature (only women writers included)

1896 catalogue

Alcott, Louisa: *Something to Do; Work; Little Women; Little Women Wedded*
Austen, Jane: *Pride and Prejudice*
Bell, Currer (= pseud. of Charlotte Brontë): *Shirley*
Bentham, Mrs. Edwards: *The Passing of the Ways*
Braddon, Miss: *The Day Will Come*
Broughton, Rhoda: *Doctor Cupid; Cometh up as a Flower*
Burnett Hogdson, Mrs: *Through One Administration*
Corelli, Marie: *Thelma*
Crawford, Marion: *Greifenstein*
Deland, Marg.: *John Ward, Preacher*
Eliot, George: *Middlemarch; Felix Holt; Impressions by Theophrastus Such; The Lifted Veil; The Mill on the Floss*
Falconer, Lanoe (pseud. of Mary Elisabeth Hawker): *Mademoiselle Ixe; The Hôtel d'Angleterre and Other Stories*
Fern, Fanny: *Fern Leaves*
Fullerton, Georina: *Lady Bird*
Giberne, Agnes: *The Curate's Home*
Grand, Sarah: *The Heavenly Twins*
Harradan, Beatrice: *Ships That Pass in the Night*
Hungerford, Miss: *A Conquering Heroine*
Kavanagh, Julia: *Nathalie*
Keeling, E. d'Esterre: *In Thoughtland and in Dreamland*
Lyall, Edna: *In the golden days* (2x); *We Two; Donovan* (2x); *A Knight-Errant*
Malet, Lucas (pseud. of Mary St Leger Kingsley): *The Wages of Sin*
Marryat, Florence: *The Fair Haired Alda*
Marshall, Emma: *Under Salisbury Spire; Penthurst Castle*
Monsdale, Marg: *Sister Dora*
Montgomery, Florence: *Misunderstood; Thwarted*
Mulock, Miss: *A Woman's Thoughts About Women*

Ouida: *Signa; Idalia; Pipistrelo; A House Party; Princess Napraxine; Two Little Wooden Shoes*
Poynter, Frances E.: *Among the Hills*
Schreiner, Olive: *The Story of an African Farm; (Ralph Iron) Dreams*
Stowe, Mrs. Beecher: *Uncle Tom's Cabin*
Thomas, Annie (Mrs. Pender Cudlip): *A Passion in Tatters*
Ward, Mrs. Humphrey: *Robert Elsmere; Marcella; The History of David Grieve; Miss Bretherton*
Wood, Mrs. Henry: *Lord Oakborn's Daughter; The Master of Greylands; Elster's Folly*
Yonge, Miss: *The Trial; The Chaplet of Pearls; The Pillars of the House; The Daisy Chain*
Wyndham, Emyla: *Evelyn Marston*

1900 catalogue

Barrett Browning, Elisabeth: *Aurora Leigh*
Bateson, M.: *Professional Women Upon their Professions*
Blissett, Nellie K.: *The Concert-Director*
Brontë, Emily: *Wuthering Heights*
Brontë, Anne: *Agnes Grey*
Broughton, Rhoda: *Not Wisely, But Too Well*
Burke, Mrs. W.A.: *The Structure of Life*
Caird, Mona: *The Morality of Marriage and Other Essays of the Status and Destiny of Women; The Daughters of Danaus*
Corelli, Marie: *The Sorrows of Satan; Ziska, the Problem of Wicked Soul*
Dickens, Mamie: *My Father, as I Recall Him*
Edwards, Amelia B.: *Unhodden Peaks and Unfrequented Valleys*
Egerton, George: *Discords; Fantasia's; Symphonies; The Wheel of God; Keynotes*
Eliot, George: *The Legend of Jubal and Other Persons*
Gerard, Dorothea: *A Spotless Reputation*
Grand, Sarah: *The Beth Book*
Harraden, Beatrice: *Hilda Strafford and the Remittanceman*
Hodgson Burnett, Francis: *A Lady of Quality*
Holdsworth, Annie E.: *Joanna Trail, Spinster; The Years,That the Locust Hath Eaten; Spindles and Oars; The Gods Arrive*
Lyall, Edna: *Derrick Vaughan, Novellist; Wayfaring Men; Hope the Hermit*
Mary E. Mann: *Moonlight*
Marryat, Florence: *Petronel; The Confessions of Gerald Estcourt; The Strange Transfiguration of Hannah Stubb*
Montgomery, Florence: *Thrown Together; The Blue Veil*
Oliphant, Mrs.: *The Greatest Heiress in England; Kinsteen, the Story of an English Family*
Ouida: *A Leaf in the storm; Cecil Castlemain's Gage; Ruffino; Toxin and Other Papers; The Massareness*
Paston, George: *A Fair Deceiver*
Perkins Stetson, Charlotte: *Women and Economics*

Rauschenbusch-Clough, Emma: *A Study of Mary Wollstonecraft*

Schreiner, Olive: *Trooper Peter Halkett of Mashonaland; An English-South-African View of the Situation*

Steel, Mrs. Flora Annie: *Red Rowans; On the Face of the Waters*

Swiney, Frances: *The Awakening of Women or Woman's Part in Evolution*

Ward, Mrs. Humphrey: *Sir George Tressady; The Story of Bessie Costrell; Helbeck of Bannisdale*

Wilkins, Mary: *Madelon*

Wood, Mrs. Henry: *Trevlyn Hold*

Appendix III:

English periodicals 1894-1900

Shafts

Studio

Review of Reviews

The Artist

The House

Weekly Times

Labour Prophet

The Speaker

English Women's Review of Industrial and Social Questions

Bibliography

Andringa, Els. "'In godsnaam en Virginia's naam waarom een vertaling?' Virginia Woolf in Nederlandse overzetting." *Textual Mobility and Cultural Transmission*. Eds. Martine de Clercq, Tom Toremans and Walter Verschueren. Leuven: Leuven University Press, 2006. 87-103.

Ardis, Ann L. *New Women, New Novels. Feminism and Early Modernism*. New Brunswick/ London: Rutgers University Press, 1990.

Duyvendak, Lizet. *'Door lezen wijder horizont' Het Haags Damesleesmuseum*. Nijmegen: Vantilt, 2003.

Duyvendak, Lizet and Diederik Grit. "Margaretha Meyboom: not only a translator." *'I have heard about you'. Foreign Women's Writing Crossing the Dutch Border*. Eds. Suzan van Dijk et al. Hilversum: Verloren, 2004. 323-330.

Egerton, George. *Keynotes & Discords*. London: Virago Press, 1983 [1893].

Flint, Kate. *The Woman Reader: 1837-1914*. New York and Oxford: Clarendon Press, 1993.

Frawley, Maria. "Victorian age, 1832-1901." *English Literature in Context*. Ed. Paul Poplawski. Cambridge: Cambridge University Press, 2008. 410-518.

van der Weel, Adriaan. "Nineteenth-Century Literary Translations from English in a Book Historical Context." *Textual Mobility and Cultural Transmission*. Eds. Martine de Clercq, Tom Toremans and Walter Verschueren. Leuven: Leuven University Press, 2006. 27-40.

van Deventer, Charles. "Robert Louis Stevenson." *De Gids* (1896): 476-509. [*Digitale Bibliotheek voor de Nederlandse Letteren*. Stichting DBNL, Leiden. 21 February 2008. http://www.dbnl.org/tekst/_gid001189601_01/_gid001189601_01_0029.htm

Vicinus, Martha. "Introduction." *Keynotes & Discords*. George Egerton. London: Virago Press, 1983. vii-xix.

Notes

[1] From the period after 1945, a large number of the recommendations of the reading committee have been preserved. These assessments constitute a unique source by "ordinary' readers" opinions, as distinct from reception documents that were mainly written by literary professionals.

[2] These were mainly in Dutch.

[3] "*The New Woman* is een thema om misselijk van te worden." (478)

[4] The lending library of C.C. van der Hoek (1792/93-1876) was started in 1822. Van der Hoek began business by taking over an existing lending library and in 1856 he in turn transferred the company to two of his sons. In 1897 and 1899 the brothers retired from the firm. The library was carried on until 1946 by new owners, though still under the name of Van der Hoek, but died a lingering death. Various catalogues and a section of the books belonging to Van der Hoek's lending library have survived. These catalogues and books are housed in Leiden's Municipal Archives (Gemeentearchief). The lending agency's commercial basis suggests that Van der Hoek's firm tailored its purchasing and investment policy to its clients' tastes. Whether Van der Hoek's books were actually read, whether they were borrowed often or only sporadically, and by whom, such questions of course remain unanswered. The fact, however, that the Van der Hoek brothers depended on the firm for a living suggests, that these were sought-after books, books that attracted enough customers.

Laura Kirkley (University of Cambridge)

Feminism in Translation: Re-writing the *Rights of Woman*

In 1792, Mary Wollstonecraft published her Revolutionary feminist manifesto, *A Vindication of the Rights of Woman*. Provoking outrage amongst conservatives and admiration in progressive circles, the *Rights of Woman* was translated into French and German in the same year and brought the author fame in Europe. At the hands of each translator, however, Wollstonecraft's feminist message underwent distinct transformations. The anonymous French translator uses his translational choices and paratextual commentary to promote Wollstonecraft's feminist message. A note of utopian possibility sounds throughout *Défense des droits des femmes* [*Defence of the Rights of Woman*], aligning it with the deluge of political tracts and pamphlets that flooded the French literary market in the early years of the Revolution. The German translation, *Rettung der Rechte des Weibes* [*Rescuing the Rights of Woman*] was the work of the pedagogue Christian Gotthilf Salzmann and his employee and future son-in-law, Georg Friedrich Christian Weissenborn. By 1796, the radical Batavian, Ysbrand van Hamelsveld, had published a Dutch version, *Verdediging van de Rechten der Vrouwen* [*Vindication of the Rights of Women*]. The few scholars to discuss this latter translation have presumed that Van Hamelsveld muted Wollstonecraft's feminist voice to mollify the Dutch public. In fact, the most thoroughgoing transformation of the text occurred earlier, in the conservative ethos of the German Nation. This article will argue that the successive translational mutations of the *Rights of Woman* reflect the cultural clashes and affinities of Revolutionary Europe.

Europe is not, and never has been, a homogeneous entity. The cosmopolitan spirit of the Republic of Letters was offset in the 18th century by the formation of distinct national and cultural identities, which developed in opposition to stereotypes of rival nations. In the Netherlands, for instance, stereotypes included the shallow Frenchman, the arrogant Englishman, and the dim-witted German. The Germans, for their part, mocked the Dutch for their Low German language and their flat land. The latter, moreover, became increasingly outmoded as Gothic and antiquarian literature fuelled public enthusiasm for untamed, rugged landscapes. Political turbulence following the revolutions in North America, the Netherlands, and France contributed to this climate of inter-national factionalism. Each revolution was fired by the Rights of Man discourse which decreed that all men were born free and equal. By the time *Verdediging van de Rechten der Vrouwen* appeared, the short-lived Batavian Republic had been established in Holland under French occupation. The shock waves created by this unrest reverberated through Europe, sparking a conservative backlash in neighbouring Germany, where the ruling classes panicked and turned to literary censorship to stem the tidal wave of revolution.

The political and cultural heterogeneity of 18th-century Europe suggests that Wollstonecraft's tract would draw accolades from some quarters and derision from others. Political and civil rights for women and French Republicanism were, after all, closely linked. This article will consider, in succession, the versions of Wollstonecraft's feminism found in *Défense des droits des femmes*, *Verdediging van de Rechten der Vrouwen*, and *Rettung der Rechte des Weibes*.

Défense des Droits des Femmes

The *Rights of Woman* is a political manifesto with its roots in the *Declaration of the Rights of Man and the Citizen*, and the French translator's version is even more entrenched in that political context, associating male supremacy with the despotism of the monarchy and amplifying Wollstonecraft's republican sentiments. Although Wollstonecraft denounces hereditary power, she couches her criticisms in language which acknowledges that monarchs, as well as their subjects, are victims of an iniquitous system. When she writes of the "crimes that have elevated men to the supreme dignity" (5: 85), the passive verb form distances the "men" from the "crimes", so that the men do not sound like the specific or sole perpetrators of injustice. The French translator, however, interpolates an adjective lest we forget the severity of these "crimes atroces", and favours an active construction in which "des méchants se sont frayés un chemin au trône" ["evil men forced their way to the throne"]. (13) Whereas Wollstonecraft describes kings simply as "men", he exploits the French practice of making adjectives nounal to describe them as "méchants", while barely disrupting the rhythm of the sentence. Similarly, whilst Wollstonecraft concedes that the "very station" of the king "sinks him *neces-*

sarily below the meanest of his subjects" (5: 85), mitigating his guilt if, not absolving him altogether, the French translator emphasises his misdeeds: "que ses vices rabaissent presque toujours au-dessous du dernier de ses sujets!" ["whose vices almost always sink him beneath the meanest of his subjects!"] (14).

Before the Terror, the most progressive exponents of women's rights were the Girondin members of the "Cercle Social" club in Paris. These included Condorcet, Olympe de Gouges, and the Dutchwoman Etta Palm, who campaigned for French-style women's clubs when she returned to the Netherlands in 1795. The French translator of the *Rights of Woman* links the cause of female emancipation explicitly to the political events unfolding in France. When Wollstonecraft calls women "slaves" in a political and civil sense, and hopes that changes in the legal and educational systems of "an enlightened nation" will "bring them back to nature", the translator is eager to point out that the "enlightened nation" in question is France. His footnote continues at some length, arguing that women deserve "une meilleure éducation" ["a better education"], "le divorce, que la tyrannie seule des prêtres a pu leur ravir" ["divorce, which only the tyranny of priests could take from them"]; and "des réparations de tous les crimes gothiques de la féodalité" ["compensations for all the gothic crimes of feudalism"]. (449) Rights for women are bound up with the progress to enlightened government, and female disenfranchisement is associated with the feudal hierarchy.

Despite identifying himself as a man in one of his footnotes, the translator is largely sympathetic to Wollstonecraft's feminism. Accordingly, he alters her syntax to intensify her rousing imperatives. "Let us, my dear contemporaries, arise above such narrow prejudices!" (5: 161) becomes "O mes contemporaines! sortez de ce cercle étroit de préjugés; osez vous élever au-dessus" ["O my contemporaries! quit this narrow circle of prejudices; dare to raise yourselves above it"]. (224) The tripartite structure remains, but the exclamation mark and semi-colon make each clause succinct and dramatic, with imperative verbal modes like "osez" bringing an extra thrill of daring to the prose. Wollstonecraft hopes that "the Rights of Woman may be respected." (5: 69) The translator confidently declares that "les droits de la Femme seront enfin comptés pour quelque chose et respectés comme ils doivent l'être" ["the rights of Woman will finally count for something and be respected as they should be"]. (16)

The word "Femme" is capitalised throughout the translation, signalling the translator's respect for the writer and the women she seeks to liberate. Similarly, while Wollstonecraft argues that education "raise[s] females in the scale of animal being" (5: 74), the translator writes that "les Femmes" are raised "dans la balance des êtres animés jusques à leur vraie place" ["in the scale of living creatures to their rightful place"]. (5) He strikes the same ardent note throughout, often transforming passages of speculative enquiry with the unequivocal language of a political manifesto in order to supra-radicalise Wollstonecraft's already controversial message.

The translator also invests intellectually in Wollstonecraft's argument that gender is a social construction. Whereas Wollstonecraft suggests that women who transgress socially-prescribed gender roles may be "hunted out of society as masculine" (5: 103), the translator unpacks the "masculine" label in language that touches on the issues of essential gender, gendered self-representation, and the unequal distribution of political rights between the sexes. The fact that liberated women risk public slander and the loss of their reputations is expressed with the verb "se dénaturer", which literally means "to misrepresent" but has its etymological roots in the idea of an essential, gendered "nature", so that misrepresentation carries connotations of literal denaturing. Appearing "masculine", meanwhile, connotes for the translator an aggressive encroachment on the rights of the male, so that women may be "rejetées de la société comme empiétant sur les droits de l'autre sexe" ["rejected from society for encroaching on the rights of the other sex"]. (66) Similarly, when Wollstonecraft scoffs at Rousseau's claim that women are constantly aware of their sexuality, while men are only sexual when aroused by some object of desire, the translator intervenes to emphasise that any apparent difference must arise from social construction: "Les hommes ne sont pas toujours hommes dans la compagnie des Femmes, les Femmes ne se souviendront pas toujours non plus qu'elles sont Femmes, si l'usage leur permettait d'acquérir plus de bon sens et de connaissances."[1] (317)

In spite of the translator's apparent determination to engage with questions of gender representation, however, the forceful language and impactful syntax of the French translation are not always favourable to Wollstonecraft's feminism. Countless critics have expressed concern that her critical attitude to women prohibits the female solidarity which, for many modern feminists, is a pre-requisite for political, social, and psychological change.[2] The problem is increased by the translator's emphatic style. Women's "cunning tricks" (5: 68) become "de petites finesses, puériles mais gênantes" ["little niceties, puerile but embarrassing"] and "a smattering of accomplishments" (5: 76) becomes "une teinture de connaissances, un vernis agréable mais léger" ["a tincture of knowledge, a pleasing but light varnish"]. (12) The embellishment of these criticisms of women does not, however, align Wollstonecraft with their male oppressors. In fact, the same emphasis is applied to descriptions of the sexual exploitation of women. When, for instance, Wollstonecraft complains that men consider "females rather as women than human creatures" (5: 73), the translator presumes a very specific and troubling interpretation of the word "women", which emphasises their disenfranchised status as objects of desire: "considérant les femmes plutôt comme les instruments de plaisir de l'autre sexe, que comme des créatures humaines" ["considering women rather as instruments of pleasure for the opposite sex than as human creatures"]. (2) The result is pronounced shifts between recognisable positions of gender-identification, so that the textual voice never has a sustained bias.

Verdediging van de Rechten der Vrouwen

The question of women's natural equality with men was a commonplace of Dutch public debate and, although the French debated the issue more fervently than the Dutch, the arguments for female emancipation advanced by Batavian and French women were virtually identical. An anonymous pamphlet, possibly by Etta Palm, was published in the Netherlands in 1795, "in support of the proposition that women should participate in the government of the country". Catharina Heybroek and Lieve van Ollefen edited the *Nationale Bataafsche Courant* from 1797 onward and women with literary reputations were invited to join literary societies. Even left-wing parliamentary representatives, however, only occasionally suggested that women should be given the vote. For the most part, the Netherlands was not as radical as France, and Van Hamelsveld's changeable feminist convictions are a case in point. In 1795, his journal, *De Vraag-al* [*The Obstinate Questioner*] proposed cutting the sentence from the Reformed marriage service which required wives to submit to their husbands, on the grounds that it was incompatible with "true Enlightenment". But it seems that Van Hamelsveld was reluctant to commit to a firm feminist position: the next edition of *De Vraag-al* contained a refutation of the original argument. Although there is no surviving copy of *Verdediging van de Rechten der Vrouwen*, extensive quotations from a 1797 review in the *Vaderlandsche Letteroefeningen* suggest that the Dutch translation had a more conservative inflection than the *Défense*.

The reviewer also furnishes significant evidence that Van Hamelsveld was influenced, to some extent, by Christian Gotthilf Salzmann's extensive paratext, and the translational choices of Weissenborn. The reviewer mentions both a Dutch and a German translator and, according to the title of the review, Salzmann's *Einleitung* formed part of the Dutch edition. Van Hamelsveld also refers to the German paratext in his "Introduction". It was common practice in the 18th century for foreign texts to enter a language via an existing translation. It is therefore probable that Van Hamelsveld was working from the German translation rather than the English original.

The Introduction to *Verdediging van de Rechten der Vrouwen* establishes his radical credentials, significantly with scathing reference to neighbouring Germany: "Eer wy eindigen", he writes, "moeten wy nog zeggen [...] dat Mrs. WOLLSTONECRAFT eene warme voorstanderes der vryheid is, eene vyandin van alle willekeurige heerschappye, en alle erflyke regeering afkeurt" ["Before concluding, one must say [...] that Mrs. WOLLSTONECRAFT defends liberty passionately, that she is the enemy of all arbitrary governments, and that she disapproves of hereditary rule"]. Like Salzmann, however, Van Hamelsveld uses his "Introduction" to recommend a specific reading of the feminist message in the *Rights of Woman*. He calls attention, in particular, to Wollstonecraft's claim that the virtues of the two sexes must be the same in quality, if not in degree. This statement, he writes, is "den sleutel van het geheele Werk" ["the key to the entire work"] and "den regel, tot welken de gezegden van Mrs. WOLLSTONECRAFT moeten terug gebragt worden, wanneer zy, in haaren yver voor de eere haarer kunne, somtyds hare eischen merkelyk verder schynt te driven" ["the principle to which all of Wollstonecraft's remarks can be reduced, even if in her enthusiasm for her sex, she sometimes seems to push her demands too far"].[3] A cursory knowledge of Wollstonecraft's original, heterogeneous tract contradicts any suggestion that the *Rights of Woman* might be "reduced" to a single axiom. Yet Van Hamelsveld determinedly prescribes a single view of the text, which focuses on one of Wollstonecraft's least radical statements. She admittedly concedes that women might not have the same "degree" of virtue as men; but elsewhere in the text she insists that women could match men both morally and intellectually, if given access to the appropriate education and opportunities. Extolling Wollstonecraft's eloquent description of women's domestic role, Van Hamelsveld assures the reader that, although she protests against draconian limits on women's freedom, she does not insist on complete equality.

To a certain extent, Van Hamelsveld panders to conventional attitudes to women in the Netherlands in 1796, where even the most influential women's periodicals accepted that the duties of female citizenship were best fulfilled in the home. If he was working from the German translation, however, it is unsurprising that he regarded Wollstonecraft as a moderate advocate of women's rights, whose most revolutionary statements could be dismissed as excessive enthusiasm. The remainder of this article considers the impact of the German translation on the feminism of the *Rights of Woman*.

Rettung der Rechte des Weibes

In 1790, Wollstonecraft translated Salzmann's *Moralisches Elementarbuch* (1785) into *Elements of Morality for the use of young children*. It was a conduct book for children, which delineated the Rousseauvian pedagogical theories practised at Salzmann's school in Schnepfenthal. In his *Memoirs of the Author of "The Rights of Woman"* (226), William Godwin records a correspondence between Wollstonecraft and Salzmann which unfortunately does not survive, but appears to have grown out of the commercial success of her translation. When she sent a copy of the *Rights of Woman* to Schnepfenthal in 1792, a translation appeared that same year, accompanied by Salzmann's *Einleitung* and thirty-seven footnotes. The paratext constitutes a critical commentary on the *Rights of Woman*, which at times supports and at times gainsays Wollstonecraft's ideas. The translator, Weissenborn, was a twenty-eight-year-old teacher at Schnepfenthal. In 1796, he married Salzmann's daughter, Wilhelmine, and in 1800 published an article "Über die bisherige Zurücksetzung des weiblichen Geschlechts", arguing for improvements in the condition of women. It seems that Revolutionary feminist demands found a sympathetic ear in Weissenborn. Whatever his readerly response might have been, however, his position as Salzmann's employee and his ideological context combined to curtail his freedom as a translator.

Unlike Britain and France, the German nation did not see any significant protest against female disenfranchisement until 1800. Although some few of the various states, principalities, and duchies were reasonably enlightened, many were still autocratic and would not have permitted the sale or reprinting of a feminist text within their borders, particularly if the local censors considered it seditious. In such a climate, Salzmann appears progressive in publishing a translation of the *Rights of Woman* at all; but his paratext marks him out as less radical than Wollstonecraft, who addressed the original English text to Talleyrand, the president of the French National Assembly.

Wollstonecraft argued that in the wake of the Revolution, men were freer, while women were still everywhere in chains. She envisaged a future for women as rational and desiring subjects and politically-active citizens, calling for improvements in female education, honesty in sexual relationships, and parliamentary representation for women. Salzmann cut the dedication to Talleyrand and used his *Einleitung* to circumscribe the feminist message intended for the German readership. Like Wollstonecraft, he equates the balance of power between the ruler and the ruled to that between husband and wife. It behoves each despot, he argues, to teach his subordinates to think rationally. This is an ingenious case for improving female education, but it also allows Salzmann to undercut Wollstonecraft's demand that women learn to live independently, by suggesting that the proper maintenance of the private and political status quo will benefit their education.

During the Revolution, which consolidated the idea of the bourgeois family as a microcosmic state, the mother became a symbolic guarantor of the social order, her devotion to maternal duty ensuring the physical and moral soundness of her children. Women were seen as cogs in the socio-political machine, granted or denied rights according to their impact on others. Underpinned by these ideas, Salzmann's highly pedagogical "Einleitung" presents *Rettung der Rechte* as a conduct-book for men educating female dependents to safeguard domestic tranquillity. This pedagogical focus, both in the "Einleitung" and in a series of substantial footnotes, characterises Salzmann as a progressive educationalist but belies the political thrust of the original text. He hopes that *Rettung der Rechte* "bey vielen Weibern und Maedchen, Gefühl ihrer Würde wirken, und sie zu dem Entschlüsse bringen möge, die ehrenvolle Stufe zu behaupten, zu welcher sie der

Schöpfer benimmt hat, Freundinnen, Rathgeberinnen, Freudgeberinnen, dem Manne, kluge Wirthinnen ihrem Hause, Erzieherinnen und Muster ihren Kindern zu seyn."[4] (1: xix) In other words, women are encouraged to fulfil their current duties virtuously and rationally, and not to challenge their place in the social order.

Although Salzmann often endorses and expands Wollstonecraft's pedagogical ideas, he admits that he also uses his footnotes to dissent from her most controversial statements. When Wollstonecraft "declare[s] against all power built on prejudices" (5: 170), for instance, he intervenes to restore confidence in her agenda:

> Man stösse sich nicht an diese starken Ausdrücke! Wenn man weiter lieset: so wird man finden, dass es die Verfasserin nicht so böse meynt, als es das Ansehn hat.[5] (2: 31-32)

Salzmann goes on to claim that Wollstonecraft is incapable of advocating total independence for women, vehemently reaffirming the role of the husband as "der Versorger, der Schutz der Familie!". Calming his male readers' fears of emasculation, he goes on to reassure them that Wollstonecraft "eifert nur gegen jene entehrende Abhängigkeit, durch welche das Weib nur zum Ziele sinnlicher Wünsche und zur schönen Sclaven gemacht wird".[6] (2: 31) The footnote closes with a narrower definition of the terms at stake than Wollstonecraft's original text offers, so that "Unabhängigkeit" ["independence"] is understood as freedom from slavery, rather than personal and economic self-determination. Salzmann's footnotes dominate the page, so that his counter-arguments are often developed more extensively than the arguments of Wollstonecraft's original text. The textual debate is therefore weighted heavily in his favour.

The cumulative effect of the footnotes is such that the reader experiences a hybrid text, rather than a political manifesto. Three voices emerge from the translation: Wollstonecraft, the author; Weissenborn, the translator; and Salzmann, the editor and commentator. The struggle for dominance between these voices radically re-shapes Wollstonecraft's text. Readers in Germany and the Netherlands therefore experienced, not the *Rights of Woman*, but a manifestly different text from the English original.

Working in tandem with Salzmann, Weissenborn frequently tones down the original text, inserting qualifying adjectives to dilute divisive passages. Wollstonecraft makes her conception of "masculine women" clear in the "Introduction":

> If by this appellation men mean to inveigh against their ardour in hunting, shooting, and gaming, I shall most cordially join in the cry; but if it be against the imitation of manly virtues, or, more properly speaking, the attainment of those talents and virtues, the exercise of which ennobles the human character, and which raise females in the scale of animal being, when they are comprehensively termed mankind; - all those who view them with a philosophical eye must, I should think, wish with me, that they may every day grow more and more masculine. (5: 74)

In Weissenborn's translation, the call for "more and more masculine" women sounds less provocative by virtue of the qualifying phrase "in diesem Sinne" ["in this sense"], which emphasises that this masculinity should be confined to "those talents and virtues, the exercise of which ennobles the human character." (1: 7) Similarly, when Wollstonecraft claims "I may be allowed to doubt whether woman were created for man" (5: 148), Weissenborn inserts the qualifying adjective "bloss" ["simply"] which dampens Wollstonecraft's fiery statement and aligns her prose more easily with the softness thought natural to women: "so wird man mir doch erlauben, den Satz, dass das Weib bloss um des Mannes Willen geschaffen sey, für's erste noch zu bezweifeln" ["for a start, I may be allowed to call into question the statement that woman was created simply for the sake of man"]. (1: 288)

Conclusion

Where Weissenborn's translation fails to subdue Wollstonecraft's feminism, Salzmann's "Einleitung" and footnotes mitigate or dissent from her most revolutionary statements. The net result is a German version of the *Rights of Woman* which, while appearing to engage in dialogue with Wollstonecraft, diminishes her radicalism. It was this enfeebled text that Van Hamelsveld encountered. It is clear that *Rettung der Rechte des Weibes* influenced his perception of Wollstonecraft's feminism and, as a result, the version of the *Rights of Woman* made available to the Dutch readership. By contrast, the anonymous French creator of *Défense des droits des femmes* makes Wollstonecraft's feminism even more radical, on the whole, than that of the *Rights of Woman*. His translational strategy reflects the utopian spirit of the early days of the French Revolution. The cosmopolitan ethos of the Enlightenment ostensibly ensures that Wollstonecraft's feminist ideas cross national and linguistic borders, but as they meet and clash with the diverse ideologies and political systems of 18th-century Europe, the distinctive language of her Revolutionary feminism is transformed. Consequently, her emancipatory message is at times amplified and at times subdued, but always distorted.

Bibliography

Défense des droits des femmes, suivie de quelques considerations sur des sujets politiques et Moraux. Paris: Buisson, 1792.

Godwin, William. *Memoirs of the Author of the Rights of Woman, A Short Residence in Sweden and Memoirs of the Author of "The Rights of Woman"*. Ed. Richard Holmes. London: Penguin, 1987.

Kloek, Joost and Wijnand Mijnhardt. *1800: Blueprints for a National Community*. Basingstoke and New York: Palgrave Macmillan, 2004 (translation of: *1800: Blauwdrukken voor een samenleving*. The Hague: Sdu, 2001).

"Maria Wollstonecraft. Verdediging van de Rechten der Vrouwen. Benevens Aanmerkingen over Burgerlyke en Zedelyke Onderwerpen. Uit het Engelsch, volgends den IIden Druk. Met Aantekeningen en eene Voorreden van Christiaan Gotthilf Salzman. Door Ysbrand Van Hamelsveld. Eerste Deel. In den Haag, by J. C. Leeuwestyn, 1796." *Vaderlandsche Letteroefeningen*, 1797, vol. VII-1, 343-349.

Poovey, Mary. *The Proper Lady and the Woman Writer: ideology as style in the works of Mary Wollstonecraft, Mary Shelley and Jane Austen*. Chicago and London: Chicago University Press, 1984.

Salzmann, Christian Gotthilf, ed. *Moralishes Elementarbuch*. Trans. Georg Friedrich Christian Weissenborn. 2 vols. Schepfenthal: Verlag der Erziehungsanstalt: 1792.

Sapiro, Virginia. *A Vindication of Political Virtue*. Chicago: University of Chicago Press, 1992.

Wollstonecraft, Mary. *Works*. Eds. Janet Todd and Marilyn Butler. 7 vols. London: Pickering and Chatto, 1981.

Notes

1 "Men are not always men in the company of women, nor would women always remember that they are women, if custom permitted them to acquire more good sense and knowledge."

2 See, for example, Mary Poovey's *The Proper Lady and the Woman Writer* and Virginia Sapiro's *A Vindication of Political Virtue*.

3 Ibid., 347.

4 "[…] prompts a feeling of dignity in many women and girls, and might make them decide to claim the noble roles for which the creator destined them, to be friends, advisors, joy-givers of man, sensible managers of their households, educators and models for their children."

[5] "Do not be offended by these strong expressions! If you read on: then you will find that the authoress's meaning is not as wicked as it seems."

[6] "He is after all the provider, the protector of the family! She only inveighs against that degrading dependence, through which the woman is merely made into a lovely slave and object of lascivious desires."

Stephanie Walker and Suzan van Dijk (Universiteit Utrecht)

What Literary Historians 'Forgot': American Women Authors in the 19th-Century Netherlands

In 1982 J.G. Riewald and J. Bakker published *The Critical Reception of American Literature in the Netherlands 1824-1900*. At the time, reception studies were still referred to in German as "Rezeptionsforschung" and were only starting to be recognized "as an important part of comparative studies" (6). The authors did have some predecessors who had worked on the reception of American literature in Germany and Russia, but were quite confident that their book-length study on the Netherlands was the first of its kind, unique in its scope and approach in an until then "much neglected field" (1). Right at the beginning of their preface, Riewald and Bakker make substantial claims regarding their project: "The purpose of this book is to explore the contemporaneous recognition of American literature in 19th-century Dutch periodicals and to assess its quality." (1) They specifically emphasize that "in order to present a realistic picture of the Dutch response, it was vital to aim at *complete coverage*" (1, our italics). In the remainder of the preface, the authors continue to make reference to the uniqueness of their study, emphasising the inclusiveness of their research. They call it a "systematic presentation and analysis of a hitherto unexplored wealth of data" (3) in which "all known translations, including subsequent printings [...] have been recorded" (2). They also describe the way in which they have proceeded:

> To locate the documentary evidence – mainly reviews, many of them anonymous and untitled, and scattered in defunct journals – we have read through the relevant magazines of the period, most of which had apparently not been so scrutinized by other investigators, and printed *all* those materials that seemed to be of *any* importance. (1, our italics)

This commitment to completeness and to thorough research will have inspired confidence. The book has long been (and possibly still is) considered as an important source of information regarding the reception of American literature in the Netherlands. In fact, research carried out in the context of a preceding phase of our own project concerning the presence of foreign women's writing in the Netherlands, had also used this book in order to account for the international female context surrounding and possibly inspiring Dutch women who wanted to become authors.[1]

However, since 1982 book history and reception studies have continued to develop, in particular since the expansion of the *WomenWriters* database (since 2004[2]), which made evidence concerning women authors' international reception more easily accessible. So much so that comparison between the listings provided in Riewald and Bakker's book and the present content of this database reveals that quite a number of traces of Dutch reception of American writers are, for one reason or another, lacking in this 'complete' inventory. The question to be discussed in this contribution, then, is double:

(1) as we are concerned with the reception of *women* authors, we need to investigate whether the work of these two male researchers is possibly gender biased as they were working in a period when issues regarding gender were less prominent than they are in 2008;

(2) as this Riewald-Bakker case is probably not an exception, what is the value, in this electronic age, of older 'hand-made' inventories which we still might want to use, and which might indeed be important enough to be transposed into online databases?[3]

American women authors in the Netherlands

The Critical Reception of American Literature is basically an inventory, per author, of references to articles published in the Dutch literary and 'general/cultural' press between 1824 and 1900. In a general introduction, the authors present their approach and comment on the most striking results (5-38), in particular a 'ranking' in which Harriet Beecher Stowe "with sixty reviews and articles to her name, scores the highest number of Dutch contributions devoted to a 19th-century American writer" (10), while Herman Melville and Edgar Allan Poe seem to be neglected (for each of them only two articles had been found (28)). The authors provide a list (39-297) containing references to, and "critical synopses" of, the 360 articles that had been found in 36 periodicals. For each American author there is also "a preliminary checklist of Dutch translations", established in part thanks to the review articles, most of which concern Dutch versions of the works and provide references to the translations commented upon. The list contains 37 American authors whose works had been received in the Netherlands.

The number of women authors included in this list seems small: *six* out of the 37; 60 out of the 360 articles discuss their works. It may be objected that proportions do not differ very much from those on the production side: the online *American Literature Anthology Writers' Index* mentions 53 names of authors, born between 1750 and 1850, who may be supposed to have been active during the 19th century – ten of whom are women[4]. However, the recent increase of authors' names referenced in the database *WomenWriters*, as well as Riewald/Bakker's insistence on completeness,[5] has necessitated comparison: therefore, let us have a look at the details, in both listings, concerning women.

Table 1:
Female authors referenced by Riewald and Bakker

Names (list 1982)	*articles in the literary press*	*translations*	*period concerned*
Sedgwick, Catharine Maria	**3**	**2**	**1837-1841**
Sedgwick, Susan Ann Livingston	**1**	**1**	**1840**
Stowe, Harriet Beecher	**60**	**36**	**1852-1896**
Alcott, Louisa May	**14**	**37**[6]	**1873-1897**
Phelps, Elisabeth Stuart	**1**	**1**	**1900**
Hitchcock, Mary E.	**1**	–	**1900**

To begin with, *The Critical Reception of American Literature* lists 60 articles about the ever famous Harriet Beecher Stowe (1811-1896), and 14 on Louisa May Alcott (1832-1888), whose work is also still in print and requested by readers even now. As stated in the introduction, Stowe is regarded to be more popular than authors such as James Fenimore Cooper, Longfellow, Emerson and Hawthorne, while Alcott is on the same level as Mark Twain and still within the ten most 'popular' (with the Dutch public) American authors. The four other women would have been much less commented on in the Dutch press: three articles about Catherine Sedgwick

(1789-1867) and one for each of the following three: Susan Sedgwick (1788-1867), Elizabeth Stuart Phelps (1844-1911) and Mary Hitchcock (publishing *Two Women in the Klondike* in 1899). It is perhaps important to briefly note that certain male writers (nine in fact) also received only one article…

On the other hand, it is noteworthy that such names as Maria Susanna Cummins (1827-1866, author of *The Lamplighter*) and Fanny Fern (1811-1872) are lacking. Indeed, to anyone more or less familiar with Dutch 19th-century library successes, or with the literary taste of leading critic Conrad Busken Huet, it seems difficult to admit that neither Cummins nor Fern would have found any response in the Dutch press. And indeed, the *WomenWriters* database does inform us about the actual presence of their names in the Dutch press: their works are mentioned, commented upon, and discussed in several of the very periodicals perused by Riewald and Bakker: *Tijdspiegel* and *Vaderlandsche Letteroefeningen*.

Database outcome

Cummins and Fern are not the only ones missing: information included as of November 2007 in the *WomenWriters* database has provided the following overview of American women writers' presence in the 19th-century Netherlands. Table 2 follows the chronological order of publication of Dutch commentaries.

This overview shows a substantial increase. According to these data, between 1838 and 1899, 21 women authors had articles published about themselves, or were mentioned in articles discussing other authors, or even subjects other than those regarding American literature. Stowe, Alcott and Sedgwick still remain 'leaders', but it appears now that the two authors searched for in vain, Cummins and Fern, did in fact generate response with Dutch critics. Clearly, the corpus analysed is not identical with Riewald and Bakker's,[7] as two of their authors are not present in this list (Susan Sedgwick and Mary E. Hitchcock).

Why these 17 names have been left out is not clear. The articles about them were, again, published in those very periodicals which Riewald and Bakker used and included in their list (329-336): *De Gids*, *De Portefeuille*, *De Tijd*, *Nederlandsche Spectator*, among other. Were the authors not really interested in women's literature? A broad and quite informative article they had found about "Woman in North American Literature", written by the

Table 2:
American WomenWriters' presence in the 19th-century Dutch press, as referenced in the WomenWriters database (November 2007)

Names	*number of articles/ mentions in general/ literary press*	*period concerned*
Reed, Rebecca Theresa	2 art.	1838
Sigourney, Lydia	1 ment.	1838
Sedgwick, Catharine Maria	**8 art./1 ment.**	**1838-1855**
Macintosh, Maria Jane	4 art./1 ment.	1852-1859
James, Maria	1 art.	1852
Wheatley, Phyllis	1 art.	1852
Stowe, Harriet Beecher	**29 art./25 ment.**	**1853-1887**
Warner, Susan Bogert	2 art./2 ment.	1855-1863
Southworth, Emma D. E. Nevitte	1 art.	1855
Pike, Mary Hayden	2 art.	1855
Hale, Lucretia Peabody	1 ment.	1855
Parton, Sarah Payson Willis (Fern Fanny)	4 art./3 ment.	1857-1872
Cummins, Maria Susanna	3 art./2 ment.	1858-1865
Dorr, Julia Caroline Ripley	1 art.	1858
Lothrop, Amy	1 ment.	1858
Lewis, Harriet O'Brien	2 art./2 ment.	1872-1882
Alcott, Louisa May	**14 art./4 ment**	**1873-1899**
Prentiss, Elizabeth	2 art./1 ment.	1873-1876
Whitney, Adeline Dutton Train	1 art.	1875
Campbell Deland, Margaret Wade	2 art.	1890
Phelps, Elisabeth Stuart	**1 art.**	**1890**

American poet Helen Gray Cone (1859-1934) and presented in Dutch translation in *De Portefeuille* in 1891, is only abstracted and not used – as could have been done – to provide a context for their six women's names. Cone's 25 supplementary names of women authors are merely documented in their footnotes (306-309), but Riewald and Bakker simply dismiss some of her statements about them, considering these to have been "inspired by feminist zeal rather than by a balanced judgment" (29).

So possibly, we must indeed dare to speak of a gender bias in this book.[8] It seems manifest in the introduction, where the most important texts are highlighted in different ways, depending on gender. Riewald and

Bakker show a tendency towards comparing articles on male authors to modern, positive, appreciation: 19th-century reactions to Walt Whitman for instance, "sound surprisingly modern" in their "broadminded and understanding attitude toward Whitman's supposed immorality" (20), while D.E.W. Wolff's "evaluation of Emerson as thinker and essayist still makes eminent sense" (21). For the female authors, those articles where a negative slant is predominant seem to receive more attention. Considering probably that their works are now outdated, the authors cite an 1853 comment of the *Leeskabinet*, which claimed that *Uncle Tom's Cabin* "as a work of art, shows serious flows. There is no unity" (10). Also, an 1879 article from the same journal about Alcott is quoted: "The plot [of *Work*] lacks harmony and unity, while the style is vulgar" (24). So much so that these two male historians, probably unhelped by sisters or daughters[9] and in complete innocence as to recent editions, state "that her [Alcott's] fame did not last much beyond the 19th century, neither in her own country, nor in the Netherlands" (24). The gender-bias is probably not particular to them, and may also be a sign of their adherence to the established literary canon, which kept them from recognizing those works whose existence they did not know of before.[10]

Anyway, it is evident from their own material that women – Dutch women in particular – had played a certain role. Although translators' names are often unknown, clearly an important proportion of the translating – about 25 % – is known to have been done by women: Aleida Doedes and H. Koorders-Boeke, for instance, were particularly productive, translating books by men and women, from English as well as other languages. This could have invited Riewald and Bakker to not only to consider the general press, but also the female and feminist press, which was then emerging in the Netherlands.[11] It could have, but clearly it did not and it is fair also to accept the fact that their focus was different from that of the *WomenWriters* database.

By the inclusion of a third list based on the *present* content (July 2008) of this database, we want to show that in order to approach something like 'completeness' it can be important, in reception studies, not to restrict the sources to one type – such as the 'critical reception' –, but to also include other categories of evidence, which can complement the overall impression.

Table 3:
American women writers' presence in the 19th-century Netherlands (press and translations), as referenced in *the WomenWriters database* (July 2008)

Names	articles/ mentions in the press	translations[12]	presence in library	*period concerned*
Reed, Rebecca Theresa	2	1	–	1837-1838
Sedgwick, Catharine Maria	**9**	**2**	**–**	**1837-1855**
Sigourney, Lydia	1	1	–	1838
Sedgwick, Susan Ann Livingston	***1***	***1***	**–**	***1840***
Kirkland, Caroline Matilda Stansbury	*2*	–	–	*1841-1842*
Ward, Maria	*2*	–	–	*1851*
Macintosh, Maria Jane	5	4	3	1851-1859
James, Maria	1	–	–	1852
Lippincott, Sarah Jane	*1*	–	–	*1852*
Moreton, Clara	*2*	–	–	*1852*
Wheatley, Phyllis	1	–	–	1852
Stowe, Harriet Beecher	**97**	**22**	**31**	**1852-1896**
Southworth, E.D.E.N.	1	3	3	1854-1861
Cummins, Maria Susanna	5	5	10	1854-1886
Pike, Mary Hayden	2	2	3	1855-1860
Hale, Lucretia Peabody	1	–	–	1855
Parton, Sarah Payson Willis (Fern, F.)	14	8	12	1855-1886
Warner, Susan Bogert	4	4	10	1855-1866
Dorr, Julia Caroline Ripley	1	1	1	1858-1859
Lothrop, Amy	1	–	–	1858
Lewis, Harriet O'Brien	4	4	4	1859-1882
Evans Wilson, Augusta Jane	–	*1*	*1*	*1860-1861*
Prentiss, Elizabeth	3	2	–	1871-1876
Phelps, Elisabeth Stuart	**4**	**2**	**–**	**1871-1900**
Alcott, Louisa May	**31**	**17**	**16**	**1873-1899**
Whitney, Adeline Dutton Train	1	–	–	1875
Paton, Agnes	*1*	–	–	*1886*
Campbell Deland, Margaret Wade	2	1	1	1889-1896
Cone, Helen Gray	*1*	–	–	*1891*
Barnett, Edith A.	–	*1*	*1*	*1895-1900*
Gilman, Charlotte Perkins	–	*1*	–	*1899*
Hitchcock, Mary E.	***1***	**–**	**–**	***1900***

Compared to Riewald and Bakker's initial list of six authors as well as to the previous database listing containing 21 authors' names, this table again shows a considerable increase of and contains no less than 32 names. The two most appreciated authors are visibly maintaining their position, but it is less and less clear why the four other authors were selected, rather than Susan Warner or Maria Jane Macintosh.

The new figures are more impressive for several reasons. Firstly, a greater variety of source materials have been included. In particular, the database includes publications from the women's press, as well as translations that were published not as volumes but in the periodical press (addressing the general public as well as female audiences). This provides a more complete impression, although further analysis with regard to specific authors is still needed. What we show in the rest of the paper are just two short examples that might further illustrate our argument. Secondly, the information as provided by Riewald and Bakker has, of course, also been included in this database – the principle being that any information be integrated, with due reference to its origins. Still, this is certainly a provisional view of the matter. In the near future it will, for instance be possible to also benefit from online accessible daily newspapers, which must be considered to provide further evidence.

Fanny Fern (1811-1872) and Maria Susanna Cummins (1827-1866)

In this last section we want to show the relevance of pursuing an account complete as possible of the reception of 19th-century American women's literature in the Netherlands – and in particular of going beyond relatively 'innocent' cases as those of Harriet Beecher Stowe (about whose work the consensus was global) and of Louisa Alcott (addressing young girls). By way of examples, we will discuss very briefly some aspects of the Dutch reception of Fanny Fern and Maria Susanna Cummins. Their published output was considerably smaller than those of Stowe, Alcott and others, which of course contributed to their apparently 'smaller' reception, and must be kept in mind in order to understand the figures. These observations, based on the present database content, are supposed to show how this database provides a first overview and stepping stone for further research.

We are following Nina Baym's interpretation of American women's fiction of the period 1820-1870, which she presents as "a protest against long-entrenched trivializing and contemptuous views of women that animated the fiction of Richardson and other later 18th-century fiction of sensibility" (29). These authors were so numerous that Nathaniel Hawthorne complained that

> America is now wholly given over to a d–d mob of scribbling women, and I should have no chance of success while the public taste is occupied with their trash – and should be ashamed of myself if I did succeed. What is the mystery of these innumerable editions of the *Lamplighter*, and other books neither better nor worse? – worse they could not be, and better they need not be, when they sell by 100,000.[13]

The situation in the Netherlands was completely different and critics were bound to be surprised at the great number of women writing in the United States (as well as in other countries). In the Netherlands, women generally did not write with the express goal to earn money,[14] while in contrast "most of the American authors were middle-class women who needed money. As a general rule […] only middle-class women had sufficient education to know how to write books, and only those who needed money attempted it" (30). Because of this, it is not surprising that "most of their heroines had to support themselves and often dependents as well for some period of time. Examples of professional women, such as teachers and authors, are found in the fiction frequently and are presented with the greatest respect and admiration" (28). The content of these novels could have been seen as conflicting with dominant Dutch customs and practices of the time. It is therefore important to know whether the reception of these authors was indeed so limited, or if their works may have contributed to the first feminist wave, visible also in the Netherlands at the end of the 19th century.

Maria Susanna Cummins, the author of *The Lamplighter* (1854) and whom Hawthorne did not admire, was also very successful in the Netherlands. All four of her novels were translated immediately, but especially *The Lamplighter* was reprinted many times, well into the 20th century; was translated time and again, and adapted into a version for children. Copies of her books were present in the commercial library of the Van der Hoek brothers in Leiden – not only in Dutch, the original English versions and French translations were present as well. *The Lamplighter* was also, somewhat later, part of the collection of the Ladies Reading Museum in Amsterdam.

Critics did not always agree with the general preferences of the readers for *The Lamplighter*. For example, in the *Vaderlandsche Letteroefeningen*, Cummins' second novel, *Mabel Vaughan*, received higher praise.[15] In the same periodical, *Haunted Hearts* was predominantly appreciated because the subject of love was approached and treated differently than in French novels. Cummins' work is admired for its "pure, thoroughly healthy morality" and for the "powerfully sound religious life," that "speaks to us from almost every page".[16] At least from these references it seems clear that there was little attention for what Baym considers to have been Cummins' intention: "to persuade women that she is responsible for saving herself and equal to the demand" (166).

With regard to Fanny Fern, the information that is now available in the *WomenWriters* database tells the following story. Her newspaper columns, which were collected and published in book form from 1853 onwards, were quite popular with the Dutch readers. Starting in 1855, translations of these collections were also available. The same was true regarding her novels, *Ruth Hall* (1855) and *Rose Clark* (1856). Both appeared in Dutch translations (by still unknown translators) in the same years as their American publication. The magazine *Europa* published her texts regularly between 1856 and 1875. Eight copies of her books were present in the Van der Hoek commercial library, both in translation and the original English version. The later established women's libraries in The Hague and Amsterdam also carried her work. It is interesting to note here that the library in The Hague, which was certainly more sophisticated than the one in Amsterdam, however, did not carry Cummins' work.

At the time, various translators – positively evaluated by critics – were publishing Fern in Dutch, and as a result several volumes were published. Some of these may have contained, at least partially, the same texts. Fern's writings for children were published in 1856 in a translation by the well-known poet J.J.A. Goeverneur. As there appeared to be a female audience who appreciated Fern's writing, there were also several women who took it upon themselves to translate her work. This is perhaps not surprising in view of the way Fanny Fern presented herself in her preface:

> I never had the slightest intention of writing a book. Had such a thought entered my mind, I should not long have entertained it. It would have seemed presumptuous. What! *I*, Fanny Fern, write a book? I never could have believed it possible. [...] (v)

Here it is clear that she is parodying the longstanding topos of feminine modesty – and it is important to keep in mind that she and her two children lived from her pen, and quite well at that, due to the success of her writing.[17]

One of Fern's women translators was the wife of Conrad Busken Huet, Anne van der Tholl. She had also decided to use her pen to earn money and was greatly enthusiastic about *Fern Leaves*. She was, however, *really* insecure, which allowed for her husband to intervene in the translation to such an extent that it was eventually published under his name.[18] This, in turn, strongly suggests that he himself was also interested in Fern's work.

Dutch reviewers emphasized the American roots and Fern's work was favourably compared to fiction coming from France. The perceived difference between American and Dutch women is implicitly present: the Dutch publishers are urged "to offer the masculine work of the American beauties to our own women and girls, who are fortunately still feminine".[19] In 1859, reviews stated that "Fanny Fern, for quite some time now, has become familiar to us", and that "her multi-faceted talent, her utterly captivating style, her insightful view into human nature, and especially her fine, deep sense of humor that so masterfully plays the stings of our hearts, has found numerous Dutch admirers."[20] Many of these admirers were women: the feminist journal *Ons Streven* regularly praised Fern's work in the 1870s and valued, more than other periodicals, her "portrayal of a woman as the self-reliant American individualist," as well as the fact that *Ruth Hall* ends, not with the protagonist's marriage, "but with her acquisition of ten thousand dollars in bank stock" (Warren 2). Both contemporaneous periodicals, *Ons Streven* and *Onze Roeping*, were of the opinion that women had the right to an independent income derived from their work. Fern served as a good role model indeed. However, it is relevant to note that men also wrote for these women's journals: sometimes they clearly felt under attack by Fern's writing.[21]

To be continued

It is clear that these two women writers cannot be missed in a survey of American literary presence in 19th-century Netherlands. This is what the increase in the number of sources leads us to conclude. However, this increase in sources also makes research more complex. What we have shown here is just a beginning; even more so as the database *WomenWriters* continues to accumulate data.

Bibliography

Baym, Nina. *Woman's Fiction. A Guide to Novels by and about Women in America 1820-70.* 2nd ed. Chicago: University of Illinois Press, 1993. [1st ed. Ithaca: Cornell University Press, 1978.]

Fern, Fanny. *Fern Leaves from Fanny's Portfolio.* Auburn: Durby and Miller, 1853.

Fleming, Bill, *Sources in American literature.* Sam Houston State University. 5 July 2008 <http://www.shsu.edu/~eng_wpf/amlit-sources.html>.

Jensen, Lotte. "*Bij uitsluiting voor de vrouwelijke sekse geschikt.*" *Vrouwentijdschriften en journalistes in Nederland in de achttiende en negentiende eeuw.* Hilversum: Verloren, 2001.

NEWW project (New approaches to European Women's Writing, dir. Suzan van Dijk). *Women Writers' Networks.* Utrecht, Igitur Utrecht Publishing & Archiving <http://www.womenwriters.nl>.

Praamstra, Olf. *Busken Huet. Een biografie.* Amsterdam: SUN, 2007.

Riewald, J.G. and J. Bakker, eds. *The Critical Reception of American Literature in the Netherlands 1824-1900. A Documentary Conspectus from Contemporary Periodicals.* Amsterdam: Rodopi, 1982.

Visser, Irene. "American women writers in the Dutch literary world 1824-1900." *"I have heard about you". Foreign women's writing crossing the Dutch border: from Sappho to Selma Lagerlöf.* Eds. Suzan van Dijk, et al. Hilversum: Verloren, 2004. 281-299.

Warren, Joyce. *Fanny Fern: An Independent Woman.* New Brunswick, NJ: Rutgers University Press, 1992.

Notes

[1] See, for example, Irene Visser's essay on "American women writers in the Dutch literary world".

[2] Thanks to the digitizing project "The International Reception of Women's Writing", funded by the Netherlands Organisation for Scientific Research (NWO) from 2004 until 2007. In this context a number of Dutch large-scale reception sources was perused and data were integrated in the database. See also the introductory article of the present section.

[3] Actually, at the Huygens Institute in The Hague, a project is now being prepared that aims to digitize information found in Dutch literary press of 1760-1840 and stored in a card system prepared in the 1960s and 70s.

[4] *Sources in American literature.* This list corresponds, of course, to present perspectives on the literary canon: 12 out of the 31 male authors received in the 19th-century Netherlands do *not* figure there, for example.

[5] The "completeness" is qualified by the scrutinizing of "well over a hundred and fifty Dutch periodicals", of which "thirty-six were found to yield material of interest. The most important of these [sixteen] have been selected for inclusion" in an "Annotated list", in order "give the reader an adequate idea of their character and quality" (329).

[6] Translations were also checked checked in national library catalogues, which explains the important numbers.

[7] For information about the sources used, see the section on "Sources" on the corresponding website: *Women Writers' Networks.*

[8] Probably the category of male authors has equally suffered, see for example the difference between the Riewald-Bakker list and the online presentation of American literature (n. 4).

[9] Exceptions do exist, however. Berteke Waaldijk, studying the authorship of Anne Frank, held the female gaze of the German translator responsible for the detection of an important female influence on her diary: the one exerted by a Dutch woman author, writing for girls, Cissy van Marxveldt, in particular by her *De H.B.S. tijd van Joop ter Heul*, published in

1919, and still in print today (cf. Berteke Waaldijk, "Reading Anne Frank as a Woman", in *Women's Studies International Forum* (Autumn 1993), and reprinted in: Hyman A. Enzer and Sandra Solotaroff-Enzer (eds.), *Anne Frank. Reflections on Her Life and Legacy* (Chicago/Urbana: UIP, 2000. 110-120).. Later on Gerrold van der Stroom demonstrated that in fact Theodor Holman was the one who discovered the link between Van Marxveldt and Frank (cf. Gerrold van der Stroom, *De vele gezichten van Anne Frank; visies op een fenomeen*, (Amsterdam: De Prom, 2003. 106-122)). We thank Monica Soeting for these details.

[10] Most of these novelists were presented and discussed in Nina Baym's *Woman's Fiction. A Guide to Novels by and about Women in America 1820-70*, the first edition of which had been published (Cornell University Press) in 1978; the second (University of Illinois Press) in 1993.

[11] Admittedly, this press was not yet much studied in 1982. See Jensen *"Bij uitsluiting voor de vrouwelijke sekse geschikt". Vrouwentijdschriften en journalistes in Nederland in de achttiende en negentiende eeuw*. Hilversum: Verloren, 2001.

[12] Figures according to current database content, not yet systematically checked in national library catalogues.

[13] Letter to his publisher and friend William D. Ticknor on January 19, 1855.

[14] There were some exceptions, such as Barbara van Meerten-Schilperoort.

[15] *Vaderlandsche Letteroefeningen* (1859-1): 91.

[16] "Zuivere, door en door gezonde moraal zit er niet *op*, maar *in* de gansche voorstelling. [...] Krachtig, gezond godsdienstig leven spreekt ons bijna van elke bladzijde toe" (*Vaderlandsche Letteroefeningen* (1865-1): 437).

[17] It is also important to realize that Hawthorne, after getting to Fanny Fern's work, partially retracted his previous statement regarding the "scribbling women": "In my last, I recollect, I bestowed some vituperation on female authors. I have since been reading *Ruth Hall*; and I must say I enjoyed it a good deal. The woman writes as if the devil was in her; and that is the only condition under which a woman ever writes anything worth reading. [...] Can you tell me anything about this Fanny Fern? If you meet her, I wish you would let her know how much I admire her" (Letter to William Ticknor, 1855, quoted in Warren (1).

[18] See Praamstra's *Busken Huet* (217).

[19] "Wat mij betreft, men ga gerust voort, mits niet al te doldriftig om den mannelijken arbeid der Amerikaansche schoonen, aan onze, gelukkig nog vrouwelijke, vrouwen en meisjes aan te bieden" (*Vaderlandsche Letteroefeningen* (1857-1): 244-45).

[20] "Al is gelukkig Fanny Fern ook sinds lang geene vreemde meer in ons midden; al heeft haar veelzijdig talent, haar uiterst boeijende schrijftrant, haar geoefende menschkundige blik en vooral haar fijne, diepe humor, waardoor zij zoo meesterlijk de toetsen van ons hart weet te bespelen, reeds sinds geruimen tijd ook hier te lande eene menigte bewonderaars uitgelokt [...]" (*Vaderlandsche Letteroefeningen* (1859-1): 189).

[21] *Ons Streven* (25 May 1870, 75): "[...] ik heb werkelijk eene ernstige beschuldiging tegen Fanny Fern in te brengen. Ik beschuldig haar namelijk van onrechtvaardigheid jegens de mannen. [...]". See also Jensen (205).

Contributors

Susanna De Schepper studied English and German language and literature at the Katholieke Universiteit Brussel (2002-2004) and the Katholieke Universiteit Leuven (2004-2006). For her MA in Book and Digital Media Studies at Leiden University (2006-2007) she focussed on book and publishing history. She is currently a Ph.D. student at the University of Warwick's Centre for the Study of the Renaissance, researching the social networks surrounding English translations of navigation manuals (1500-1640).

Lieven D'hulst teaches modern French and Francophone literatures and translation studies at the Katholieke Universiteit Leuven. He has published widely on French and Belgian Francophone literature in general, translation studies, Shakespeare in French translation (with D. Delabastita) and on French Caribbean literature.

Lizet Duyvendak studied Dutch language and literature at the University of Utrecht. Since 1984 she has worked at Open Universiteit Nederland, where she currently holds a senior lectureship in literature and cultural studies. Her current research focuses on 19th- and 20th-century literature, in particular women's literature and the history of reading. *Door lezen wijder horizont, het Haags Damesleesmuseum* was awarded the Victoria van Schaick Prize in 2004.

Laura Kirkley studied English and Modern Languages at the University of Oxford. She is currently pursuing doctoral studies at the University of Cambridge. Her research draws on contemporary theories of translation, feminism, and cosmopolitanism to situate Mary Wollstonecraft's work as a linguistic and cultural translator in the context of Revolutionary Europe. She also considers Wollstonecraft's translation and reception in Europe in the 18th and 19th centuries.

Cees Koster teaches translation studies and English translation at the University of Utrecht. His research focuses on 19th-century translation history. In 2002 he published *De Hollandsche vertaalmolen. Nederlandse beschouwingen over vertalen, 1820-1885* (Reeks vertaalhistorie, deel 5a) and (with Ton Naaijkens) *Een vorm van lezen. Nederlandse beschouwingen over vertalen, 1885-1946* (Reeks vertaalhistorie deel 5b). He also publishes on Shakespeare in Dutch translation and children's literature in translation. He is member of the editorial board of the Dutch journal on translation *Filter*.

Francis Mus is research assistant at the Katholieke Universiteit Leuven. He is preparing a Ph.D. on the dynamics (cultural transfers, identity construction, literary dialogues) of modernism and historical avant-garde literature in Belgian literary magazines. Within that framework, the position of language, bilingualism and translated literature constitute a crucial research item

Kris Steyaert is Senior Lecturer in Dutch literature at the University of Liège. He obtained his Ph.D. at University College London with a dissertation on P.B. Shelley and Willem Kloos. His research interests include British Romanticism, the Eighties Movement (Tachtigers), and the history of Dutch Studies in Wallonia.

Tom Toremans is Lecturer in English literature and literary theory at the Catholic University of Brussels (partner in Hogeschool-Universiteit Brussel and affiliated researcher at the Katholieke Universiteit Leuven.). He obtained his doctoral degree at the KU Leuven and the KU Brussel with a dissertation entitled *Ghosts of Defunct Bodies: Aesthetics, Ideology and Materiality in the Work of Thomas Carlyle*. Apart from articles on Carlyle, he has also published on contemporary Scottish literature, literary theory and reception studies. He is co-founder and member of the steering committee of the Centre for European Reception Studies (CERES).

Anne van Buul studied Dutch Language and Culture at Radboud University Nijmegen. For the research master 'Literary Studies: New Philology' at Nijmegen, she wrote a thesis about the reception of Dante Gabriël Rossetti in the Netherlands. During her internship at the Huygens Institute, she investigated the relationship between Dutch and English book design around 1900. She is currently preparing a Ph.D. at the University of Groningen on the reception of Pre-Raphaelite literature, art and design in the Netherlands during the *fin de siècle*.

Karen Vandemeulebroucke is a research and teaching assistant at the Katholieke Universiteit Leuven (Campus Kortrijk). She is preparing a Ph.D. on Belgian Francophone poetry in literary periodicals during the second half of the 19th century, with special attention to the place and function of translation.

Liselotte Vandenbussche studied English and Dutch literature and linguistics at Ghent University and literary theory at Katholieke Universiteit Leuven. She obtained her Ph.D. in 2006 at the Center for Gender Studies with a dissertation on liberal women writers in Flemish literary and cultural journals (1870-1914). It is published as *Het veld der verbeelding. Vrijzinnige vrouwen in Vlaamse literaire en algemeen-culturele tijdschriften (1870-1914)* by the Royal Academy for Dutch Literature and Linguistics (KANTL, 2008). It was awarded the Jozef Vercoullie Prize 1998-2006, the Provincial Prize for History 2008 and nominated for the Frans van Cauwelaert Prize 2008. She published among others in *Tijdschrift voor Nederlandse Taal- en Letterkunde, Nederlandse Letterkunde*, *Spiegel der Letteren* and *Yang*, and contributed to several books with articles on gender and literature in 19th and early 20th century Flanders. She is currently a postdoctoral research assistant at the Department of Translation Studies of University College Ghent and affiliated researcher at Ghent University. Her postdoctoral research focuses on literary translators in Flanders, 1830-1914.

Suzan van Dijk is director of the international collaborative project 'New approaches to European Women's Writing', based at Utrecht University. She has published widely on French 18th- and 19th-century press and novel writing, particularly in relation to the reception of women novelists. She is (co-)editor of several volumes, including *Writing the History of Women's Writing: Toward an International Approach* (Amsterdam, 2001), and "*I have heard about you": Foreign Women's Writing Crossing the Dutch Border* (Hilversum, 2004).

Ton van Kalmthout obtained his doctoral degree for his thesis entitled *Muzentempels, Multidisciplinaire kunst-kringen in Nederland tussen 1880 en 1914* [*Temples of the Muses. Multi-disciplinary art clubs in the Netherlands from 1880 to 1914*] (1998). In 2005 he was appointed as senior researcher at the Huygens Institute of the Royal Netherlands Academy of Arts and Sciences. He is co-editor of the cultural-historical journal *De Negentiende Eeuw* and of *Tijdschrift voor Nederlandse Taal- en Letterkunde* .

Walter Verschueren teaches American literature and translation studies at the Faculty of Language and Literature of the Hogeschool-Universiteit Brussel. His present main interest is in translation and reception studies, in particular 19th-century literary dynamics between English literatures and the Dutch-speaking Low Countries. With Tom Toremans, he is co-founder and member of the steering committee of the Centre for European Reception Studies (CERES).

Stephanie Walker holds a BA degree from Kent State University(US), where she majored in English Literature and Writing with a focus on American (Second Wave) feminist poets. After moving to the Netherlands in 1994, she paused her university career until September 2005 when she resumed her studies at the University of Amsterdam. In August 2007, she received her BA in English Language and Culture from the University of Amsterdam with a minor in Women's Studies from Utrecht University. She is currently completing the Master program in Comparative Women's Studies in Culture and Politics at Utrecht University.